WORLD SPORTS

Selected Titles in ABC-CLIO's
CONTEMPORARY
WORLD ISSUES
Series

Books in the Contemporary World Issues series address vital issues in today's society such as genetic engineering, pollution, and biodiversity. Written by professional writers, scholars, and nonacademic experts, these books are authoritative, clearly written, up-to-date, and objective. They provide a good starting point for research by high school and college students, scholars, and general readers as well as by legislators, businesspeople, activists, and others.

Each book, carefully organized and easy to use, contains an overview of the subject, a detailed chronology, biographical sketches, facts and data and/or documents and other primary source material, a directory of organizations and agencies, annotated lists of print and nonprint resources, and an index.

Readers of books in the Contemporary World Issues series will find the information they need in order to have a better understanding of the social, political, environmental, and economic issues facing the world today.

WORLD SPORTS

A Reference Handbook

Maylon Hanold

**CONTEMPORARY
WORLD ISSUES**

 ABC-CLIO

Santa Barbara, California • Denver, Colorado • Oxford, England

Library of Congress Cataloging-in-Publication Data

Hanold, Maylon.
  World sports : a reference handbook / Maylon Hanold.
    p. cm. — (ABC-CLIO's contemporary world issues)
  Includes index.
  ISBN 978-1-59884-778-9 (hardback) — ISBN 978-1-59884-779-6
(ebook) 1. Sports—Cross-cultural studies. 2. Sports—Sociological aspects—Handbooks, manuals, etc. I. Title.
  GV706.8.H36 2012
  796—dc23   2012014150

ISBN: 978-1-59884-778-9
EISBN: 978-1-59884-779-6

16 15 14 13 12   1 2 3 4 5

This book is also available on the World Wide Web as an eBook.
Visit www.abc-clio.com for details.

ABC-CLIO, LLC
130 Cremona Drive, P.O. Box 1911
Santa Barbara, California 93116-1911

This book is printed on acid-free paper ∞
Manufactured in the United States of America

Contents

List of Tables

List of Figures

Preface

An Introduction to World Sports

"World sports" in the context of this book pertains to understanding those sports and those issues that are of global concern. Specifically, the aim of this book is to acquaint the reader with how sport came to be an internationally significant cultural practice and which issues remain important for sport administrators, athletes, and spectators to understand. Appreciating modern world sports requires a focus on the history of Western sport and its economic, political, technological, and sociological developments. While the author recognizes that this particular perspective leaves out many other valid perspectives in sport development, the Western world dominates "world sports" in terms of the values they reinforce, the forms they take, and the organizations that control them.

Chapter 1 provides a historical background to the issues presented in the remainder of the book. This chapter shows how sport has been aligned with cultural, religious, and violent practices since its earliest forms. Moving into the modern era, Chapter 1 discusses how competitive sport became the dominant form of sport, growing quickly by being associated with the values and aims of white, upper class people as well as the through the demands of the industrial revolution. In addition, this historical perspective frames how sport became more than a cultural activity and grew into a global business. Finally, this chapter takes a look at how sport has traditionally marginalized various groups based on gender, sexuality, race, ethnicity, and social class. These perspectives show how the current issues in sport have grown out of a long history of sport being intricately integrated with cultural practices, economics, and dominant ideologies.

Chapter 2 focuses on a worldwide perspective of the ongoing issues in sport. In the first two sections, the alignment of sport with politics is discussed as a general phenomenon, then this relationship is considered in the specific sport for development movement. The third section is an overview of what it takes to bid for and host the Olympics. The next two sections show several sides of the debate about performance enhancing drugs and technology in sport, revealing the complexity of decision making in sport that these advances present. The next four sections are aimed at explaining how issues around race and ethnicity, masculinity, violence, unsportsmanlike conduct, and gender are still present in modern day sport. The chapter ends with a look at the dynamic and symbiotic relationship between the media and sport.

In Chapter 3, the perspective turns to North American sport in which several of the issues above are detailed in this context while new topics are explored. The first section highlights the politics and business of hosting a Super Bowl. Further issues with North American professional sport become clear in the next section about player salaries and league revenue. From this vantage point, the North American phenomenon of intercollegiate sport as a business and highly commercialized endeavor is examined. The next two sections take a look at race, ethnicity, and gender issues in North American sport. Next, the difficulties of globalizing a "local" sport are explored through a discussion of NASCAR. Then, growing concerns about concussion and brain trauma are considered in light of the growing demand for high-performing athletes. Finally, the lifestyle sports of skateboarding and ultra-running illustrate how and why these sports attract participants who desire a "different" kind of sporting experience as well as how they reproduce many of the same values found in mainstream sport.

Chapter 4 is a chronology of major events in sport regarding the growth of sport; sport as a business; the growth of sport professionals; and significant political, social, and ethical concerns. The establishment of major sport organizations, leagues, and sport events are chronicled to contextualize the various avenues through which sport grows, and 25 examples of events that have shaped the sport industry—along with 10 important developments signifying the expansion of sport professionals—are presented. This chapter also highlights 25 political, social, and ethical issues and developments in sport.

Chapter 5 offers the reader 32 biographical sketches of people who have shaped modern sport. Sport sociologists, physicians, physiologists, publishers, presidents of sport organizations, CEOs of sports media companies, athletes, coaches, sports commentators, sports magazine editors, and social activists comprise the list of noteworthy sport leaders. Each profile shows how these individuals have either helped open up opportunities for more people to play sport, moved sport into a highly commercial enterprise, or brought social and ethical concerns to the forefront.

Chapter 6 includes 2 documents, 19 figures, and 14 tables that present evidence of the global significance of sport. Data and statistics show how sport has developed into a global phenomenon as well as an international business. The social and ethical issues that arise out of this growth are supported in this chapter though detailed information. These data are contextualized and expanded upon in order to allow the reader to develop a deeper understanding of the complexities of the controversial and social issues in sport.

Chapter 7 features descriptions of 95 sport or sport-related organizations. Professional leagues, amateur sport-governing bodies, youth sports organizations, business and media associations, organizations devoted to medical or psychological health of athletes and sport participants, groups that promote character development through sport, sportsmanship, and ethical decision making in sport, and those organizations dedicated to increasing participation and enhancing the sport experience for marginalized people are described in this chapter. Contact information and Web sites are provided for each organization.

Chapter 8 provides over 120 annotated bibliographies of reference works, books, magazine and journal articles, other print works, DVDs, videotapes, databases, and Internet sites. These print and nonprint resources have been strategically selected to present the most significant historical events and the most current information about the growth of sport and the associated controversies regarding the economic, political, and social implications of sport. These resources help the reader become more knowledgeable about the issues presented in this book, allowing her/him to consider sport in a new light.

The glossary includes over 75 entries connected to the growth, business, and social, political, and ethical aspects of sport.

Acknowledgments

My passion for sport began with my parents who always believed in me and is sustained by my partner, Kaj Bune, and son. I am grateful to my family without whom I would not be able to remain physically active and take on the task of helping make sport a better place. I would also like to express my sincere thanks to my good friend, Bonnie Wharton, whose research and graphic skills were crucial to moving this project along.

1

Background and History

The Meaning and Cultural Significance of Sport

Robert R. Sands (see Baker 1988) reminds us that sport is one of the significant constants in human history. Scholars from various disciplines point out many reasons why sports may have been and continue to be what Sands refers to as a "cultural universal." Some scholars emphasize certain "natural" aspects of sport that contribute to its worldwide appeal. For example, Baker (1988) suggests that sports are rooted in an inherent competitive nature in humans, proposing that sport can be identified as a physical contest in which rules govern a particular competitive form. Others (e.g., Ford and Brown 2006 and Mumford 2012) remark that sports are an inherently aesthetic experience for both spectators and participants. Still other scholars suggest that sports have been an integral activity across cultures and time because they reinforce cultural values (Coakley 2008). In this latter context, sport has been associated with religious, military, and economic values and activities throughout history. Many scholars argue that there is no single definition of and reason for participating in sports. Instead, people shape different meanings of sport depending on sport's social significance, all of which depends upon history and context. They argue that meanings of sport are contested terrain, stressing that it is important to understand what constitutes sport for particular groups, which sports receive more attention and funding, and who is either advantaged or marginalized in the process (Coakley 2008). A closer look into these cultural aspects throughout the history of sport provides a starting point from which to make sense of contemporary world sports.

Competitive Nature

William J. Baker (1998) proposes that humans have a "competitive impulse" that forms the basis for modern sport practices. He notes that humans were in competition with other animals for survival. Such circumstances led humans to work together to kill animals for food or to fight off predators for survival. Baker explains that as communities developed, rewards were bestowed upon the most skilled hunter or the most proficient warrior. Hunters gained notoriety within their tribes by bringing home the most food for their families, which established a stable social order. Aggressive behavior among individuals within these isolated tribes was rare because roles and relationships were clearly defined in these types of societies. When tribes encountered other tribes or individuals, aggressive behavior often resulted because of disruption to the social order. Individuals lower in social status vied for better positions in society over the newly arrived. Baker contends that such aggression heightened as humans became agriculturally based. Farming meant that communities became attached to specific places. Property such as land, huts, farming tools, domesticated animals, and cooking and eating utensils had to be protected. With these changes, honor was given to warriors who demonstrated the most bravery in battle for the sake of protecting the community. Baker concludes that competition for glory among hunters and warriors was a natural consequence of early survival strategies of humans. He argues that such a "competitive impulse" remains evident in modern sport contests in which rewards and social status are given to those who rise above others in physical contests.

Aesthetics of Movement

The ancient Olympics celebrated the aesthetics of physical movement (Baker 1988). The grace and beauty of physical movements and perfectly trained bodies represented discipline and perfect symmetry for the ancient Greeks. Since beauty and aesthetic sensibility were values of the ancient Greeks, Olympic athletes became models for painters, fresco makers, and sculptors. While the athletes of the ancient Olympics were sometimes criticized for spending too much time on physical strengths to the detriment of intellectual and spiritual development, many Greek philosophers such as Socrates, Plato, and Aristotle admired the grace and beauty of the Olympians. In their writings, they extolled the virtues of having a strong, fit body but warned of the excess. These philosophers viewed physical development as complementary to intellectual development. Today, spectators are drawn to sporting events for many reasons, including the fascination with physical movement (Mumford 2012). Sports requiring finesse and graceful movements such as volleyball, gymnastics, and figure skating are among the most watched sports during Olympic coverage today (McComb 2007).

Additionally, the joy of moving appears to align with our sense of play. Yi-Fu Tuan, noted Chinese-American geographer, highlights the power of this body experience when he says, "consider those moments which seem to have only a sensual or emotional-aesthetic character: for instance running barefoot on the sand [a] common delight in bodily movement—a biological exuberance" (as cited in Bale 2004, 12). Whether engaging in play, recreation, or achievement sport, this physical pleasure seems to ground the sport experience for those participating. Roger Bannister, the first person to break the four-minute mile barrier, is widely quoted from his memoirs because of how well he captures the joy of running. He says:

> In this supreme moment I leapt in sheer joy. I was startled, and frightened, by the tremendous excitement that so few steps could create. I glanced around uneasily to see if anyone was watching. A few more steps—self consciously now and firmly gripping the original excitement. The earth seemed almost to move with me. I was running now, and a fresh rhythm entered my body. No longer conscious of my movement I discovered a new unity with nature. I had found a new source of power I never dreamt existed. (as cited in Bale 2004, 11)

For Bannister, the joy of running remained central to his success. Fascinated by these types of peak experiences, the humanistic psychologist Abraham Maslow (1968) researched and identified specific aspects of such experiences. He proposed that peak experiences are comprised of sensations such as total harmony with the environment, total absorption in the experience, and heightened senses. Psychologist Csikszentmihalyi (1990) furthered Maslow's inquiry by studying the relationship between peak experiences and high performance in elite competition. He suggests that this state, which he calls flow, is an optimal balance between capabilities and demands of the activity. Such findings may partly account for why athletes seek greater challenges either in physical form or with increased competition. From this perspective, athletes are less driven by the outcome than they are by aesthetics or the feeling they experience when challenged. In these ways, the aesthetics of movement seem integral to sport: whether watching sport, participating in sport for fun, or competing at an elite level.

Sociocultural Basis of Sport in the Pre-Modern World

Historically, sports have had religious significance (McComb 2007). Through religious ritual and ceremony, sports have historically been woven into the fabric of societies in intricate ways. For instance, the Aztecs and Incas played a ball game in stone courts. Losers and sometimes winners of these ball games would be sacrificed to the gods. Hoping the gods would be pleased by this sacrifice, Aztecs and Incas relied on this sport ritual for the promise of healthy crops, healthy children, and victory in wars. Zuni Indians from the North American Southwest played a less violent ball game. The game consisted of throwing darts at a ball. Whoever struck the ball first raised it in prayer for rains to arrive in springtime. In addition, several running events functioned as ceremonial rites of passage for young boys in the Apache and Tarahumara tribes. Today, the Tarahumara still live in the same canyons they moved to 400 years ago and continue these ultra-distance running races as a rite of passage and cultural event (McDougall 2009).

The most well-known ancient athletic contest also has its roots in religious ceremony (Baker 1988 and McComb 2007). The ancient Olympic Games was first recorded in 776 BC and continued for 1,000 years. The athletic contests were few in the beginning, but by 472 BC, the games were reorganized to include more events along with the religious ceremonies. For the next 800 years, the games took place over a five-day period with two and one-half days devoted to athletic contests and two and one-half days dedicated to ceremonies, religious rituals, and prayers. The first day was entirely comprised of religious prayers, sacrifices, and hymn singing. Equestrian events and pentathlon occurred on the second day, followed by a religious feast and sacrifice in the evening. The afternoon of the third day marked a return to athletic events with the foot races. Various forms of wrestling took place on the fourth day followed by a fifth day of prize giving, prayers to Zeus, and a closing banquet in which all the sacrificed animals were eaten. With the rise of Christianity around AD 400, the Greek games were abolished because all ceremonies having to do with pagan gods were forbidden.

While religious at its core, the ancient Olympic Games was also a display of brute strength and toughness. Wrestling, boxing, and the pancratium were some of the most violent athletic contests. For instance, wrestling events had few rules. While biting and gouging out the eyes were banned, any other means to subdue an opponent were allowed. Boxing was even more brutal as competitors could strike the head and neck or even slap the opponent. The pancratium was an event that combined wrestling, boxing, and judo-like moves. Choking an opponent, breaking fingers and toes, and pulling on ears and noses were not uncommon. The victor was declared when his opponent gave the signal of defeat. Although much more violent than today's games, the Greek athletic contests were relatively mild compared to ancient Rome's spectacles.

While the Romans admired many aspects of Greek culture, the Greek athletic contests did not appeal to them. Given that they were concerned with conquering the Mediterranean world, Romans were much more interested in contests that highlighted the practical skills of military combat. Their games were more like their predecessors, the Etruscans, who preferred bloody contests between men or between men and animals. As such, the Colosseum became a site for extreme contests of skill and strength in the form of fighting until death. Even if an opponent gave the sign that he was defeated, the crowd had the choice of whether the gladiator would live or not. If the gladiator fought well, his life would be spared, at least until some future fight. If he did not fight well, his life would end right there in front of crowds numbering almost 50,000. Later on during the Roman Empire, these gladiatorial contests became an important form of entertainment. In addition, the competitors were often criminals or slaves and therefore not considered worthy of living anyway. As the living conditions of Rome fell and unemployment rose, more holidays were declared in order to amuse the masses and keep them from revolting. In AD 300, the emperor declared 200 days of public holidays, of which 175 were dedicated to games. During this period, sporting contests in the spirit of the ancient Greeks waned, and the violent spectacle of the Romans emerged as dominant.

Although the Greek Olympics and the Roman gladiatorial contests were the official physical contests of their time, only a select few individuals actually participated in such events. During the early years, only the wealthy, aristocratic families could afford the time for training. Later on, lower-class men participated, but only if they had a wealthy patron to pay for all the expenses associated with training for and competing in the Olympic Games. Women were forbidden to participate in the Olympic Games. Because of this exclusion, women organized their own games in honor of the Greek goddess, Hera. Still, the masses of people—including men, women and children—in both civilizations participated in physical exercise in some form. For the Greeks, developing a healthy body became part of the approved way of living. Gymnasiums and palaestrae, spaces dedicated to wrestling activities, were built throughout the Greek world for the everyday person. In contrast, the Romans had a very different view of physical activity, and they never constructed buildings specific to physical development. Nevertheless, they did construct numerous baths throughout their empire. Near the entrances to these baths, grassy fields or official anterooms became sites for informal ball games, running, jumping, and wrestling. The baths were a social experience in which people gathered for recreation, conversation, and reading. While quite different in practice and meaning, the underlying belief that physical exercise complemented other life pursuits was part of the common peoples' experiences for both ancient Greece and Rome. After the Greek games disappeared, sport became largely a pastime for local people during the Middle Ages.

The Industrial Revolution and the Development of Physical Culture in the Modern World

The Industrial Revolution brought widespread change, moving sport from pastime to an important social and economic activity (Keys 2006). Driven by the need for a strong, healthy labor force, physical culture became valued on several levels. Moving from a pastime of the Middle Ages, sport developed into an economic and ideological imperative during the Industrial Revolution.

The notion of the "productive body" spread throughout the Western nations. Not only was a strong workforce needed, but also a fear developed that male bodies were becoming soft and unfit as more men were sitting in offices rather than working in the fields. For these reasons, physical activity was promoted in various forms. Physical education became part of schools, private sporting clubs developed, and public stadiums and playgrounds were built. Physical culture flourished during the latter part of the 19th century and early part of the 20th century, predominantly taking two forms.

In Europe, the gymnastics movement dominated physical culture. Turnen in Germany and the Ling system in Sweden were popular forms of physical activity and recreation based on the idea that a nation's people should be healthy (Keys 2006). Fearing biological weakness after the Franco-Prussian War, the French adopted the Swedish system of gymnastics as a way to strengthen their nation. These forms of sport were distinctly anticompetitive, focusing on group identity, precision of movements, and the aesthetics of movement. These forms of physical exercise were institutionalized in the educational systems, becoming a model upon which U.S. physical education programs would later be based. The rationale for such programs was largely related to health, military conditioning, moral character, and national pride. Although preferred by most of Europe, this type of exercise remained localized and nationalistic. Such local focus would ultimately account for the subordination of this type of physical activity. While gymnastics provided a strong physical fitness program, it could not garner the international attention that competitive sport could.

In contrast to most of Europe, Great Britain and the United States favored a more competitive form of sport. Grounded in similar beliefs that physical activity could produce a healthy, physically fit nation as well as develop moral character, the competitive form of sport offered an international component that the practice of gymnastics could not. Political and military leaders noticed that the competitive forms of sport found in Great Britain produced stronger, more muscled and balanced physical bodies. In contrast, the gymnastics program appeared to create less vigorous and physically strong bodies. Whether or not there is fact to these purported observations, it remains that competitive sport was viewed as producing bodies that had military and economic value. Furthermore, the idea that nations could compete with each other and prove national superiority through sport made competitive sport an appealing international activity. While focusing on nationalistic pride, an international sport community could develop. Soon, European nations began to imitate and adopt competitive sport within their own countries. The voluntary spread of competitive sport throughout Europe and the attraction of international competition resulted in the exponential growth of competitive sport as compared to the gymnastics tradition. By the early part of the 20th century, modern sport was clearly built around the competitive form and gaining more economic and political importance.

Globalization and Sports

Despite the turmoil of the 1930s, sport historian Barbara Keys (2006) cogently argues that this time period was perhaps the most significant with respect to the solidification and growth of modern sport. Worldwide collapse of economies and two world wars brought strength to the sport movement. Keys argues that competitive sport had the unique ability to develop national identities while simultaneously encouraging international solidarity.

The 1930s: Bringing Sport into the Modern Age

The Industrial Revolution brought forth physical cultures that slowly became attached to national identities. Human resources such as healthy, strong bodies became just as important to national identity as economics and national resources. Along with the hard-working bodies needed for the Industrial Revolution, leisure time increased, and sport became one of the primary modes through which nations sought to build character and develop moral qualities. Given the rising tension in Europe during the interwar years, national pride rose to high levels. One of the more striking results was the staging of the 1936 Olympics in Berlin under Hitler's regime. Despite being ideologically opposed to competitive sport because he desired a more cohesive, collaborative, and obedient society, Hitler was drawn into international competition. His hope was that the Olympics would provide a stage upon which he could demonstrate Aryan superiority. He hoped to prove that his form of leadership promoted a healthy and robust society, both bodily and economically. Many European nations were eager to participate in this proving ground, which consisted of demonstrating national pride and expertise through sport. The desire to express national pride and prove superiority continued throughout the Cold War years in which the battle between democracy and socialism remained a powerful undercurrent. As a result, international competitions rose dramatically during this time, and the Olympic Games, along with World Cup soccer, became two of the premier events.

The Rise of International Sport Organizations

As the demand for more international competitions grew, so did the need for organizing these events. The wide appeal of competitive sport partly resulted from the sense that these events could objectively determine superiority. Such perceived objectivity fit the values associated with the Industrial Revolution. Such ideals as standardization, measurement, and uniform rules and regulations were needed in an international sport environment (Keys 2006). In other words, in order for nations to compete fairly with each other, rules and regulations had to be standardized. As a result, such international governing bodies as the International Olympic Committee (IOC) and the Fédération Internationale de Football Association (FIFA) grew slowly but steadily. Fields, stadia, distances, and ways of measuring had to be codified in order for the comparison of nations to occur. These standards were not necessarily easy to establish because each nation already had localized forms, rules, and measurements in many sports. Yet, given the desire to establish sport more globally, the institutionalization of sport began to take shape.

The power that these governing bodies possessed grew steadily with the popularity of international events. International sport organizations also demanded the development of national governing bodies to serve as liaisons between national sport and international competition. These early international sport organizations possessed relatively unlimited power because they were not governed by any one nation. Such organizations as the IOC and FIFA were free to function as they saw fit and oversee the rules and regulations they imposed on national governing bodies. Thus, their power to create the content and symbolism of world sport was unfettered by national politics. They operated beyond such political boundaries. Instead, economic opportunity became a strong guiding force for these international organizations.

International Sport, Economics, and the "Golden Triangle"

Improved transportation and technological developments aided the growth of international sport. With better roads, steamships, and airplanes, international travel for athletes was no longer burdensome. In addition, spectators could also travel more easily to support their favorite teams. The ease with which athletes and spectators could travel made international sport a reality. International competitions grew tremendously during the first half of the 20th century, and corporations were on the move to associate themselves with events that promised a global audience.

As international competition grew, the belief that sport was a universal practice, appealing to everyone, strengthened (Keys 2006). Sporting events were broadcast through radio and television. Not only was this beneficial to fans, but more significantly, corporations began to see these media broadcasts as opportunities to develop global recognition of their products. Sport became globally significant not only as a cultural form but also as an economic endeavor. Slowly but surely, professional sport, media, and corporations began to understand that there was a symbiotic relationship from which each group could benefit. Aris (1990) coined the term "golden triangle" to refer to the lucrative relationship among professional sport, media, and corporate sponsorship. With a captive audience and emotions that were tied up in international sport, the golden triangle dramatically changed the direction of modern sport.

Horst Dassler of Adidas was perhaps one of the most influential people with respect to corporatizing sport. As interest in the World Cup grew, he saw a global customer base that had yet to be tapped. Using his inside political connections, Dassler negotiated contracts with FIFA that helped support existing teams with shoes as well as gave money to developing African nations. FIFA provided the means for Adidas to be able to reach more people. Athletes were happy to be wearing "free" shoes, and developing nations were able to grow sport programs, all of which led to a larger market for both FIFA and Adidas. The IOC also saw corporate sponsorship as a way to increase public interest in the Olympics. Today, the IOC benefits primarily from media bids.

The emergence of sport-media companies has made this type of sponsorship highly competitive. In fact, the IOC postponed allocating its media rights for the 2012 Olympics in London in order to wait for the economy to rebound, hoping that higher rates could be obtained.

Certainly, other international organizations benefited from this perspective as well. The International Rugby Football Board was established in 1886 so that rugby tournaments could be hosted worldwide. The establishment of the Davis Cup in tennis in 1904 put tennis on the international scene. Soon, other tournaments popped up as the upper class wanted to be associated with high performance sport. In addition, as British colonialism proceeded, cricket became an international sport. The more interesting result that occurred throughout these movements, and especially evident in cricket, was the way in which colonists reproduced specific sports as their own form of physical identity, embracing them as their own. A good example of this phenomenon is C. L. R. James's seminal book on West Indies identity formation around cricket. This phenomenon is no less true of soccer and rugby in such countries as New Zealand, South Africa, and Australia.

Sports and Business: Major Historical Trends of This Symbiotic Relationship

In ancient Rome, chariot racing was the most watched sport. As entertainment, chariot racing became a business (Rosner and Shropshire 2004). In the Circus Maximus, thousands of spectators paid to view the charioteers race laps around the oval. The drivers of the chariots were often former slaves, who were sponsored by businesses. Teams were divided into four basic colors with fans being loyal to a specific color. As competition became more intense and winning became associated with profits, drivers became commodities. Offering attractive salaries was a regular part of luring drivers to new teams. Such practices resulted in salaries of these drivers exceeding most other professions. A historian from the time period noted that the salary of a driver was 100 times that of the entire Senate. As chariot racing was more commercialized and the Republic of Rome transformed into an empire, many franchises formed, resulting in the formation and expansion of leagues. As races increased in number, profits from ticket sales made selling franchises profitable. Violence became an ordinary part of the spectacles and was allowed to continue because audiences seemed to approve. Investors were not interested in ethical action when nonaction resulted in greater profits. Thus, for thousands of years, sport as entertainment has been aligned with more than aesthetics, the pursuit of excellence, and competition. In short, sport is a business.

In the modern era, the business of sport has most notably centered on sport as entertainment (Rosner and Shropshire 2004). Since the late 1800s, sport and sport business have experienced tremendous growth. As of 1999, the total revenue generated by the sports industry is estimated at $213 billion (Mahoney and Howard 2001). Money spent on sports facilities during the 1990s increased 800 percent over the previous decade with over $16 billion being spent on 160 new ballparks, stadiums, arenas, and racetracks in the United States alone (Mahoney and Howard 2001). In addition, the last two decades of the 20th century saw 170 new professional sports teams and 13 new leagues, including sunbelt hockey; women's professional sports; and as recently as 2010, Street League Skateboarding, a niche market, lifestyle sport. By the end of the 1990s, there were over 600 professional sports teams in North America. Coinciding with the growth of sports was triple growth in corporate sponsorship (Silk, Andrews, and Cole 2005). By 1999, corporations were sponsoring sports to the tune of $5.1 billion. Naming rights and luxury suite sales were responsible for a large percentage of these sponsorships. Given the growth in sport and corporate sponsorship of it, sport as entertainment has evolved from being controlled and run as a top-down local activity to being controlled by a large number of stakeholders involved in a complex web of relationships and interests. The history of sport business is best approached as a web of negotiations among various stakeholders with divergent interests and shifting rules, policies, and regulations (Giulianotti and Robertson 2007 and Tomlinson and Young 2006). The purpose of this brief overview of sport business is to follow a few of the major trends during the 20th century. To illustrate some of these trends, this section focuses on European cycling, North American professional leagues and franchises, and governance issues of North American intercollegiate sports. Specific issues that arise from the complex relationships among stakeholders are addressed throughout.

In Europe, the control that sport governing bodies have over how sport is played, who gets to play it, and who benefits from sport has experienced many shifts since the 1930s. One example of the shift in how races are run, financed, and controlled is that of professional cycling. During the late 1800s, bicycle racing had taken hold in Europe. During these early years, companies began seeking more publicity sponsored riders. The most famous race today, the *Tour de France*, began in 1903 as a business idea for the newspaper, *L'Auto* (Morrow and Idle 2008). Although city-to-city cycling races were common during the latter part of the 19th century, *L'Auto*'s sports writer suggested a multistage race that would take riders all over France. He thought that coverage of this epic race would increase newspaper sales. The owner gave the go ahead, and the Tour de France was born. In these early years, the stages were extremely long, and riders typically rode during the night. With prize money offered for every stage in the amount six times a normal person's annual salary, cheating was rampant. Such behavior almost meant the end of the Tour de France. Realizing this, stages were run only during the day by the third year. As integrity of the race improved, *L'Auto* grew into a very profitable newspaper. By 1930, independent riders were replaced by national teams. Yet, because riders wore national colors but had loyalties to their sponsors who supported them throughout the year, issues arose. First, national team members could not necessarily trust each other because of their diverse corporate allegiances. Second, bicycle factories were experiencing declining sales and put pressure on the organization to return to trade teams. Trade teams were allowed to advertise on bikes and jerseys, increasing the visibility of companies during this prestigious race. As a result, trade teams were once again allowed to compete in 1962. By this time, *L'Equipe*, a newspaper established after World War II when *L'Auto* was terminated, organized the Tour de France. With the return of trade teams, other controversies arose around doping and overt commercialism. Such controversy led to the establishment of national teams again in 1967 and 1968. Yet, pressures from sponsors, who wanted exposure during the most prestigious race in Europe, as well as the purchase of *L'Equipe* newspaper by Amaury Sports Organization (ASO) helped swing the pendulum back to trade teams in 1969, which is the primary form the Tour de France takes today. While the primary organizer for the Tour de France has been relatively stable since the 1960s, the history of the Tour de France demonstrates the various ways in which multiple stakeholders can influence the ways fans experience sport, the relative power of corporate sponsors, and the ways in which athletes get to compete.

A turn to North American sport shows other reasons people invest in sport as a business (Rosner and Shropshire 2004). By the turn of the 19th century, wealthy entrepreneurs emerged from the Industrial Revolution and began to take interest in sport as a business. Entrepreneurs wanted to acquire sport franchises for such various reasons as profits, positive association with sport, and personal interest. History shows that owning a professional sports team can satisfy personal interests and also result in greater public exposure through positive association. In terms of the bottom line, however, franchise ownership rarely turns out to be profitable.

A closer look at the specific and unique aspects of sport finance shows that owners benefit in other ways (Rosner and Shropshire 2004). Primarily, accounting practices and occasional exemption from antitrust laws that occurs in the sport business makes it financially attractive to wealthy people. First, owners are allowed to be on the payroll, allowing them to be subject to more favorable tax laws. Second, if the owners happen to be broadcasting companies, they can easily shift money from one enterprise to the other by charging themselves broadcast fees, which affects the bottom lines for both the sport franchise and the broadcast company. Depending on the tax laws, owners can adjust the accounting to be in their favor. For instance, there are many incentives that encourage showing the "value" of TV rights as broadcast revenue rather than team revenue. Complicating the matter is the fact that teams share the revenue generated by leagues. Thus, if revenues are transferred to the broadcast companies, who are also owners, the team loses money and does not contribute to league revenue. Teams that show a loss can benefit from the league's revenue sharing rules. In addition, owners are allowed to use depreciation as part of their accounting strategies. For instance, a before tax loss is easy to show because players' contracts can be depreciated, which is simply a book value, not real cash. This depreciation then appears as a loss. This strategy effectively lowers the tax rate owners are in because it can substantially reduce their total income for the year. Not only, then, do the owners essentially "earn" the depreciation difference as real after tax income, but what they save on taxes effectively becomes additional after tax income. Despite the fact that most professional teams do not make a profit, ownership of sports teams provides multiple avenues for the wealthy to effectively retain and increase wealth.

Essential to the success of professional sports is the formation of leagues (Rosner and Shropshire 2004). In general, leagues were created to bring standardization to the rules, establish dependable competitions among teams, and bring stability to sport finances. The most prominent leagues in North America are Major League Baseball (MLB), the National Hockey League (NHL), the National Football League (NFL), and the National Basketball Association (NBA), established in 1876, 1917, 1920, and 1949 respectively. One of the earliest functions that leagues served was to codify rules that all franchises must follow in the name of fairness. Today, leagues create and enforce all season play rules as well as those for postseason play and championships. By deciding which teams play each other in regular season, leagues establish predictable competition among individual teams. Also, leagues exist to provide some element of financial stability by earning revenue that is then distributed to the franchises after expenses. In these ways, leagues have grown from strictly organizational entities to profit-oriented businesses. By controlling broadcasting rights and revenue from merchandising, leagues have considerable control over revenue distribution. With the Sports Broadcasting Act in 1961, leagues were given exclusive negotiating privileges with broadcasters. In addition, since the 1980s, the MLB, NFL, NBA, and NHL have become exclusive negotiators in merchandise agreements. This system allows leagues to negotiate bigger media and merchandising deals, maximizing revenue streams because the product is a series of games rather than a single competition. Since leagues are exempt from antitrust laws, they are allowed to continue as the sole negotiator of media and merchandising rights.

While many feel that leagues help franchises survive by distributing revenue from these sources, other sports businessmen believe that leagues restrict franchise revenue and reduce the level of competition, which results in fan disinterest (Rosner and Shropshire 2004). Theoretically, the distribution of revenue earned by leagues equalizes each team's opportunity to win by prohibiting wealthy teams from capitalizing on their performance to increase their wealth to the extent that they can lure the best athletes. If this were to happen, some sport businessmen argue that the wealthiest teams would always win, taking away the uncertainty of winning, which is arguably an important aspect of competition. Thus, the impetus behind revenue distribution is to protect the competitive balance: the idea that in any given game, the outcome is unpredictable. But other sport scholars point out several issues with this system. First, it can create disincentives for teams to win because teams do not get the full benefit of winning. Instead, when teams win, it does not result in a greater share of the league's revenue. A franchise's share of league revenue remains constant. As a result, for franchises to do well, they are compelled to lower costs. In turn, teams are willing to hire less talented players at lower costs than select the best. Some scholars argue that this ultimately reduces the level of play and competition. Second, there is a "free rider effect" in that lower market teams are supported by the sharing revenue system. Such support leaves no incentive for these teams to market themselves. In other words, given that they will receive their share of league revenue without extra marketing, they do not spend money on this. Instead, they rely on the efforts of other, more successful teams to spend the time and money to promote the sport in general.

While leagues have prospered, franchise profitability continues to be ambiguous (Rosner and Shropshire 2004). In response to the league's control over significant revenue, franchises have historically turned to enhancement of stadiums and arenas in order to attract more fans and benefit directly. Legally, stadium ticket sales, luxury suite sales, and concession sales are revenue for local teams, not leagues. Many lower market teams have built new stadiums in hopes of bringing them more on par with the higher market teams, but the higher market teams have also built new stadiums. Therefore, despite revenue sharing, the financial gap between these two tiers of teams continues to increase. For example, the Dallas Cowboys have historically been able to sell their luxury suites for considerably more than other teams, resulting in revenue often three to four times that of lower market teams. Beginning in the early 1990s, creative tactics were used to build more attractive and fan-friendly sports facilities. One strategy included getting the public to finance the construction of stadiums through taxation by convincing cities that new stadiums would produce jobs and additional revenue. By 1999, however, taxpayers were not convinced that new stadiums would result in more jobs and produce significant revenue; in fact, 9 out of 13 proposals for stadiums to be built with taxpayer money were rejected that year. As a result, more teams have had to pay for their stadiums, leaving one-quarter to one-third of North American professional teams in debt. From these examples, it is clear that North American professional sports is based on a complex web of relationships in which various entities rely on, as well as compete with, each other.

North American collegiate sports are unique in that a wide variety of stakeholders are involved in its production (Rosner and Shropshire 2004). While other collegiate sports programs exist worldwide, no other collegiate programs compare in popularity to those of North America. Unlike all other collegiate sports programs, North American collegiate sports are solidly a business. Although located within institutions of learning, collegiate sports have historically been affiliated with corporate sponsorship as well as some of the issues that come with pairing money and sport. Even though students initially organized and facilitated collegiate sports, corporations have sponsored collegiate teams since the first collegiate competition in 1852, the rowing regatta between Yale and Harvard. Elkin Rail Line financed the famous rowing regatta between Harvard and Yale for years. Successful teams and athletes often received money or nicer accommodations than other students. Sometimes the desire to win was so great that cheating occurred. One notable account was when Harvard tried to hire a nonstudent coxswain. Another notable abuse occurred when Rutgers beat Princeton in football by playing four freshman who had all failed algebra and were not technically eligible to play. Concerns over safety escalated in 1905 when there were 13 deaths and over 100 serious injuries in college football. Such events collectively contributed to the increased demand for the institutionalization of collegiate sport. Discussions between 1840 and 1910 revealed that many constituents thought that there should be more control over intercollegiate sport. Simultaneously, student-athletes were calling for professional coaching and improved facilities. Finally, university presidents began to see revenue opportunities associated with a strong athletics program.

Although conferences had been formed, the concern for safety and fairness combined with the potential for financial gains prompted university administrators to help establish the International Athletic Association (IAA). The primary role of the IAA was to provide consistent rules and regulations aimed at improving the safety for student-athletes. In 1910, the IAA was renamed the National Collegiate Athletic Association (NCAA).

Since that time, the NCAA has grown significantly and currently provides a wide variety of support services for collegiate sports. In doing so, the NCAA has become a significant stakeholder in the business of intercollegiate sport. Growing from an organization that helped create new sport opportunities and established rules, the NCAA now negotiates media rights and is more prominent in the oversight and enforcement of athlete eligibility. Given the complexity of corporate sponsorship, concerns over student-athlete graduation rates, recruiting policies, media rights, Title IX requirements, and conference championships, it is clear how the NCAA has become a powerful and important stakeholder in intercollegiate sport, markedly shaping the sport experience for many North American collegiate athletes.

Sports business has been an integral part of sport for hundreds of years, but the growth of sport since the Industrial Revolution has resulted in sports business being distinguished by intricate webs of relationships (Giulianotti and Robertson 2007 and Thibault 2009). In essence, the "golden triangle" consisting of codependent relationships between media, corporations, and sport has been facilitated by sport governing bodies. Cooperation and tensions among these various constituents characterizes sports business, making it a dynamic and complex enterprise. As more sports are created, developed, and commercialized, it is important to consider the trends noted above (Mahoney and Howard 2001). While athletes have increased opportunities to play because of sport functioning as a business, drawing attention to the tensions among stakeholders emphasizes the extent to which sport experiences are shaped by sport business.

The Marginalizing and Privileging Power of Sport: A Historical Perspective of Social Issues

Women and Sport

Historically, women have struggled to find an equal place in sport. In ancient Greece, women were in subordinate societal roles (Nixon 2008). They had to sleep in different parts of the home than men and were not allowed to be educated. Their duties included running the affairs of the home and childbearing.

Sport participation was extremely limited for women. The most notable ancient sporting event, the ancient Olympic Games, was for men only. This prestigious event excluded women as participants and spectators for its entire 1,000-year history. Wanting to take part in some sort of physical contest, Greek women organized the Herean Games in honor of the Greek goddess, Hera. Ancient Greeks approved of the Herean Games to the extent that they were grounded in a fertility ritual. In other words, physical activity for women was accepted as long as it was thought to aid in childbirth. When the modern Olympic Games were instituted in 1896 by Pierre de Coubertin, women were excluded. Coubertin believed that it was unsightly and unhealthy for women to compete in strenuous exercise. Because of women's growing desires to play sport, 11 women were allowed to compete in lawn tennis and golf in the 1900 Olympic Games. Gradually, women's desires to participate in sport grew, especially in track and field. As a result, the Women's Olympic Games were organized in 1922 in Paris. Due to the success of these games, the IOC lobbied for the inclusion of track and field events and the admittance of more women for the 1928 Games. Women's inclusion in the Olympic Games has since increased every year. In 1952, women comprised 10 percent of the total athletes. By 1976, that number rose to 20.2 percent and continued to rise to 40 percent during the 2004 Summer Games in Athens (Nixon 2008).

The rise in participation rates for women in international competition is only a recent phenomenon; but it grows out of a long, sometimes tumultuous history of various sport opportunities that women had (Nixon 2008). During the Middle Ages, women did not hold a particularly high place in society. Fortunately for women, sport was much less organized. Competitive sport during ancient times gave way to less competitive ball games and pastimes. Everyone, including men, women, and children, participated in these informal games. In fact, historical documents show that milkmaids invented and played stoolball, a ball game thought to be a precursor to cricket. In stoolball, a pitcher threw a ball at a milking stool, attempting to knock it over, while a batter tried to defend it. It was the responsibility of the batter to keep the ball from knocking it over. The batter was allowed to use only her hands in defense of the stool. The development of stoolball is one example of how women may have helped shape modern sport games. While sport as a pastime remained open to women as the modern age commenced, women's participation in competitive sport was challenged throughout the early 20th century.

The 1920s marked a time of unprecedented change in the United States. In addition to music, poetry, and technology, sport captured Americans as both participants and spectators. The 1920s were viewed as the time when men and women were cutting loose from Victorian values and embracing new lifestyles. Understandably, many women wanted more opportunities to participate in sport just as they wanted to attain equal status in other such areas of life as voting. With the growing desire of women wanting to participate in athletics, sport programs emerged in women's colleges (Cahn 1994). Women physical educators were staunch supporters of women's sports although they supported a specific kind of participation by women. These female leaders helped organize and support women-only clubs and extracurricular physical activities in female-only colleges. Various sports were supported, but they varied in social acceptability throughout the years. In general, the more strenuous the activity, the more problematic the sport was for women. Such sports as golf, equestrian events, and tennis were much less problematic because they ostensibly did not require as much pure strength or raw fitness. Sports requiring less perceived exertion were more acceptable because they were considered more appropriate for women's bodies, which were thought to be more fragile and delicate. Women physical educators were key in the promotion of socially acceptable women's sports, helping women enter into the physically active milieu in the early part of the 20th century.

The control of women's sports by primarily female physical educators helped, as well as hindered, women's participation in competitive sport (Cahn 1994). Despite promoting sport for women, physical education instructors were concerned about overexertion, a compromised female identity, and loss of control over female sports. For years, female physical education instructors warned of the "dangers" of too much physical exertion for women. They viewed this exertion as being harmful to the health of female athletes. There was fear that sport would create "manly" women. Thus, while they advocated for more women's sporting opportunities, the type of physical activity they were willing to support remained largely participative and anticompetitive. These educators were particularly concerned about the reputation of elite white women in finishing schools. In their minds, competitive sport went too far in putting these "nice girls" and their bodies on display for others. They opposed competitive sport because they thought that this type of activity sexualized women's bodies. More importantly, these educators were very concerned about losing control of female sports to men and having women's sports be defined by them.

During the first half of the 20th century, most women's sports were separate from men's sports and predominantly controlled by women (Cahn 1994). One notable exception during this period was the All-American Girls Baseball League, which began in the 1940s by men and continued for 12 years. Men's control over this female-only baseball league resulted in women experiencing cultural tensions that they would continue to experience for decades to come and foreshadowed who would ultimately control women's sport. One example of the cultural tensions these women experienced was the conflict between sport-required masculine athleticism and societal expectations of femininity. Women wanted to play baseball as aggressively as the men, but the male promoters of the league wanted to highlight the athletes' femininity in order to sell more tickets. The league required that the women wear pastel-skirted uniforms, put on makeup, keep their hair long, and behave in "feminine" ways while off the field. The existence of this league manifested the physical educators' fears. Women's bodies were being put on display, and men controlled the league. Debates about to what extent women's sport should conform to men's standards and who should control women's sport would go on for at least four decades. Today, the outcome of those debates is clear. Women's sports have taken the form of men's competitive sport and are primarily controlled by men.

Sexuality and Sport

Given that sport historically has been associated with masculine values and attributes, it serves as a powerful site for reinforcing particular notions of gender. Specific notions of gender are inextricably tied to unequivocal ideas about sexuality (Coakley 2008 and Nixon 2008). One of the most significant ways to prove one's masculinity is to assert one's heterosexuality (Anderson 2009 and Nixon 2008). Because sports reinforce masculine values and attributes, male athletes are repeatedly compelled to confirm their heterosexuality. Because homosexuality has been viewed as the antithesis of masculinity and what it means to be a "real man," gay athletes have traditionally had no legitimate space in sport.

Enormous pressure for male athletes to prove their heterosexuality has made it next to impossible for gay athletes to come out in sport. Compulsory heterosexuality in sport practically obliges male athletes not only to distance themselves from gay athletes, but in many cases to express hatred toward gay athletes. Many male heterosexual athletes, as well as society in general, feel threatened by gays in sport, especially in more aggressive "masculine" sports, because gay athletes do not conform to society's specific notions about gender, particularly as reinforced through sport.

Today, many people feel that sexuality has become less of an issue in society overall, but it remains unclear what they think when it comes to sport. While homophobic enunciations occur daily in sport, Anderson (2010) suggests that the reality of how athletes respond to openly gay teammates is far from the myth. Typically, people think that openly gay male athletes would be respected less and hurt the team. Anderson's research shows that many gay collegiate athletes have had empowering, positive experiences coming out to their teams. Professional gay athletes may have such greater fears as losing sponsorship deals. In 2005, out of the 3,500 professional athletes from men's basketball, football, baseball, and hockey, none openly identified being gay (Nixon 2008). As of 2011, there are still no professional athletes who are openly gay, but many feel that 2011 marked a significant change and that sports have become less homophobic than historically has been the case.

For women, sports participation presented slightly different issues with respect to sexuality (Cahn 1994). With the pairing of sport and masculinity, people feared that women would be "masculinized" through the process. Such fears of masculinization resulted in fears that sport would produce lesbians. The fear of being labeled a lesbian produced all kinds of tension for female athletes. Female athletes often went to great extremes to show their femininity. Early on in women's sport development, many women felt compelled to participate in only those sports that were considered "feminine" such as swimming, figure skating, tennis, and golf. As a result, the growth of women in more aggressive such sports as soccer and rugby has been slow.

During the 1940s and onward, there were many lesbians in sport, but being overtly lesbian was not socially acceptable (Cahn 1994). Sport provided a very comfortable environment for lesbians. Some historians argue that the high percentage of lesbians in these early years is attributed to sport being a site in which aggressive, strong, athletic behavior was required, thus permitting these women to cross gender boundaries. In addition, the desires of heterosexual women to avoid being labeled lesbian may also account for these high percentages since heterosexual women may have avoided sport for these very reasons. Despite the fact that sport provided such a comfortable space, there were "unwritten rules" among these women to deny lesbianism in public. Indeed, this attitude pervaded well into the late 20th century. During the early years, the Women's National Basketball Association (WNBA) maintained a dubious attitude toward lesbian athletes. While some players self-identified as lesbian, the WNBA's early campaign promoted family, wholesomeness, and feminine beauty. This was a clear attempt to counter the idea that female athletes were lesbians for fear of alienating potential fans.

Sports have also been "gendered" such that less aggressive sports are considered feminine, and highly aggressive sports are considered masculine (Coakley 2008 and Nixon 2008). The gendering of sport has implications for gay and lesbian athletes, especially in today's sport world. Some such athletes as Olympic diver Matthew Mitcham have come out, even during their competitive career, because they participated in less aggressive sports. As a diver, Mitcham's homosexuality was more acceptable to society in 2008. Alternately, as a tennis player Martina Navratilova was able to come out as early as 1981 because it was not a surprise to society that athletic women might be lesbian. While different for men and women, the result of socially constructed ideas about gender have had real implications for both men and women in terms of how they participate (or not) in sport and whether they can fully be themselves when they do.

Race and Ethnicity

Despite the idea that sports unites people of different racial and ethnic backgrounds, racism in sports has a long history and remains evident in today's sporting world (Coakley 2008 and Nixon 2008). In the early 1900s, as competitive sport took hold in the United States and Europe, racial exclusion and segregation were the norm when organizing sports. Such organization reflected the social status appointed minorities in society at large. As sport grew during the 20th century in the United States and Europe, minorities participated in sport just like the majority of whites partly because of corporations' desires to have a healthy, productive work force. Company sponsored sports programs grew as a result of this focus, especially in the United States. With many immigrants entering the United States and joining the workforce, company sports programs were also seen as ways to Americanize "outsiders." Such minorities as blacks from the southern states were included in this group. The Great Migration during the 1920s resulted in a million African Americans migrating to the North for work opportunities in the factories. Due to this influx of African Americans, segregated leagues began to form. During this time, the Negro Leagues were created, allowing African American athletes to play baseball under their own league rules.

Segregation was the norm for many institutions throughout the Industrial Revolution. For example, all-black colleges became places for African Americans to receive an education. One of the more famous colleges was Tuskegee, founded in 1881 in Alabama. While segregated, Tuskegee provided a unique experience for female African American athletes (Cahn 1994). African American female athletes in colleges like Tuskegee had a few easier paths to a select number of competitive sports than did some of their white counterparts. Such black colleges as Tuskegee often had programs for women's track and field and basketball, competitive sports often ignored or not offered in the "finishing" colleges for white women. Tuskegee became well known for its women's track and field team. These all-black colleges provided a safe place for women to participate in competitive sport. Many Tuskegee black female athletes reported having much support from family, friends, and coaches (Cahn 1994). The school community was proud of their female athletes. Such an environment insulated these women from the larger social criticisms about women becoming too "mannish" through sport. In many ways, this isolation allowed these women to compete without the tensions felt by many other white women who were a more visible and accepted part of society. From the black perspective, the success of their female athletes was a point of pride and represented black cultural achievement. While these early programs laid the foundation for sports that African American women pursued in later years, they also tended to limit the views of what sports black female athletes felt they could pursue. Today, African American female athletes are overly represented in basketball and track and field compared to other sports.

Even when racial integration occurred, the history of racial ideology and segregation has meant that racial tensions continue to exist despite the ever growing integration in at least a few of the world's more popular sports (Coakley 2008 and Nixon 2008). Jackie Robinson's debut into MLB started the integration of minorities into professional sports. Some scholars argue that this event helped America realize the possibility and benefits of racial integration. Other such scholars as William Rhoden (2006) criticize this integration because at this juncture in history, African Americans had become part of a sport system run by white wealthy males. In this move, Rhoden argues that African American baseball players were lured by the Major Leagues, which resulted in the demise of the Negro Leagues. Rhoden's view is that when Branch Rickey, owner of the Brooklyn Dodgers, selectively chose Jackie Robinson from the Negro Leagues to be the first black player in MLB, the blueprint of how blacks would be integrated was established. Institutional integration was circumvented by the fact that the Negro Leagues, along with its black owners, managers, staff, and coaches was not brought into MLB as an equal institution. Instead, black athletes were brought into Major League Baseball as individual athletes. By 1956, the multimillion dollar business that the Negro Leagues had once been ceased to exist.

The collapse of the Negro Leagues meant that opportunities for African American male athletes to compete professionally were more limited at this point in history (Nixon 2008). As a result, African American males began seeking white, more prestigious universities to attend in order to get greater national exposure and enhance their opportunities for playing in the professional leagues. Similar to professional baseball, black athletic administrators, coaches, and staff did not follow these athletes into the white institutions. Thus, although college campuses became more integrated with respect to student populations, African American athletes experienced cultural isolation and lacked adult role models and mentors in this environment. Rhoden argues that during this period of time, African Americans failed to advocate for opportunities to be part of the power structure in collegiate and professional sport. Instead, African Americans and other minorities were integrated to the extent that they helped produce successful teams for white men to control. Ironically, as minorities have been recruited into professional American football, baseball, and basketball, the public has the impression that minorities have been fully integrated into sports. Yet, these professional sports are a mere fraction of the number of sports played around the world. Considering the power structures and breadth of sport, full integration is far from the truth.

Despite the fact that sports are more diverse than ever worldwide, minorities struggle to gain full acceptance (Nixon 2008). Analysis of baseball and soccer in other such parts of the world as Europe, Japan, and Korea suggest that minorities have been marginalized in both Western and Eastern societies. For instance, blacks playing soccer in England have historically been subject to racial slurs and discrimination. In countries where the population is largely homogeneous, minorities have faced similar forms of discrimination. For example, Japan has been slow to accept international players, and Japanese baseball remains comprised mostly of Japanese players. Even when minority players are well liked, the general population's view of minorities does not necessarily improve. Even as late as the year 2000, Major League Baseball fans appreciated such particular Latino players as Edgar Martinez of the Seattle Mariners, but research showed that such appreciation did little to alter general views of Latinos. Conversely, many Latino fans reported that they attend games to support Latino players but had little interest in the overall welfare of the team. As both soccer and baseball have become globalized, players from diverse backgrounds have frequently been united and celebrated under national identities. Zinedine Zidane, an Algerian, is a good example of how a country highlighted national identity over racial identity. For years, Zidane represented the success with which an ethnically and racially diverse French national team could exist as a unified national team. Yet, when Zidane head-butted another player during the 2006 World Cup, the reactions of the French immediately focused on his Algerian background as a problem and primary reason for his behavior. On these grounds, he was rejected as a hero although he had held hero status for years. Although sport has become much more diverse throughout much of the 1900s, racial and ethnic tensions remain evident.

Social Class

The historical significance of the ancient Olympic Games being largely for the wealthy remains a significant aspect of modern sport (Coakley 2008 and Nixon 2008). When Coubertin initiated the process for reviving the ancient games, his vision was to promote character and values associated with the upper classes so that they would be fit to govern the people. In addition, the popularity of competitive sport was driven largely by the institutionalization of sport in the elite British physical education programs. These programs were created out of the desire to produce men of character who would one day be leaders in British society. Competitive sport boomed under this rationale for decades. In North America, competitive sport in colleges and universities grew out of this same reasoning. Throughout the Industrial Revolution, elite schools promoted competition as a way for the upper class to promote character building and values associated with their class. For the middle and upper classes, sport has historically been seen as an amateur pursuit. It was considered a temporary achievement until real life happened. The meaning of sport in today's elite colleges and universities remains grounded in these historical roots.

Alternately, for the lower and middle classes, sport participation grew out of very different motivations. As noted before, corporations were interested in developing a physically fit working class during the Industrial Revolution. There was also some fear that with the growth of leisure time for all people, the working class might become unruly. Companies were partly interested in providing sports for their employees to keep them occupied. Not only was participation promoted by corporations, but also by local organizations such as the Young Men's Christian Association (YMCA). Baseball and basketball were invented to fill these needs, and track and field became integrated into sports for the middle and lower classes through female African American participation in all-black colleges. While these programs opened up sport to more people, their growth only served to strengthen the gap between upper class and lower to middle classes.

Class issues have historically intersected with racial and ethnic issues. Many middle and lower class participants consisted of minorities. Class-segregated sport led to racially segregated sport. As a result, many minorities developed very limited views of which sports they felt they could play. As professional sport developed, these limited views propagated beliefs that certain sports were avenues toward breaking down class barriers for certain minorities. For instance, African American males were largely exposed to basketball, football, and track and field. When young males witnessed the success of professional African American players, they became more convinced that sport was their way out of poverty. Research (Coakley 2008 and Nixon 2008) today suggests that lower class minority youth believe that sport is their savior. Such ideas have partly resulted in the overrepresentation of minorities in such sports such football, baseball, basketball, and track and field. Ironically, such overrepresentation leaves the impression that middle to lower classes and minorities are gaining ground in sport. Yet, when looking at sport from the broadest view, sport remains dominated by wealthier, typically white people who have access to leisure time and discretionary money. Indeed, race, ethnicity, and social class have historically intertwined in ways that promote and limit sport participation by these groups of people in significant ways.

References

Anderson, Eric. 2009. *Inclusive masculinities: The changing nature of masculinities.* New York: Routledge.

Anderson, Eric. 2010. *Sport, theory and social problems: A critical introduction.* New York: Routledge.

Aris, Stephen. 1990. *Sportsbiz: Inside the sports business.* London; United Kingdom: Hutchinson.

Baker, William J. 1988. *Sports in the Western world.* Chicago: University of Illinois Press.

Bale, John. 2004. *Running cultures: Racing in time and space.* New York: Frank Cass Publishers.

Cahn, Susan K. 1994. *Coming on strong.* Cambridge, MA: Harvard University Press.

Coakley, Jay. 2008. *Sports in society: Issues and controversies.* New York: McGraw-Hill.

Csikszentmihalyi, Mihaly. 1990. *Flow: The psychology of optimal experience.* New York: Harper & Row.

Ford, Nicholas and David Brown. 2006. *Surfing and social theory: Experience, embodiment and narrative of the dream glide.* New York: Routledge.

Giulianotti, Richard and Roland Robertson, eds. 2007. *Globalization and sport.* Malden, MA: Blackwell Publishing.

Keys, Barbara. 2006. *Globalizing sport: National rivalry and international community in the 1930s*. Cambridge, MA: Harvard University Press.

Mahony, Daniel F. and Dennis R. Howard. 2001. Sport business in the next decade: A general overview of expected trends. *Journal of Sport Management* 15: 275–96.

Maslow, Abraham. 1968. *Towards a psychology of being*. New York: John Wiley & Sons Inc.

McComb, David G. 2007. *Sports in world history*. UK: Taylor & Francis. Kindle edition.

McDougall, Christopher. 2009. *Born to run: A hidden tribe, superathletes, and the greatest race the world has never seen*. New York: Vintage.

Morrow, Stephen and Catherine Idle. 2008. Understanding change in professional road cycling. *European Sport Management Quarterly* 8(4): 315–35.

Mumford, Stephen. 2012. *Watching sport: aesthetics, ethics and emotion*. New York: Routledge.

Nixon, Howard L. 2008. *Sport in a changing world*. Boulder, CO: Paradigm Publishers.

Rhoden, William. 2006. *Forty million dollar slaves*. New York: Three Rivers Press.

Rosner, Scott R. and Kenneth L. Shropshire. 2004. *The business of sports*. Boston: Jones and Bartlett Publishers.

Silk, Michael L., David L. Andrews, and Cheryl L. Cole, eds. 2005. *Sport and corporate nationalisms*. New York: Berg.

Thibault, Lucie. 2009. Globalization of sport: An inconvenient truth. *Journal of Sport Management* 23: 1–20.

Tomlinson, Alan and Christopher Young, eds. 2006. *National identity and global sports events: Culture, politics, and spectacle in the Olympics and the Football World Cup*. Albany: State University of New York Press.

2

Sport Issues Worldwide

Sport and Politics

Despite the fact that the majority of people hold the belief that sport and politics do not mix, there has never been an instance in which sport and politics have been separate. Defining politics is complex, but at its most basic level, politics is concerned with power. In this light, it is easy to see the primary ways that politics and sport are entwined. Relationships between sport and politics often have the following purposes: (1) provide direct support for sports through government intervention, (2) provide symbolic support for issues of fairness, (3) promote identities and status among disparate groups, and (4) assist in social development. When sport and politics are entwined in each of these ways, different groups have various levels of power and control over how sport is played, who gets to play, and what values are supported through sports participation. Local, state, and national governments; sport-governing bodies, corporations, special interest groups, and individuals carry out these purposes. While complex, examination of these purposes sheds light on the intricate ways that sport and politics are inexorably linked, for better or for worse.

Perhaps the most obvious link between sport and politics is government support for sports participation. Municipal governments are the gatekeepers to sporting events that take place within their jurisdiction. Approving permits for sports events is a major area of control for municipalities. In addition, support in the form of blockades and police protection is standard for such

31

sports events as marathons, triathlons, cyclo-cross, and cycling. At the recreational level, governments play a key role in deciding where people can practice sports. Stadiums, public parks, no-skateboarding signs, skateboard parks, designated trail systems, and fitness stops along paved pathways are ways that governments control where physical activity takes place. Certainly, the role of governments varies nationally and culturally. For instance, in European, African, South American, and Asian countries, elite sport is often developed through government-supported recreational sport. In Scandinavia, national governments provide funds to municipalities for developing sport programs (Bergsgard and Norberg 2010). In turn, municipalities create sport clubs and encourage widespread participation. In the United Kingdom, Sport England is the government agency specifically tasked with promoting health and fitness in this country. Inspired by the London 2012 Olympic Games, Sport England was created with the purpose of leaving a legacy greater than Olympic facilities (Sport England 2011). Its purpose is to change attitudes toward health and increase sports participation. Funding for sports is directly tied to whether or not specific sports reach their target participation rates (Gibson 2011). In this way, the control of money for sports in the United Kingdom lies in the hands of the government. While facilities are often tied to governments in the United States, money for sports programs is primarily provided through private funds. In fact, the United States Olympic Team is the only team in the world supported entirely by private funding. Corporations who sponsor Olympic teams in the United States hold some power as to which sports get what types of funding, which affects participation rates and experiences.

Another link between sport and politics is based on issues of fairness. Political statements about social justice come in the form of boycotts and the inclusionary and exclusionary practices of sport-governing bodies such as the International Olympic Committee (IOC) and the Fédération Internationale de Football (FIFA). Sport boycotts have historically been a way for countries to show either their solidarity with or disapproval of the actions of other nations. For instance, from 1956 to 1988, boycotts occurred at every summer Olympic Games (Global Peace Support Group 2011). The summer Olympic Games in 1992 was the first Olympics to take place without boycotts. In 2011, a boycott was called to raise awareness of the genocide in Sri Lanka (Global Peace Support Group 2011). While they were not suggesting Sri Lanka be denied participation in the Olympics, the Global Peace Support Group was suggesting that they be denied access to major world cricket tournaments. Exclusion and inclusion regarding worldwide sporting events carry major political overtones. South Africa was banned from participation in the Olympic Games beginning in 1964 because of national policies, known as apartheid, designed to segregate people based on race. When South Africa was allowed to compete in the 1992 Olympic Games in Barcelona, it marked the end of a 32-year exclusion and was a significant political move that celebrated the end of apartheid in South Africa. Yet, as Houlihan (2007) suggests, it is unclear what impact these actions have on larger political discourse among nations. He remarks that the actions are symbolic at the time, but few diplomats capitalize on these political symbols. Houlihan suggests that diplomats prefer to make political statements within sport because it is relatively less serious than worldwide "real" issues, which are arguably much more difficult to address. Houlihan also makes the point that some nations may use these tactics as a way to divert attention from more immediate and pressing forms of discrimination within their own countries. Still, there is some feeling that such actions raise awareness and may contribute to citizen pressure for change in the long term.

Additionally, sport has been used as a venue to promote political agendas, including the promotion of identity and status among nations. The Olympics have been tied to national identities since 1906 when athletes competed under nations. In this intermediate Olympics in Greece, athletes marched into the stadium holding national flags, and flags were raised during medal ceremonies. Today, audiences hear the national anthems of all the gold medalists. Also, hosting a worldwide sporting event brings prestige to the hosting country. South Africa's hosting of the World Cup in 2010 was a point of pride. South Africa wanted to showcase their progress since the end of apartheid to the rest of the world. After years of exclusion, this sporting event symbolized worldwide acceptance and was framed as a victory for human justice. The reality is that worldwide competitions such as the Olympics and the World Cup claim to be about international solidarity, but in reality they often accentuate national boundaries and promote national identity and prestige.

Finally, politics in sport take various forms regarding social issues. In the case of the IOC, its public political agenda with respect to social issues is summed up in the Olympic Charter

(2011), which states, "Any form of discrimination with regard to a country or a person on grounds of race, religion, politics, gender or otherwise is incompatible with belonging to the Olympic Movement." Yet, when political relations and corporate sponsorship alliances are at stake, the IOC is less enthusiastic about supporting these ideals. For instance, during the 2008 Olympic Games in Beijing, athletes were asked to refrain from expressing any political views regarding social injustice, especially if it was critical of the Chinese government. Still, the relationship between sport and politics is complex. While critique of China was officially forbidden, the Beijing Olympics ended up being a notable, worldwide stage for raising awareness and making progress with respect to sexuality. In this instance, the personal became the political when Matthew Mitcham became the first openly gay Olympic athlete to win a medal (Outsports 2011). His gold medal made him a public figure, but it was his openly being gay that was political. In the process of becoming an Australian "hero," Mitcham helped tear down stereotypes of male athletes and reshape the relationship between sexuality and sport. Even when the personal has the potential to become the political, many professional athletes are reluctant to speak out. For example, when LeBron James had an opportunity to join an athlete petition regarding the thousands killed and millions displaced in Sudan, he refused. It was China's relations with the Sudanese government that kept James from speaking out. James did not want to upset China, the country where Nike shoes are made. James's position is not unusual in the modern, corporatized sport context in which politics and self-interest are often at odds. In contrast, sports events and organizations often exist precisely for the purpose of addressing social issues. The Gay Games, gay football clubs (soccer) in the United Kingdom (Jones and McCarthy 2010), and the focus on equal opportunity for women in sport as promoted by the United Nations World Conferences are excellent examples of how sport is deliberately aligned with justice issues. The worldwide attention to women's rights via the United Nations's efforts helped secure the inclusion of women's boxing in the London 2012 Olympic Games, making it the first Olympics in its history to have men and women represented in every sport. Although not the dominant form, sport has been, is, and can be used as a political vehicle for social change.

Issues and Controversies with the "Sport for Development" Movement

The Sport for Development or "sport, development and peace" (SDP) movement has been growing steadily since the late 1990s. At its core, SDP is aimed at promoting social betterment and economic growth in poorer countries in which internal conflict has contributed to national unrest and instability (Black 2010, Coalter 2010, Darnell 2010, and Giulionatti 2011). Sport for Development Programs center on bringing divided people together in the context of sport so that they may interact in positive ways (Giulianotti 2011). Other aims include helping youth learn skills of responsibility and teamwork so that they may thrive as adults and eventually become leaders, helping their countries grow in positive directions. The SDP movement has been implemented at all levels. The United Nations backed sport as a means for development in struggling nations in 2003. Then, in 2005, the United Nations dedicated that year to be its International Year of Sport and Physical Education as part of its larger Millennium Development Goals. This support of the United Nations invigorated the widespread inclusion of Sport for Development programs within national development organizations (Black 2010 and Darnell 2010). For instance, governmental agencies such as Norway's Norwegian Agency for Development Cooperation (NORAD), the United Kingdom's Department for International development (DFID), and Canada's Canadian International Development Agency (CIDA) have contributed to these efforts with specific programs in sport (Black 2010). The forms these programs take have involved both top-down and bottom-up or grassroots efforts. Top-down efforts have been associated with the growth of larger scale resources being allocated to the development of sport programs for greater numbers of youth while the bottom-up efforts have focused more on involving the local people in the development of sport. In the bottom-up efforts, the programs' meanings and forms are aligned with the local culture. Even the corporate sector has recently contributed to these efforts . For example, for the years 2007–2009, Nike contributed a total of $315 million to worldwide efforts to improve lives and help build healthier communities worldwide (Nike CR Report 2008).

The common thread among these efforts is the widely held belief that sports are inherently good. In addition to the obvious goal of improving health worldwide, sport scholars suggest that development through sport has gained more footing in recent years due to the ideological attributes associated with sport (Coalter 2010). For instance, the President's Council on Physical Fitness and Sport has highlighted the notion that sports build "character" and promote morality through developing personal and social skills, which consist of hard work, discipline, honesty, generosity, and trustworthiness. Such ideals prevail because sport is unambiguously associated with the idea that sport is a "level" playing field. Such thinking positions sport as apolitical and naturally suited to producing positive experiences through the concept of meritocracy. Several Canadian interns working in Sport for Development programs reflected this attitude and viewed sport as a social site in which inequalities could be transcended, leadership and responsibility could be practiced, and social mobility enhanced (Black 2010).

For all the positives that are attributed to sport and used to promote the SDP movement, sport scholars (e.g., Giulianotti 2011) insist that this movement has failed to take a critical look into the issues that go along with this movement. They claim that these programs might not be achieving what they set out to achieve. First, sport scholars question the notion of "development" itself as an ambiguous term that gets in the way of being able to fully operationalize the mission and vision of these organizations. Second, they claim that the SDP movement is uncoordinated, which leads to issues of sustainability once the initial programs leave. Finally, critical sport scholars assert that these programs only serve to reinforce many of the injustices that they purport to overcome by reinforcing a social and political system that sustains inequality.

According to Jan Nederveen Pieterse (2001), development as a concept has two key features. One feature is that development is initiated with a purpose in mind. In other words, it is a purposeful pursuit that is initiated as an intervention to change the status quo. The second important feature is that development is thought to bring about improvement. Historically, there have been many development programs that followed this framework. Rotary's recent work with the Gates Foundation to eradicate polio is a good example of development interventions in health aimed at improving human conditions for all people. At the same time, development movements have inadvertently served a distinctly destructive purpose. Consider the attempts to "civilize" indigenous peoples through colonization. Beyond the ambiguous definition and practice of development as a concept, the SDP movement has nevertheless been instituted in a variety of ways with the intention of improving human conditions.

One important characteristic of development through sport programs is that they have often been initiated with multiple, seemingly conflicting purposes. Some such efforts as the FIFA 2010 World Cup in South Africa and the 2010 Winter Olympic Games in Vancouver are examples of how countries hoped to parlay the hosting of a large-scale event into positive developmental results for their respective nations and cities while increasing national prestige (Burnett 2010). In each of these nations, governments used these events to initiate large-scale sports programs with multiple aims. These aims included getting more youth participating in sport, addressing internal social concerns, showcasing their country in hopes of increasing tourism, and encouraging business investments. These large-scale efforts have a double-edged quality to them because most SDP programs exist to help poorer nations overcome more socially and politically oriented issues rather than enhance the status of a developed nation. South Africa hoped to use the 2010 World Cup as both an internal as well as external intervention. Sport and Recreation South Africa hoped to show the world that they were improving conditions for all South Africans by establishing the following goals: (1) increase the number of youth participating in sport, (2) minimize the effects of other social inequalities through these youth sport programs, (3) use sport to educate their youth about HIV/AIDS issues as well as reduce crime, and (4) increase their chances of doing well in sport on an international level. Despite public rhetoric about improving internal social conditions, efforts in Canada leading to the 2010 Olympics were much more directed toward national prestige. Canada dedicated over $110 million into the "Own the Podium" campaign, which resulted in the most number of gold medals ever won by Canada in a winter Olympics. Other efforts such as the Mathare Youth Sports Association (MYSA), Right to Play, Athletes for Africa/Gulu Walk, Commonwealth Games Canada (CGC), and International Development through Sport (IDS) operate as small-scale interventions at the local level and are aimed at directly supporting people less privileged. These programs are not without their issues. Sometimes the push for SDP programs results in local residents and sponsoring organizations becoming skeptical because intentions are misinterpreted.

Given these various agendas and the large number of people and organizations involved, SDP programs are often characterized by a high degree of uncoordinated efforts. Such varying efforts serve only to increase the ambiguity surrounding purpose. An example of how efforts can fail due to uncoordinated efforts is South Africa's School Sport Mass Participation Programme during the lead-up to the 2010 World Cup. The School Sport Mass Participation Programme was aimed at increasing sport participation at the broadest level. Sport staff were hired and instructed to introduce this program in local schools. The tensions between the sport staff who were seen as relatively uneducated and the teachers created difficulties in the implementation of this program. In addition, governmental regulations required certain paperwork to be filled in order for students to participate. After an initial increase, many poorer students were not able to fill out the paperwork because of limited support. Failure to comply with the paperwork caused many to drop out of these programs. Thus, coordination between sport organizations, educational institutions, and governmental agencies was lacking, causing these efforts to have limited success. Unfortunately, situations along these lines are not uncommon in SDP global efforts because they involve very complex relationships that are not always anticipated.

Finally, critical sport scholars remind that when well-intentioned "first world" nations reach out to help "third world" countries, the social values and structures they impose may have paradoxical consequences. On the one hand, supporters of SDP programs argue that many of the values they teach are beneficial to struggling communities. When Canadians helped establish sport programs in Africa, they witnessed a positive change in youth. Many participants of the program began to take on more individual responsibility and make better decisions regarding health practices (Black 2010). On the other hand, some scholars suggest that if empowerment and education are presumed to solve the issues of these countries, then other contributors to inequity such as social structures get ignored in the analysis (Darnell 2010 and Giulianotti 2011). Social structures of organized sport are reproduced in these programs, which often reinforce injustices along the lines of gender, sexuality, and race. Some scholars suggest that ignoring these larger social and political aspects of sport for development programs only serves to help participants be better prepared to engage and uncritically believe in these systems that reproduce inequity in other ways. Put simply, SDP programs aimed at bringing people out of unjust and inequitable systems may ironically serve to make them better citizens of an alternate, yet just as inequitable, system.

Several scholars (e.g., Darnell 2010 and Giulianotti 2011) argue that given the ambiguous history of development projects, SDP movements need to be scrutinized in order to ensure that they are benefiting communities. Several strategies have been proposed to avoid many of the pitfalls outlined above. First, the notion that development and global interconnectedness are inevitable suggests that development through sport programs ought to be continued. In other words, doing nothing and opposing these programs is not a viable strategy. Next, improvement as a concept should be considered as local and relational. In many instances, there are local traditions that deal with local issues well. Being able to identify and incorporate these practices into the improvement interventions through sport is key to integrating the "outside" values with the local values. Following this idea, peacemaking and political engagement through sport should be contextual. Coordinating already established local organizations and the intervening sport organizations is paramount to working effectively as well as establishing sustainability. Historically, the programs that emphasized community ownership of the programs have been more successful and long lasting.

The Business of Hosting the Olympic Games

Hosting the Olympic Games is a complex enterprise involving pride, prestige, and money. Most cities are interested in two aspects of undertaking such an endeavor. First, hosting the most prestigious sporting event in the world is about civic pride. Cities bidding on the Olympic Games hope to increase civic pride and prestige by bringing their city to the world's stage. Their hope is that such visibility will eventually translate into increased job opportunities and new business investments in the short run and increased tourism in the long run (Berkes 2010). Second, host cities are often interested in using the Olympic Games as a way to improve the infrastructure of their city. While considerable costs are still incurred by the host city, the influx of corporate and media sponsors often allows cities to build roads, expand public transportation, and improve or build various facilities in a much shorter time frame than they would be able to do with only local money (Cashman 2002). As such, hosting an Olympic Games is a social, political, and economic undertaking. While hosting the Games may turn out to be of social and political benefit, the economic impact of the Olympic Games is much less clear.

Organizations that are interested in promoting business within an area often show that hosting the Olympic Games turns out to be economically beneficial. For instance, when Barcelona hosted the Olympic Games in 1992, the Games were frequently cited as a successful example of how the infrastructural improvements revitalized a city (Cashman 2002). Indeed, in preparation for the Olympics, Barcelona improved roads, airports, sewage systems, and waterfront properties. The athlete's village was part of a renovation project in the harbor that is now prime real estate for homeowners. Also, the commercial zones were improved in this area as well, bringing more business to Barcelona as a Mediterranean port. Atlanta asserts that hosting the 1996 Olympic Games has brought more sporting events there as well. Atlanta boasts the fact that as of 2005, they host more sporting events each year than any other city in the world. In addition, the city's growth has continued since 1996 as more than $2.6 billion have been invested in constructing hotels, office buildings, high-rise residential buildings, and entertainment venues. Finally, PricewaterhouseCoopers estimates that the 2000 Olympic Games in Sydney created $350 million in new business investments and $1.2 billion in postgames infrastructure and service contracts. In addition, the total tourism dollars for Sydney one year post-Olympics was estimated at over $3.2 billion.

The most expensive Olympics to date are the 2008 Olympics in Beijing. China parlayed the Olympic opportunity into vast improvements in infrastructure, buildings, and environmental cleanup (Cummings 2009). Politically, the Beijing Olympics seemed to be about presenting a progressive nation to the world, especially since China had emerged as a world economic power. Final costs are estimated to range from $40 to $50 billion, almost $10–$20 billion over the originally estimated costs. Compared to the $16 billion spent on the 2004 Olympic Games in Athens, the Beijing Olympics marked a significant increase in funds directed toward the most prestigious sporting event. As a city, Beijing gained many new features. Transportation facilities were considerably improved. For instance, many roads were improved, and the new airport terminal provided yet another city benefit. At least $1 billion was spent in cleaning up the environment. Facilities and landscape improvements were other major costs. Around $2.5 billion went toward building stadiums and specific venues, including the Olympic Stadium and Water Cube.

While it remains to be seen whether or not Beijing will benefit economically in the long run, history shows that hosting the Olympics does not always bring prosperity. For instance, Greece is still paying off $11.2 billion from the 2004 Olympic Games while most of their Olympic structures are going into disrepair because maintenance costs exceed what the government can presently afford (Cashman 2002).

Despite improved infrastructure and increased business, scholars suggest that profitability of the Olympics is questionable because predictions of profitability during the bidding process rarely pan out, and post-Olympic studies are not thorough enough to assess real economic impact (Crompton 2006 and Kirkup and Major 2006). In particular, scholars point out that accounting procedures used in the bidding process always favor hosting the Olympics because it is always in the potential host city's interest. For instance, construction costs are often moved to the benefits side of the ledger, showing that they are an infrastructural benefit rather than a real cost to taxpayers. Monies paid by federal and local governments toward the Olympic Games are shown as income by the organizing committee rather than expenses to the taxpayer. Other tactics include not showing certain expenses at all or moving them to other budgets. For instance, the Olympics of the past three decades show on paper that they have been profitable events. Profitability is created on official reports by including only the operating costs of the 16-day period of the Olympics compared to total revenue. The costs for pre-Olympics infrastructure are detailed in a different budget. Such accounting practices show the Olympic Games to be an economically sound investment; however, after the fact, the only Olympic Games to actually be profitable has been the 1984 Olympics in Los Angeles.

Another reason that the Olympic Games are likely to be a net loss has to do with timeline (Kirkup and Major 2006). The bidding process for the Olympic Games must occur years prior to the actual vote. The actual vote occurs nine years prior to the Olympics for which they are bidding. The bidding process itself is an expensive undertaking. For example, both Sydney 2008 and London 2012 spent approximately $25 million on the bid alone. As seen in such recent Olympics as Salt Lake City and Sydney, some of these costs are directed toward wooing IOC members. Many host cities also employ people who specialize in bridging "cultural" barriers in order to have the committee members better understand the host city. As Olympic Games scholar Helen Lenskyj points out, these people are essentially hired to gain votes for their city because of their personal connections to IOC members. Practices in the bidding process that have recently gone under scrutiny are the large amounts of money that bidding cities give to smaller countries in the name of improving sport within their respective countries. Lenskyj (2000) argues that these funds are nothing less than monetary bribes for votes. Once the Games are awarded, construction and preparations begin. With almost a decade passing between bidding for and hosting the actual event, construction costs almost always rise dramatically, increasing the actual costs by significance percentages. A case in point is the construction costs for the London 2012 Olympic Games. At present, the Olympic Stadium is costing at least 50 percent more than originally budgeted from an original estimate of $22 million to $35 million. Other venues are similarly affected. In addition, venues for the Vancouver 2010 Olympic Games had a similar rise in costs due to an energized economy. Facility construction costs increased by C$195 million, a significant increase given the original estimate of C$470 million made in 2002 (Bobby 2010).

Given the rising costs of Olympics, it is becoming more difficult for smaller nations and cities to host an Olympic Games (Silk, Andrews, and Cole 2005). One reason for the rising costs is the dramatic expansion of the Olympics. Participation has increased exponentially from 1980s to the present with the addition of sports, increased opportunities for women, and the increase in participating nations. For instance, from the 1984 Los Angeles Olympics to the 2008 Beijing Olympics, the total number of events increased from 226 to 312 (Coakley 2008). Events for women went from 73 to 137, and the total number of nations competing increased from 140 nations to 204 (Coakley 2008). The demands of the IOC also increase costs. The IOC requires outstanding transportation, accommodation, and venue operations. Such demands often require extensive infrastructure improvements as noted above. Smaller cities often struggle with the cost of these requirements. For instance, the light rail improvements promised as part of the Torino 2006 winter Olympics bid have yet to be realized.

Rising costs of the Olympic Games result in higher fees for corporate sponsorship and media rights (Berkes 2010). For instance, The Olympic Partner (TOP) program allows sponsors to use the Olympic rings in advertising. During the Vancouver Olympics, there were nine corporate sponsors at this level. While companies do not reveal actual numbers, the minimum amount needed to be a TOP sponsor is $20 million per year. Companies like Proctor and Gamble, Coca-Cola, and McDonald's have been involved for many years. Some studies suggest that there is a short-term increase in sales when companies advertise at this level, but long-term effects are less easily attributable to Olympic investment. It also appears that the United States contributes more in corporate sponsorship than any other country. United States sponsorship support for Beijing was more than double than all the European countries combined. In addition, the media rights continue to increase, which partly drives advertising costs. The broadcasting rights for the 1996 Atlanta Olympic Games were $456 million compared to the $2 billion that NBC paid to cover the Vancouver 2010 winter Olympics (Olympics and Television 2012).

The Controversy and Complexity of Performance Enhancing Drugs in Sport

While performance enhancing drugs (PEDs) appear to be a concern of the modern era, PEDs have been part of elite sport since the ancient Olympic Games (Mazanov 2008). During and after World War II, the nation-state rivalries brought forth widespread use of PEDs among elite athletes. Initial concern over fairness turned into a health concern when several elite athletes died in the 1960s (Mazanov 2008). In response to these untimely deaths, the Olympic Movement instituted an anti-doping policy. These efforts were handed over to the World Anti-Doping Agency (WADA). WADA was founded in 1999 as an independent agency under the IOC's initiative but funded through the sport movement and national governments (WADA 2011). Its purpose is to coordinate worldwide efforts to educate and enforce the anti-doping code. WADA also maintains the list of banned substances and methods (WADA 2011). Although performance enhancing drug use is historically not new, there are complex cultural and social sensibilities that give rise to PED usage being one of the most controversial aspects of modern elite sports.

Key arguments used to support anti-doping efforts are based on the notions of naturalness, health, and fairness (Hemphill 2009). Elite sport is predicated on the idea that athletes are testing natural abilities. PEDs are considered "unnatural" because they are foreign substances introduced into the body to achieve a higher level of performance than could be achieved in a "natural" state. From this view, PED use is considered immoral because it interferes with the naturalness that is implied in competition. Additionally, anti-doping efforts are defensible because the use of PEDs may create short- and/or long-term health issues, the most serious being death. As such, sport authorities feel a legal obligation under tort law's "duty of care" to uphold anti-doping efforts. Finally, antidrug proponents often frame PED usage as an issue of fairness. That is, the use of PEDs breaks a mutual understanding that implies athletes are duty bound to abide by rules of the game, which strongly rely on the notion of a "level playing field." The use of PED is effectively a rule violation on the grounds that users have changed the conditions under which all other athletes have agreed to play. As such, users have transgressed in two ways: by gaining an unfair advantage and by breaking implicit rules.

Others contend that these key arguments are tightly constructed around loose terms. In other words, there is inherent difficulty in determining what is natural, healthy, or fair (Hemphill 2009). First, the question of natural versus unnatural does not seem to hold the same level of concern when considering the use of prescription and over-the-counter drugs. For instance, the use of "unnatural" prescription drugs in daily life raises no question of morality while usage of unnatural substances in sport elicits moral judgment. The inconsistent use of natural and unnatural weakens the argument against PED use. Second, the definition of "health" is easily questioned with respect to elite athletes. It is difficult to define what health means for athletes as they push their bodies, experience injury, and are asked to "risk" their bodies. In other words, is it hypocritical to argue against PED in the name of health when many other practices of elite sport could be considered unhealthy? Finally, the fairness argument is similarly incongruous. Given that there are so many other inequalities in sport along the lines of access to training methods and facilities, sports medicine, technological advances, high-level coaching, and funding and support from sport organizations, why should PED use be singled out?

The controversy becomes more complex when looking at the notion of self-determination. Self-determination is a concept that values individual effort. It implies that taking on all challenges using one's own resilience, perseverance, and hard work is noble. On the one hand, the use of PEDs would take away this basic value because a foreign substance effectively replaces the "self." Simply put, one would not be self-determined but rather "substance"-determined if PED use were allowed. On the other hand, elite sport is predicated on the idea that athletes are pushing the limits of performance. If PED usage could enhance recovery, strength, and rehabilitation, then it is argued that such usage would help, not hinder, an athlete's self-determination. In this view, anti-doping policies restrict an athlete's personal self-determination in their efforts to reach their own personal limits of performance.

PED usage is controversial among athletes. Some athletes believe that PED usage is unnecessary for top-level performance (Judge et al. 2010). They also believe that the number of athletes using PEDs is far greater than the number of athletes who get caught, which is around 2–3 percent (Opaszowski 2008). In 1995, a poll was conducted of Olympic athletes, in which 198 of them were asked if they would take PEDs if they knew they would not get caught *and* would win. All but three athletes said they would take the drugs (Bamberger and Yaeger 1997). A similar question was asked of collegiate athletes a decade later without the guarantee of winning, and over 80 percent said they would not take PEDs (Judge et al. 2010). Are sentiments changing in support of anti-doping efforts, or are athletes saying one thing and doing another? The rate at which professional baseball players constantly move on and off the suspended list for use of banned substances (MLB 2011) and the continued controversy surrounding drug use in professional cycling (Tucker and Dugas 2007) point rather solidly toward the latter. Certainly, the sport context in which athletes compete and personal desires influence athletes' approval and use of PEDs.

Among the general public, there is a pervasive sense that PEDs are immoral (Mazanov 2008, Morgan 2009, and Opaszowski 2008), but this sense is not without its own controversy. Morgan

(2009) reminds us that the media, who reports transgressions and criminalizes athletes in the process, feels obligated to appeal to this perceived sense of morality with respect to PEDs because they are a powerful special interest group within sport. The media makes billions of dollars reporting sport events and wants to ensure continued support from fans. Yet, Morgan also points out that there may be a disconnect between what these sport entities say and what the general public really thinks about PEDs. He thinks the general public may be shifting in their tolerance of PED use. He notes that PED use has become a more accepted practice in general, citing the increased use of amphetamines, low doses of testosterone, Prozac, and beta-blockers (e.g., for musicians who have stage fright) to improve performance in all realms of life including educational, personal, and professional lives. He then argues that the public is highly accepting of PED usage because of their admiration and demand for extraordinary athletic performances. Pointing out examples from 300-pound linebackers to the pace at which cyclists ride during the 21-day Tour de France, Morgan makes the case that these athletic bodies could not exist without PEDs. He argues that no one is calling for the reduction in size of football players nor are they calling for the end of the Tour de France. More important, he observes that the public has made no indication that they are enjoying these performances less.

Aside from issues of language pliability and metaphysical matters, pragmatic and social perspectives complicate the matter of PEDs even further. For instance, enforcing the banned substance list is daunting. The work involved is complex, involving problems with detection, reliability, financial costs, and privacy issues (Opaszowski 2008). Also, many substances such as Human Growth Hormone (HGH) are problematic because they already occur naturally within the body (Judge et al. 2010). Furthermore, the anti-doping efforts are singularly aimed at individual athletes. But Hemphill (2009) makes the case that athletes exist in very complex social structures consisting of sport scientists, nation-states, and corporate sponsors. The pressure to win emanating from these groups often rationalizes PED use. For instance, the culture of professional cycling has historically accepted drug use (Tucker and Dugas 2007). In addition, cyclists contend that this historical reality combined with more and more pressure to win makes PEDs a necessity to sustain the training required to be competitive, let alone win. Brown (1980) suggests that PED usage is essentially a social construct in which collective attitudes should determine which substances are acceptable and which are not. Morgan (2009) puts forth a cogent argument for a return to the treatment-enhancement distinction when demarcating the line between acceptable and unacceptable drugs and practices. He suggests that as long as PED use can be associated with treatment or healing, then they should be acceptable. If PED use is strictly associated with enhancement of performance, then it should remain on the banned list. Both scholars suggest that PED usage is a matter of deciding what is acceptable and what is not, according to specific understandings of what constitutes enhancement. They argue that PED usage is so complex that it needs to be constantly negotiated and determined by specific sport communities in ways that fit with their sport values at the time.

Technology in Sports: Tilting the Competitive Balance for Better and/or Worse

Similar to the debates regarding PEDs, discussions about technological advances in sport revolve around restorative versus enhancing and the natural versus artificial distinctions. In other words, are technological advances being used to help athletes gain or regain abilities, or are technologies being used to enhance performances? The answer seems to be a resounding yes to both questions, but the nuances of each answer reveals the complex controversies regarding technology and sport.

In many ways, technology tilts the competitive balance for the better when it opens up sport possibilities to people who otherwise would be left out. High-end prosthetics design firms have been making limbs that allow people to run, turn, and twist with agility (Adelson 2011). These companies are making it possible for youth and adults not only to engage in sports but also to be able to do so at fairly high levels so that competitive sport becomes a reality for persons otherwise "disabled." Technology is making it possible for more people to regain lost abilities, essentially making sport more inclusive. From another vantage point, technology is also allowing athletes to play safer and longer. Enhanced helmet technology has made it possible to reduce the number of concussions occurring in youth sports (Willis 2009). Improved scientific understanding of biomechanics through technological analyses is revolutionizing the way athletes train, often resulting in more humane ways of training, keeping them less injured, or decreasing the time injured through faster recovery methods (Willis 2009). In short, technology keeps more athletes training more of the time.

The issue of unfair advantage becomes increasingly complex when boundaries are unclear as to what constitutes enhancement technology or simply normal advances in technology. For example, such video game style simulators as the Thunder PlayAction Simulator and such analytical/tactical enhanced analysis systems as Dartfish allow athletes to practice plays, develop strategies, and self-critique movements in order to refine skills. The NFL and several universities are using these technologies to enhance athletes' training (Willis 2009). On one level, this technology could be considered a normal progression in sport technology that keeps players safe. These virtual sport worlds allow more "playing time" without the physical fatigue or risk of injury due to overtraining. On another level, they could be considered purely enhancing technologies. Advances in equipment technologies pose other issues of fairness. Special surfaced swim caps and more buoyant swimsuits are transforming swimming. Records have fallen dramatically since the introduction of these crucial pieces of equipment, but controversy remains as some of these swimsuits have been banned. Swimming is only one of many sports making use of improved equipment to gain a competitive advantage. The clap skate in speed skating revolutionized skating. Following its widespread use, skating records dropped so significantly that now everyone in the sport uses them. Even shoes have radically changed over the years. The introduction of carbon-sole shoe implants, which harness energy that might otherwise be lost in a runner's stride, is pushing the boundaries in athletics as to what is fair versus unfair advantage. One concern that is often overlooked when considering the fairness of technology is that these advanced products are expensive. To what extent are wealthy countries gaining an unfair advantage over poorer ones?

Other technological advances begin to feel as though one is solidly entering the "natural" versus "artificial" debate. For instance, blood doping is highly controversial (Munthe 2000).

Typically, blood doping is the process whereby the athlete withdraws her/his own blood when red blood cells are at a peak. Then, they reintroduce these blood cells prior to a critical competition in order to increase the blood's capacity for carrying oxygen. Although it is the athlete's own blood, blood doping is banned because it is viewed as an artificial process. Some athletes change their environment to enhance training. For example, the famous Norwegian Nordic skier and the most successful Nordic skier in history lived in a "low oxygen, low pressure house." Today, endurance athletes can rent or buy altitude tents that allow athletes at sea level to sleep at altitude, achieving similar results of more efficient oxygen uptake, lower resting pulse, and increased VO2 max.

Perhaps the most notable controversy with respect to technology and sport is the story of Oscar Pistorius, a South African sprinter. Born without tibias in either of his legs, Pistorius uses carbon prosthetics called the Cheetah Flex-Foot (Adelson 2011). Pistorius has competed in several Paralympic Games, but it was not until 2007 that he was allowed to run with able-bodied athletes. A ruling shortly afterward by the International Association of Athletics Federations (IAAF) banned Pistorius from competing alongside able-bodied athletes. The rationale was that the prosthetics gave Pistorius a 10-meter advantage in a 400-meter race. This decision was based on tests conducted in a lab in Germany. The Court of Arbitration for Sport overturned the IAAF's ruling, and Pistorius was allowed to compete for a spot on the 2008 Olympic Team. He missed making the team in 2008. Currently, Pistorius is vying for a 2012 Olympic Team spot and is on track for earning a position as the first paralympic athlete to compete in the Olympics (Vellur 2011). He must record a qualifying time within three months of the 2012 Olympic Games in order to be the first Paralympian to compete as an Olympian.

The arbitrary lines drawn to demarcate what is or is not allowable are continually contested. Andy Miah, a bioethicist, asserts that sports are about "higher, faster, stronger." He argues that this desire drives the pace at which technology is adopted into competitive sport, a pace which he contends is much faster than sport-governing bodies and that the public can currently process on ethical, cultural, and moral levels (Adelson 2011). Miah speculates that eventually high-performance athletes will need to have engineered body parts in order to remain competitive. The Swedish scholar, Jonsson (2010), posits that ultimately sport organizations and the public will have to negotiate what it means to be human. Jonsson claims that the "cyborg" athlete, perhaps reconstructed mechanically as well as genetically, is not far off, and that "cyborg" identities can only be constructed around the notion that the technologically enhanced human is authentic. Jonsson also argues that "cyborg" identities could eradicate social injustices along the lines of gender, race, and ethnicity by making these constructs nonissues. In this case, he asserts that these reconsidered humans would be competing in the purest form of sport because the athleticism, embodied in this new form, would be the defining factor in competition, not other variables. On the one hand, the reality of this future requires major paradigm shifts. On the other hand, the reality may arrive by the imperceptible redrawing of lines between what is and is not allowed over time.

Globalization of Sport: Intersections with Race and Ethnicity

Globalization is occurring as transnational corporations and national corporations try to capitalize on the world as a market. These economic movements have been no less felt in the sport world. The rise in the number of countries participating in global events has soared. In fact, the IOC and FIFA each have memberships larger than the United Nations. The IOC has 203 affiliate countries, and FIFA has 208 national members, outnumbering the United Nation's 192 members (Thibault 2009). In these respects, sport as a cultural phenomenon has more influence globally than the international body responsible for creating peace among countries. In fact, the Vatican established a sport department in 2004 under Pope John Paul II because of the recognition that sports was of cultural significance.

Globalization has made sport much more diverse than it was a couple of decades ago (Thibault 2009). Coupled with technology and ease of transportation, this trend has resulted in more countries participating in sports to which they previously had little access. For instance, countries such as Jamaica began competing in the bobsled at the 1988 Winter Olympic Games. Australia produced a speed skating champion due to indoor skating facilities. Snow domes built in such countries as Dubai allow their athletes opportunities to compete in winter sports. Muslim women are more able to compete internationally than in previous years. In these ways, the power of sport to bring together people of diverse nationalities, religions, gender, race, and ethnicities is clear.

While sport has been the site of much progress with respect to bringing diverse people together, it has simultaneously been the site of continued inequalities, especially along the lines of race and ethnicity (Coakley 2008). Before looking at some of these complexities, it is important to establish what is exactly meant by race and ethnicity. Race is often used to denote physical differences such as skin color, which becomes the basis for explaining other differences such as character or innate physical abilities. Although physiologists continue to attempt to explain performance differences among racially diverse athletes, there have been no studies that confirm there are genetic or muscular differences between races. In fact, all evidence proves the opposite. Thus, race as a category has no biological basis other than skin color. Instead, purported racial differences are rooted in sociological and ideological constructs (Coakley 2008 and Spracklen 2008). While ethnicity is used to indicate cultural differences, ethnicity and race are often entwined in complex ways. For instance, such ethnic groups as African, West Indian, and Haitian are often grouped together as part of the racial category of black (Spracklen 2008). Culture is not entirely ethnic either. It is often based on education, social status, profession, forms of play, political affiliations, and more. Thus, race and ethnicity as social constructs are complex categories that interconnect in intricate ways.

Despite no biological basis for race and the complexities involved in identifying ethnicity, race and ethnicity remain powerful organizing ideologies in society. Ideology around race and ethnicity shape the way we interact with each other in conscious and subconscious ways. As social constructs, race and ethnicity are "felt" through processes of privilege and marginalization (Coakley 2008 and Van Riemsdijk 2010). They are implicated in all our relationships, and sport is no exception. Van Riemsdijk suggests that "melting pot" is an inadequate metaphor to explain the diversity found in sport. Instead, he points out that a "kaleidoscope" more accurately represents the ways sport leaders, employees, athletes, spectators, and affiliates are grouped in sport. In other words, while there is a greater general mix of races and ethnicities, individual groupings with variable access to power and privilege remain. An important insight about how these discriminatory behaviors emerge comes from "whiteness" studies. This scholarly work (e.g., Van Riemsdijk 2010) considers the invisibility of whiteness and the unspoken privileges that come along with it. As "white" is the dominant group, this group has access to power and privilege. The benefits of whiteness include the structural and ideological reproduction of "white" as the preferred race with respect to positions of leadership and power in sport. As a result, people of color largely remain limited to positions as players while whites can more easily be both players and leaders in sport.

In order to improve the conditions of marginalized groups in sport, it is important to highlight some of the practices that keep whites in positions of power. For example, Major League Baseball (MLB) has worked hard at increasing the presence of Latino players (Vargas 2004). Such impetus has meant more exhibition and regular season games in such countries as Venezuela, Cuba, the Dominican Republic, and Mexico. Along with these greater opportunities for Latino players has been the development of baseball academies in Latin American countries. While these academies may enhance Latinos' involvement in baseball, they also are locations of MLB exploitation. For instance, many MLB teams own these academies for hiding talent. They offer baseball training to players as young as 12 years in order to keep other teams from acquiring them. The numbers of youth offered a place at the academies is very high, but most are dismissed after two years. The issue lies in the MLB's sense of responsibility toward these young players. While at these academies, athletes receive little to no education. Thus, when they are let go, they are behind other children in terms of school. In addition, while there are exceptions, the conditions are poor in most of the academies located in Venezuela and the Dominican Republic. The housing is often unsanitary, nutrition is neglected, water is often contaminated, and access to medical attention is very limited. In this way, Latino players are viewed as commodities that bring talent to an MLB team but are offered little else. Even the sense of upward mobility that playing for an MLB team might inspire is mediated by not being able to speak English and isolating practices by white team members. Thus, even if they make it to the Major Leagues, the social experiences of the players remains problematic. Furthermore, this system reproduces the idea that Latinos are good players and tacitly precludes Latinos from any leadership position. In other words, the system limits the extent to which Latinos can be involved in baseball.

In addition to structural systems that reproduce racism, ideology is another force that gives rise to a "new racism" at work (Gill 2011). "New racism" is a term used to describe the growing positive media attention given to athletes of color while ignoring other social inequities. For instance, no longer is it acceptable to segregate athletes of color from whites. Instead, other forms of racism emerge as previous forms become unacceptable. A good example of how white privilege is maintained through ideology in sport is the increasing inclusion of Indigenous players in Australian football (Halliman and Judd 2009). In the case of the Australian Football League (AFL), Indigenous players receive accolades for their physical abilities in the media. The emphasis on these athletes' "natural" quickness and skill continues to provide limiting views of what Indigenous people can do. The more positive comments regarding physical abilities of Indigenous players the media produces, the more fixed their identities become in the eyes of Australians. Furthermore, a recent study revealed that Indigenous players were often assigned noncentral field positions, which were thought to require more speed and quickness. Overrepresentation of Indigenous players in the AFL in general and periphery positions subconsciously reproduces the view that Indigenous players are not suited to leadership positions such as coaching or ownership (Halliman and Judd 2009). Put simply, the view that indigenous players are so "natural" at Australian football implies that they might not be well suited to decision-making responsibilities required of coaches. Such ideas are often reflected in what most people consider as nonracist ways of framing Indigenous players. The general Australian public has openly mentioned that Indigenous players may not be comfortable in positions requiring more than physical skills. Furthermore, the attitude that Indigenous players are not interested in money or acquiring more leadership positions is the norm.

In sum, race and ethnicity are social constructs that put into motion very real opportunities and constraints for those involved in sport at the global level. White privilege perpetuates the demographic of sport leadership through new forms of racism. The systems in place for finding new talent globally often restrict minority athletes to player positions. In addition, the kind of media attention given to minority athletes only serves to reinforce notions that people of color might make great players, but they are not equally qualified as leaders. As such, the business of sport remains in the hands of relatively few, mostly white males. To counteract this reproduction of power relations, it is important that unhealthy conditions for minority athletes be revealed and that sport institutions be held accountable for wrongdoings. The media should highlight both physical and intellectual skills equally among white and minority athletes. Finally, perhaps raising awareness about white privilege is another avenue toward change.

Masculinity: What's Sport Got To Do with It?

Worldwide, most people believe that sport has socio-positive outcomes. Most people would agree that sports participation enhances valued such social qualities as teamwork, perseverance, and leadership. While women's participation in sport has increased exponentially in recent decades, scholars agree that sport has historically been and remains a site though which men gain masculine capital (see, for example, Anderson 2009, Coakley 2008, Gee 2009, Pringle and Hickey 2010, Goig 2008, and Messner 2007). Masculine capital is acquired by displaying more behaviors and attitudes associated with masculinity, resulting in more acceptance and privilege. The more men engage in behaviors and ostensibly carry attitudes that gain them more masculine capital, the more they are rewarded with social acceptance, power positions, and a feeling that they are living out the correct script of what it means to be a man. In contrast, fewer displays of masculinity or displays associated with femininity reduce privilege and often result in marginalization. Men who engage in behaviors and attitudes that reduce their masculine capital or even question their masculinity are placed into a lower social standing; subjected to emotional battering through teasing; and, in extreme instances, physically abused to the point of death. Behaviors and attitudes that contribute positively to men's masculine capital are (1) displays of power and dominance, (2) demonstrations of strength and muscularity, (3) suppressing emotions, (4) expressing misogynistic attitudes, and (5) overt displays of heterosexuality. These behaviors and attitudes can be considered "orthodox masculinity" (Anderson 2009). It is easy to see how sport is an ideal site in which to gain masculine capital as many of these behaviors are embedded in, and indeed are, an essential part of sport. While sport may be a socio-positive activity on some levels, sport's strong alignment with masculinity perpetuates certain inequalities, narrows the construction of both masculinity and femininity, and encourages risk taking across cultures.

The masculinity-sport relationship is rarely criticized but rather simply considered "normal." The process that maintains this relationship is known as hegemonic masculinity. This process involves giving hierarchical privilege to behaviors that are deemed to closely approximate orthodox masculinity. It is a process by which "normal" comes to be defined. In many sports, aggressiveness, strength, muscularity, and physical domination are "normal" sport behaviors. This remains one of the primary reasons that sport continues to be recognized as an ideal site for boys and men to gain masculine capital. Yet, such "normalcy" associated with this particular version of masculinity creates inequalities in sport. For instance, while these behaviors are "normal" for highly physical team sports such as American football, rugby, ice hockey, and such high-risk sports as extreme skiing, they are not necessarily "normal" for figure skating, rhythmic gymnastics, or archery. As such, sports acquire hierarchical status. Some sports are deemed "real" sports and considered ideal for gaining masculine capital. Contact sports gain higher status than those sports with less visible aggression and contact. Highly valued sports are those that clearly demonstrate physical superiority. The competitive form of sport is more valued than recreational sport. Privileges that come with participating in sports at the top of this hierarchy are more media coverage, opportunities to play professionally, and better monetary rewards for doing so. Other sports are regarded less "real" and do not contribute nearly as well to masculine capital. Some sports are considered feminine, and men participating in these types of sports frequently have their masculinity questioned. Other inequalities emerge as the masculine-sport alliance intersects with race, ethnicity, and social class. While specific issues along these lines are discussed in subsequent sections and chapters, the important point is that males are stratified via the masculine capital they acquire (or not) through their participation in sport.

The masculinity-sport alliance reproduces narrow constructions of gender already present in society. Although the attributes of orthodox masculinity reinforced through sport vary in emphasis across cultures, the masculinity-sport alliance remains strong worldwide. This alliance is often used to promote ideas about gender expectations. In Japan, sport frequently promotes specific gender roles, preparing young men for work and family life and reinforcing the social order and behaviors that are ultimately expected of Japanese men and women. A respected collegiate rowing program in Japan illustrates how sport contributes to the social order. As participants expressed in one study, one of the aims of the rowing club is to develop what is known in Japan as the "salary man's" identity (MacDonald 2009). This identity is shaped by, and dependent upon, hierarchical relationships determined by age and experience. To facilitate this development and understanding, students run the entire rowing program. Seniors are the leaders and mentor juniors, who in turn carry on the traditions and mentor juniors when they are seniors. Training regimes are passed down from generation to generation. Rowing provides men with experience of the social hierarchy expected in the Japanese workplace. In addition, the valued Japanese qualities of collective identity and harmony are also developed, which shapes these young men into valued male adults (MacDonald 2009). For instance, respect is gained through commitment to the group and displays of hard work. One example MacDonald (2009) cites is the respect that a less-talented rower gains simply because he is dedicated to the team. By always showing up for practice and working harder than almost anyone else, this less-talented rower is respected as much as the winning rowers. In this way, being the best is not a prerequisite for respect but rather adherence to the Japanese expectations for men.

Furthermore, gender roles in rowing show how the Japanese masculine identity is enhanced by its relational position to that of the feminine identity (MacDonald 2009). The female rowers are separated from the male rowers on many levels. They do not live at the boathouse like the men. They follow their own training regimen, relying on male coaches outside their institution. Their attitudes toward rowing are significantly different than that of the male rowers in that rowing is a fun distraction reserved for college. They talk of looking forward to becoming wives and engaging in family life. In addition, female presence in the men's boathouse serves to further reinforce particular notions of gender. Women serve as managers for the male rowers. Their primary duty is to make meals for the male rowers. They spend most of the afternoon and early evening at the boathouse. Their significant presence at the boathouse performing duties associated with homemaking supports narrow expectations of both masculinity and femininity.

Islamic young men also value sport as a way to reinforce their culturally based masculine identities. In Islamic boarding schools, sports participation helps young men align their religious views with cultural/religious expectations in order to secure their identity as Islamic men (Farooq and Parker 2009). In particular, the young men in Farooq and Parker's study expressed that through sport, they developed physical strength, emotional control, and discipline—all of which are valued characteristics according to Islamic religious/cultural views. Muslims believe that the body is a gift from God and should be respected and properly cared for. Developing muscularity and physical strength through sport was one way these young men took care of their bodies. Also, the boys liked the multiple opportunities that sport provided for them to learn emotional control. Letting one's feelings get out of control in sports resulted in poor play and less teamwork, which was looked down upon. Finally, the boys appreciated the rules and regulations in sport. Adhering to these rules helped the boys feel as though they were practicing discipline to a high degree. They placed high value on fair play and tended to deemphasize winning. It is not as though other aspects of schooling did not reinforce these values, but the belief that the mind and body were integrated in physical movement increased the salience of sport (Farooq and Parker 2009).

Participating in sport is not the only means through which masculinity and gender roles are reinforced. Powerful cultural messages regarding orthodox masculinity are reproduced through being a sports fan and in sports advertising. In Spain, Goig (2008) found that not only do young men engage in competitive soccer to demonstrate their manhood, but also fathers take their sons to games to witness a specific type of masculinity. Goig found that fathers enthusiastically praised aggressive behavior on the field and verbalized hostility toward opponents. Fathers felt proud of their behaviors as spectators because it allowed them to model aggressiveness and emotional dominance through anger at the officials, demands for more aggressive play from the players, and hostility toward opposing team fans. In addition, sport media often reinforces similar messages. Gee (2009) followed the development of the "Inside the Warrior" campaign created to reinvigorate the NHL. The 2005 campaign deliberately incorporated Chinese warrior imagery and language to frame the game and the players. In sum, Gee notes that

> The element of physicality is evident in the "Inside the Warrior" campaign through clips of vigorous body checking, power skating, and forceful slap shots, and is indicative of naturalizing and glamorizing (to the point of Hollywoodizing) not just violence per se, but a form of violent masculinity and the specific use of men's bodies as weapons/targets (Messner, 1990). This further substantiates a powerful discourse of masculinity that is historically entrenched in, socially constructed through, and culturally reinforced by the game of hockey. (592)

Sexism is often embedded in the masculinity message in order to reproduce the dominant gender order. In one of the "Inside the Warrior" ads, a woman dressed in a white sports bra and white sheer robe attended to the player's needs before he headed out on the ice. Her purpose was to dress the "warrior" for "battle." The ad showed her dressing the player for the game. She remained in the background as he headed out onto the ice with loud cheers from the fans. Certainly the imagery was exaggerated and remained grounded in a story of mythological proportions; it nonetheless served as a visual reminder of orthodox masculinity to which men are supposed to aspire.

An inseparable link between masculinity and sports comes in the form of risk taking. In order to display toughness, athletes engage in all kinds of behaviors that risk their own health and bodies. While risk behaviors come in a multitude of forms, violence against the self through sport participation and excessive drinking in association with sports teams are common. Violence against the self occurs when athletes push their bodies past the point of training effect or when they are likely to become severely injured. The Japanese rowers valued training and racing to the point of exhaustion (MacDonald 2009). Training took place over 10 months and occurred 6 days per week. Rowers were expected to put in these exhausting hours and hard work. Doing particularly hard workouts was a sign of masculinity even when such training did not make sense physiologically according to periodization principles (MacDonald 2009). Also, Spanish soccer players were encouraged to go out and play hard even if they were injured or exhausted. Coaches controlled these settings and thought that pushing the athletes in this way made them "men" (Goig 2008). Excessive drinking is another form of risk taking frequently encouraged in sport. During post regatta celebrations, the Japanese rowers regularly engaged in excessive drinking. Being able to drink large amounts of alcohol despite throwing up was deemed admirable and provided another way that freshman could gain respect. Such behaviors were also common in rugby (Pringle and Hickey 2010). Pringle and Hickey found that initiation rites consisted of forcing a newcomer to "shotgun" a beer immediately postgame. Unfortunately, neither putting your own body through unnecessary pain nor filling it with alcohol enhances sport performance. In fact, these risk-taking behaviors jeopardize sport performance, but they offer sport participants more opportunities to reinforce their masculinity.

Recent studies have found that there are even more significant costs to using sport as a social site for reinforcing masculinity (Anderson 2009 and Pringle and Hickey 2010). Sport creates powerful in-groups and out-groups. The social "costs" of not living up to the dominant forms of masculinity reinforced through sport are high. Less-skilled male sports participants suffer derogatory labels such as "girl," "pansie," pussie," and poofta" (Pringle and Hickey 2010, 117). Name calling is particularly likely when boys express emotions, especially when they cry. Research shows that both girls and boys have needs to express emotions in various ways as children (Anderson 2009). Yet, as boys become more socialized along the lines of orthodox masculinity, they are stigmatized for crying. Sport is powerful place in which young boys are socialized *not* to cry for fear of becoming part of the out-group. Furthermore, these labels and overt disapproval of emotional outbursts place women in a subordinate position.

Yet, the process of hegemonic masculinity is not uniformly experienced. There are many ways in which men refuse to be part of this process. By behaving in ways that do not fit orthodox masculinity, some men are part of the resistance that continually expands what it means "to be a man." Pringle and Hickey's study (2010) showed how men consciously refused to push their bodies past limits, partake in drinking rituals, and use sexist language or be complicit in its usage. The men interviewed showed the various ways they questioned hypermasculine behaviors associated with their sports. These men consciously separated themselves from those types of sporting environments, helped create more equitable sporting spaces, and spoke out against such hypermasculine behaviors. Also, Goig's (2008) research revealed that on playgrounds at elementary schools, Spanish boys were not nearly as aggressive. Goig attributed these less-aggressive behaviors to the fact that female teachers were present and that soccer games included both boys and girls. Other research (Anderson 2009) has shown that the presence of women helps lessen aggressive tendencies of men. Furthermore, as the globalization of sport ensues, media language describing men's ice hockey is not emphasizing warlike language as much. Talented NHL players drafted from Europe are being hired because they possess finesse and superb technical skills (Gee 2009). In the media, their finesse and technical skills are highlighted as well. While fighting is part of hockey and the warrior motif is still applicable, the addition of technical language is one way that hockey masculinity may be expanding.

Finally, asserting one's heterosexuality is perhaps one of the strongest signifiers of masculinity. For boys and men in sport, to be gay or affiliated with gays challenges orthodox masculinity (Anderson 2010). Boys and men have such a narrow range of behaviors that are associated with proving their heterosexuality that they often overcompensate. Using "gay" as a derogatory label, expressing disapproval of gays, or resorting to violence against gays or anyone who associates with gays become common ways athletes confirm their masculinity (Anderson 2010). Anderson was the first openly gay high school coach in the United States and has a plethora of stories that illustrate the above. One notable occasion was when a male member of Anderson's high school cross-country team was badly beaten up by a football player because the football player did not like the idea that this young athlete's coach was gay. The threat that straight athletes feel from gays in sport is a fear that the presence of gays will no longer make sport the unequivocal site for proving orthodox masculinity.

Although aligning with or verifying heterosexuality is a strong marker for masculinity in sports, the issue of sexuality seems to be undergoing some significant changes in a *few* sport communities. Anderson's (2009) research into men's collegiate rugby in the United Kingdom shows that behaviors once associated with gays are accepted as "normal" for some of these male rugby players. Anderson shows how behaviors that have been previously coded as homosexual no longer hold the stigma nor ostracizing power and internal feelings of "otherness" and "out-group" status. More specifically, Anderson found that men who identified as heterosexual did not feel threatened by begin labeled as a homosexual. In other words, they were not concerned about what other people thought if they hung out with gays. More surprisingly, during postgame celebrations, these young men engaged in homoerotic behaviors such as dancing close together and kissing. The rugby players expressed no conflict between these actions and their heterosexual identities. Certainly, this is an important development, as identification with any homosexual behavior or persons often resulted in young men getting beaten up (Anderson 2010). Anderson suggests that hegemonic masculinity is insufficient to describe what is happening in this sport setting. He posits a new theory called "inclusive masculinity" to more fully explain that these athletes are more inclusive of the behaviors they consider to be part of masculinity or their heterosexual selves. These acts of resistance in sport challenge orthodox masculinity and open up a wider range of masculinities as acceptable.

Violence and (Un)Sportsmanship Behaviors in Sport

Highly aggressive acts by athletes occur both on and off the field. Sport cultures vary, and some sports condone more aggression than other sports. The range of transgressions extends from verbal heckling to fighting. On the one hand, some violence is acceptable because it draws in an audience. When fights break out among athletes, media coverage increases. Consider the publicity that John McEnroe received for being the "bad" boy on court by constantly disagreeing vociferously with umpires. Also, a certain amount of physical aggression and fighting are part of the game. Fighting is an expected part of professional ice hockey. On the other hand, if physical or verbal aggressiveness exceeds an acceptable level, then the notion of sportsmanship is violated. It is the line between what is acceptable and what is not that is constantly being negotiated in sport, whether athletes or fans.

Athletes often the pay the price when verbal or physical aggressiveness goes beyond what is allowed on the field or court, but off the field violence is much harder to control. Extreme violence while playing has led to suspension or the end of a career for some athletes. While violence in the context of playing sport is easily visible, transgressions in the context of their personal lives are more likely to be ignored. It seems as though sport organizations are much less likely to pay attention to the crimes committed outside of sport. Over the past decade, one in five NFL players was charged with a serious crime, but not one player was ever suspended. In response to a growing concern about violent athletes, Katherine Redmond founded the National Coalition Against Violent Athletes (NCAVA) in 1998. NCAVA exists to provide information, raise awareness, provide education to athletes, and assist with counseling for victims of athlete violence. A study conducted over a period of three years by NCAVA found that male student-athletes are only 3.3 percent of the entire population, but they represent 19 percent of sexual assault perpetrators and 35 percent of domestic violence perpetrators. In 1995, 36.8 percent of athletes were charged with assault, a number four times the rate at which the general population is charged with assault. Redmond believes that raising awareness about these issues is crucial to changing how athletes view themselves. She contends that athletes are put into a position of privilege and praised for their aggressive actions on the court or field. She maintains that this privileged position leads athletes to feel that nothing can happen to them because they are valued as an essential part of the team, school, or community. She argues that this privileged position makes athletes prone to bullying and violent behavior. Many scholars agree and add that overconformity to such masculine signifiers as aggression is another "cause" of violence and unsportsmanship in sport (Anderson 2009 and Coakley 2008). The recent concern that leagues and corporate sponsors have over how players are perceived has resulted in more stringent rules about aggressive behavior both within and outside of sport. For instance, the NFL recently hired Redmond of NCAVA to develop zero-tolerance policies for the league.

Athletes are not the only ones to engage in aggressive behavior. Sports fans and parents often engage in violence or unsportsmanship behavior. Some scholars (Moesche, Birrer, and Seiler 2010 and Lanter 2011) suggest that social identity theory can partially explain why fans act out in these destructive ways. Social identity theory assumes that humans want to belong to groups. Fans are emotionally attached to teams and want to make it clear which team they support. As a result, they will do almost anything to affirm their position as fans. In their study on collegiate fans, Rudd and Gordon (2010) found that abusive language and mildly abusive physical acts were considered to be appropriate by college fans as long as it was in the context of trying to help their team win. In other words, making prank phone calls to the opposing team's players, throwing popcorn on opposing team fans, and verbally degrading opponents was considered legitimate by fans. Rudd and Gordon also noted that behaviors can frequently be more severe, including derogatory chanting, fighting, and sometimes coming out onto the court or field with the intention of hurting a player or coach. Beyond fans, parents are frequently the perpetrators of violence, ranging from demeaning name calling to fighting (Mathner et al. 2010). The reasons for parental violence and unsportsmanship are complex, but many scholars agree that parents both male and female are symbolically aligning themselves with the culture of sport or proving their own masculinity. One famous case seems to stem from both imperatives. In 2002, a hockey dad, Thomas Junta, was convicted of manslaughter after he beat another father to death over a disagreement at their sons' practice in 2000 (Hockey Dad Found Guilty 2009).

In order to curtail fan and parental violence, many universities and sport organizations are implementing strategies and regulations aimed at reducing abusive behaviors (Rudd and Gordon 2010). While football (soccer) hooliganism was at its height in the 1970s and 1980s, actions taken by clubs and increased police presence at high-profile games have significantly decreased hooligan activity (Stephens 2011). Additionally, other such actions as restriction on alcohol sales, installation of surveillance cameras, and maintenance of a hooligan database to target control of specific individuals are becoming more standard in Europe (Stephens 2011). After the hockey incident in 2000 and the conviction in 2002, youth hockey implemented stricter parental rules in 2003. As a result, parents are aware of what is unacceptable behavior, and officials have clearer guidelines for banning parents from youth games.

While specific actions are being taken to reduce violent behavior related to sports, other scholars insist that a deeper understanding of sportsmanship through proactive education is needed to change the current trend of violence in sports (Feezell

2006, Rudd and Gordon 2010, and Tannenbaum et al. 2000). The first strategy involves educating coaches and parents. Given that these individuals serve as key role models for youth in sport, their behavior shapes what youth understand as acceptable both physically and verbally in sport settings. The second strategy is to rethink sportsmanship on a deeper level. For instance, many people's understandings of sportsmanship hinge on the proscriptive rules of the game. Yet, such scholars as Feezell argue that sportsmanship should not be defined by rules, but rather sportsmanship should be predicated on excellence of character. In Feezell's view, sportsmanship is not simply compliance but extends from a deeper desire to act with integrity, compassion, and mutual respect. A final strategy involves rethinking the issue of gender performance, which encourages males to engage in highly aggressive behavior as a signifier of orthodox masculinity (Anderson 2009 and 2010). Broadening what it means "to be a man" and by extension what it means to be a "good" athlete, fan or parent, will allow a greater range of behaviors to become an acceptable part of those identities. Perhaps this range of behaviors can include an excellence of character based on compassion.

Sport and Women: The Complexities of Gender

Even though the masculinity-sport alliance creates numerous issues for men in sport, it is also problematic for women. Since masculinity can be understood as a set of behaviors rather than biologically based (Butler 1990), the female body can easily be identified with masculinity. As women engage in sport more and more, they run into the following tension: sport requires "masculine" behaviors, attitudes, and muscularity, but the social construction of femininity requires different behaviors, attitudes, and body shape. As a result, women's participation in sport historically has met with resistance due to fears that sport might make women more "manly" and compromise their health, especially their reproductive health. In today's sport world, women still face tensions between masculinity and femininity although these tensions often manifest in more nuanced ways. While sentiments are changing, many physically active women report

contradictory, conflicted feelings about their athletic and feminine selves. Such tensions result in women having to constantly
negotiate society's expectations of "athletic" and "female" while
simultaneously embodying both. This constant negotiation opens
up small fissures in hegemonic gender relations and creates
more fluid and hybrid female identities. This is not to say that
there are not major challenges for women who participate in
sport. Indeed, the landscape of gender and sport is continually
contested, creating a dynamic and sometimes confusing, difficult
space for women. It can be argued that such tumultuous times
offer opportunities for reshaping relationships between gender
and sport. The changes taking place in women's sport today are
indeed challenging previous notions about women, but they are
not easily summarized. Instead, these changes are chaotic, dis-
continuous, and filled with paradox.

One change for women in sport today is the fact that so many
of them are participating in sports, creating a sense of solidarity
among a large number of physically active women. Women are taking up sports such as waterpolo, cycling, cyclo-cross, wrestling,
marathon, and "ironman" in growing numbers (Pfister 2010).
Professional opportunities for women in such sports as soccer,
basketball, and volleyball are growing as leagues develop worldwide. With growing numbers, women have a larger political voice
today than they had 20 years ago. The case of female ski jumpers illustrates how this collective political voice can exert influence over traditional views about women and sport. As recently
as 2010, sport officials held strong in their belief that women
should not ski jump. After petitioning for several years to be included in the Vancouver 2010 Winter Olympic Games, female
jumpers were denied. Reasons given for their exclusion hinged
on loosely constructed technicalities. Despite having women ski
jumpers since the 1920s, the IOC said that women's ski jumping
was too young a sport and needed more time to develop (Laurendeau and Adams 2010). Part of this argument hinged on the
number of female competitors worldwide, which the IOC suggested was insufficient. At the time there were 83 total athletes
from 14 countries competing in ski jumping. In contrast, ski-cross
was accepted in the Vancouver 2010 Olympics with only 30 skiers
total from 11 countries. In the end, the long-held belief that ski
jumping was not healthy for women's bodies seemed to sway
the vote against inclusion in 2010. Several men in key decision-
making positions brought up the historically popular view that

ski jumping was not good for women's bodies (Suddath 2010). They argued that ski jumping puts female bodies at risk. After women ski jumpers were denied access to the 2010 Olympics, women and men rallied worldwide. Petitions cropped up on the Internet, news stories openly questioned the decision, and pressure increased from women's groups. This collective political voice had an impact. After many years of formal requests for inclusion, women's ski jumping is on the program for the Sochi Games in 2014.

Even though the increase in women's sport participation is a welcome change and participation has become commonplace for young girls and adult women, research suggests that women's personal feelings about their athletic bodies is laden with tension. Studies show that while recreational and collegiate female athletes feel empowered by their athletic bodies, they frequently express discomfort because their athletic bodies are in conflict with the ideal female body that society values (Cox and Thompson 2000, Guthrie et al. 2006, and Pfister 2010). As a result, women pursue athletics and physical activity but often engage in behaviors that are meant to keep their femininity in tact. Typical behaviors include having pony tails (to avoid the butch label), dressing in "feminine" sport clothing (consider the growth of women-specific sport apparel), wearing makeup while exercising or competing, and being moderate about strength training (just enough to keep "tone"). Such tensions are clear in Markula's (2005) findings that aerobics participants desired to be "firm but shapely, fit but sexy, strong but thin." While sport requires muscularity and strength, some women view physical activity as the primary way to control their weight to maintain their femininity. Gaining athletic strength and losing weight to attain the ideal female body is frequently problematic for women, especially in competitive sport. Tenets of femininity find their way into such judged sports as gymnastics and figure skating, sports that require tremendous strength. The desire for thin bodies while still trying to attain athletic prowess results in the interrelated issues of eating disorders, bone loss, and menstrual disturbances, known as the female athlete triad. Ironically, in an effort to be good at their sports, the tension between sport performance and femininity puts both their performance and overall health at risk. In this way, being a physically active body is often a paradoxical endeavor for women.

Tensions between athletic and feminine bodies vary culturally because what it means to be feminine differs across cultures.
For instance, Chinese women in Taiwan have been subject to the
cultural devaluation of physical activity. Owing its roots to the
practice of feetbinding, femininity had the look of grace and
smallness, which led to the idea that women should not exert
themselves physically (Lu, Leaw, and Barnd 2004). In addition,
the culturally significant virtues of mild manners, tenderness, and
self-sacrifice were in opposition to behaviors required in sport.
Despite these foundations, recent trends indicate that Chinese
women are becoming more and more physically active. Lu,
Leaw, and Barnd note that the Internet has given these women
opportunities to see physically active women, whether in the
Olympics, professional leagues, or simply recreational pursuits.
Access to images of physically active women is changing their
attitudes toward physical activity. Additionally, religious views
have formed barriers to women participating in sport. Islamic
women, for example, have significant barriers to overcome in
order to participate in sport. In a recent study of Canadian Islamic women, Jiwani and Rail (2010) suggest that obstacles exist
from within their culture as well as outside. Opportunities within
their community are few. Many of the physical activities offered
are considered cultural gatherings rather than sports. On the
one hand, these women view physical activity as healthy and
regard themselves as progressive Muslims. On the other hand,
the ways in which they frame physical activity suggest that they
view it as a means to achieve a slender but toned body, a notion
reinforced by the feminine ideal. Outside their community, hijab-
wearing women are largely misunderstood and denied access
to sport because people do not think they are interested in physical activity. Sport organizations also cite safety reasons as to
why hijab-wearing women should not participate in athletics.
Although limited, these examples provide some insight into the
various ways women worldwide experience tensions as a result
of sports participation.

Given the conflict between physical activity and femininity
as well as the masculinity-sport alliance, mainstream media has
an ambivalent relationship with women's sports. Certainly, the
social construction of sport as masculine partially accounts for
the dearth of women's sports coverage in newspapers, magazines, TV, and Internet. Messner and Cooky's (2010) longitudinal

study of women's sports coverage in the U.S. media noted a decrease in women's sports coverage from 1989 to 2009. There was a gradual increase in coverage until 1999 when it piqued at 8.7 percent, but coverage since then has been in gradual decline and reached its lowest point at 1.6 percent in 2009. Ironically, sport scholars (Messner and Cooky 2010 and Harrison and Secarea 2010) show that attendance at and interest in collegiate and professional women's basketball games is increasing, so the drop in women's sports coverage is puzzling. What is notable in their study was a decline in the number of derogatory or sexualized comments made about female athletes from 1989 to 2009. Messner and Cooky suggest that this may simply be due to such a low percentage of coverage anyway. Despite these findings, there remains much research demonstrating that media coverage of women's sports remains qualitatively different than coverage of men's sports (Pfister 2010, Guthrie et al. 2006, and Harrison and Secarea 2010). Primarily, women are often not even seen doing their sports. Instead, they are sexualized, shown to be good mothers, or highlighted because of their personal lives and fan-friendly personalities.

Although mainstream media has all but eliminated women's sports from their programming, the Internet is becoming an important avenue for women to talk about sports participation on their own terms. As seen with the Taiwanese women, blogs, Web sites, and other social media are becoming powerful avenues for bringing positive images of female athletes to a larger audience (Lu, Leaw, and Barnd 2004). More important, there appears to be a qualitative change in how female athletes view their bodies that is present in social media. Third-wave feminism tries to capture the essence of these changes from a theoretical standpoint (Azzarito 2010). Third-wave feminism is grounded in the idea that more women are taking pride in who they are and what they achieve. In particular, changing attitudes toward their bodies are prevalent among physically active women. Azzarito notes these changing attitudes through the development of the "Alpha Girl" and the "Future Girl." Instead of feeling that appearance is a priority, Alpha Girls are more proud of accomplishments. They are self-confident and physically strong, feel unequivocally good about their bodies, and view sport as an ideal site for developing high-achievement skills, especially within a domain dominated by men. Furthermore, they capitalize on their athletic bodies to gain cultural and economic capital by sharing their experiences publically through social media. Future Girls are defined by multiplicity and versatility. Future Girls thrive on feeling powerful, self-determined, and unlimited in what they can accomplish. Azzarito argues that sports participation helps these women achieve a convergence of physical strength and aggressiveness with grace and aesthetic sensibilities. Thus, instead of feeling tension in their bodies, these women embrace athletic bodies *as* the ideal female body.

It is important to point out that empowerment through sport in the form of the Alpha/Future girl is primarily available to white, middle to upper class, heterosexual women (Azzarito 2010). Alpha/Future girls believe that all girls have access to the kinds of cultural capital they possess. However, minority and lower-class women do not have the same access to sport as a vehicle for empowerment. In fact, as Azzarito points out, Muslim women are identified as "losers" who possess "backwards physicalities" (270) because they do not embrace nor aim for the type of femininity valued by Alpha/Future girls. Perhaps the most poignant illustration of how this new form of empowerment marginalizes other women is the overt heterosexuality of Alpha/Future girls. The strong heterosexual identities of Alpha/Future girls serve to reinforce heterosexuality as the norm and marginalize other sexualities in the process. While there are some women's sporting spaces in which varied sexualities are openly accepted, many signifiers and behaviors associated with lesbians (butch haircut, bigger bodies, masculine ways of dressing) remain unacceptable to society at large. These types of bodies do not gain female athletes the same cultural capital as the clearly heterosexual bodies. As a result, many heterosexual athletes have a fear of being labeled lesbian because homosexuality remains a marginalized identity (Cahn 1994 and Caudwell 2003). Furthermore, hegemonic heterosexuality complicates the promotion of women's professional sports, in which many athletes are lesbian. A good example of hegemonic heterosexuality at work is the advertising focus of the Women's National Basketball Association (WNBA), which depicts the basketball players as mothers or family oriented. The ads are clearly focused on using signifiers of heterosexuality even though the athletes themselves are a mix of sexualities (Coakley 2008). Although the reshaping of femininity is occurring and facilitated through women's sport participation and images of empowered female athletes, there continues to be a need for inclusive attitudes that recognize multiple femininities as valid.

The Dynamic, Changing Landscape of the Sports and Media Relationship

Mainstream U.S. sports media has moved away from an information-focused business to an entertainment-focused one. Beyond providing scores and game reports, sports media goes further, supplying fans with background stories and social commentary. In particular, sports media personnel such as writers, producers, programmers, camerapersons, editors, and commentators work hard to transform sports action into drama (Coakley 2008). According to Coakley, drama serves at least two purposes. First, it reinforces cultural values of the middle and upper classes, the primary consumers of sport. The dominant story told in sport narratives focuses on individual achievement as well as teamwork, facing adversity, pushing through pain, and playing aggressively. These narratives serve to reproduce the heroic story. Repackaging techniques consist of slow motion, camera positioning, and editing that sensationalizes the action. The goal of these stories is to appeal to the primary consumers' values. Second, through these reinforced values, the primary consumers are more likely to keep watching sports, which serves commercial interests. Sports teams benefit from people watching sports because they generate revenue from broadcast fees. The media benefits because if viewership is strong, broadcast companies can earn more income from advertising. Thus, sport and media work together for the benefit of each.

While media repackaging and storytelling may serve both sports and media on one level, there are a number of ways that this symbiotic relationship is problematic. In particular, these reproductions seldom, if ever, reflect the lived sport experience of athletes and spectators. Diana Nyad, Olympian and reporter at the 1996 Olympic Games, notes that TV coverage selectively provides information, often leaving out whole pieces of the lived story and sometimes misrepresenting athlete relationships in order to heighten the rivalry aspect (see Coakley 2008). In this way, commercial interests are driving the content rather than any other type of interests. Furthermore, many scholars (see Coakley 2008) argue that commercially mediated sports result in real consequences in terms of who is included in these stories. Certainly the dearth of women's sports media coverage (Messner and Cooky

2010) and the fact that the Paralympics receive little to no media coverage are two results of this singular focus.

New media, sometimes referred to as user-generated media or such social media, as Facebook, blogging, YouTube, and Wikipedia, challenges the mainstream media's monopoly on sports coverage. Fans and participants can interact with all of the user-generated sites to experience and consume sport in radically different ways than before. For niche sports, which are not likely to get media coverage in mainstream, user-generated media is rich with ways for participants and fans to learn about and engage with the sport. For instance, in such sports as parkour, ultrarunning, and rogaine, virtual communities connect people, extend the teaching and learning of the sport, and provide avenues for people to participate (Facebook groups and online meetups). Even the fantasy leagues allow consumers to interact with sports on their own terms. For the fantasy players, each real game tells a specific story that uniquely informs their subsequent decisions. Thus, social media interacts with sports events in ways that bring fans or participants directly to the information they want and from the sources they choose.

Due to the power of new media, mainstream media and sport organizations have taken advantage of the consumer-directed Internet and found ways to integrate these media with their own mainstream media outlets. For instance, teams and leagues have initiated blogs in order to generate more hits on their Web site from current users (Kwak, Kim, and Zimmerman 2011). A good example is the success of ProfootballTalk.com, which tripled in page views from its launch in 2009 through 2010 (Ourand 2010). Notably, the NHL is working to distribute league content through a variety of social media outlets in order to expand their presence. In some instances, these relationships with social media sites directly bring in money. For example, the NHL made a deal with Google that they could tag NHL-related YouTube videos, 85 percent of which is uploaded by fans, and earn a percentage of advertising income (Fisher and Mickle 2010). Sports journalists appear to have a mixed relationship with social media. While many of them claim that they used Twitter to send breaking news and further promote their own mainstream Web sites, Sheffer and Schultz (2010) found that they primarily relate opinion and commentary. Sport fans do not appear to care whether or not they are getting news or opinion because while they think of mainstream media as more expert, they believe that mainstream and user-generated content are equally as trustworthy (Kwak, Kim, and Zimmerman 2011).

In other words, fans appreciate any type of information because they like connecting with their sports teams or events. Furthermore, the interaction between mainstream Web sites and social media can be used very effectively in promoting and enhancing the participant or fan experience. Schoenstedt and Reau (2010) demonstrated the ways in which this combination enhanced marathon participants' and spectators' experiences leading up to, during, and post event. As Schoenstedt and Reau point out, the advantage for local sports events organizers is that they need very little money to create this enhanced experience.

Finally, Sanderson's (2010) analysis of the power of social media to change perceptions of star athletes demonstrates the degree to which fan-generated content can help mediate mainstream commentary. Using Tiger Woods as an example, Sanderson shows that the mainstream media produced negative accounts of Woods after his extramarital activities became public. Woods's actions were framed as a tragic flaw. More notably, mainstream media relied on dominant cultural ideology by using language typical of how the black male has been depicted. For example, the media noted aggressive physicality by asserting that his actions exemplify an "insatiable sexual appetite" (445). In contrast, social media sites showed a greater array of opinions and perspectives. Many fans expressed that Woods's behavior was a private matter and simply showed that he was human. In these instances, there was a vehement call to the press to spend less time covering this aspect of Woods. Alternately, other fans expressed their disappointment, some even alluding to the fact that they were no longer fans. Sanderson explains that, in the case of Tiger Woods, social media content helped mitigate the one-way dissemination of a singular opinion, bringing the issue to a conversational level and shaping more nuanced ways of making sense of this high-profile athlete's personal life. In this way, sports mainstream media are no longer the only storytellers as their stories are now continually reshaped by user-generated content.

References

Adelson, Eric. 2011. Let 'em play. http://sports.espn.go.com/espnmag/story?id=3357051 (accessed September 1, 2011).

Anderson, Eric. 2009. *Inclusive masculinities: The changing nature of masculinities.* New York: Routledge.

Anderson, Eric. 2010. *Sport, theory and social problems: A critical introduction*. New York: Routledge.

Azzarito, Laura. 2010. "Future Girls, transcendent femininities and new pedagogies: toward girls' hybrid bodies?." *Sport, Education & Society* 15, no. 3: 261–275.

Bamberger, Michael and Don Yaeger. 1997. Over the edge: Aware that drug testing is a sham, athletes seem to rely more than ever on banned performance enhancers. *Sports Illustrated* 86(15): 60–64; 66–67; 70.

Bergsgard, Nils Asle and Johan R. Norberg. 2010. Sports policy and politics—the Scandinavian way. *Sport in Society* 13(4): 567–82.

Berkes, H. 2010. Olympic sponsors go for the golden image. *NPR*. http: www.npr.org.

Black, David R. 2010. The ambiguities of development: Implications for "development through sport." *Sport in Society* 13(1): 121–29.

Bobby, Rickey. Will the games be a golden goose or a black hole? [Web log comment]. Retrieved from http://2010vanolympics. blogspot.com/2010/02/will-games-be-golden-goose-or-black.html (accessed September 23, 2011).

Brown, William. 1980. Ethics, Drugs and Sport. *Journal of the Philosophy of Sport* 8: 15–23.

Bucy, Erik P. 2004. *Living in the information age: A new media reader*, 2nd ed. Belmont, CA: Wadsworth Publishing.

Burnett, Cora. 2010. Sport-for-development approaches in the South African context: A case study analysis. *South African Journal for Research in Sport, Physical Education and Recreation* 32(1): 29–42.

Butler, Judith. 1990. *Gender trouble: Feminism and the subversion of identity*. New York: Routledge.

Cahn, Susan. 1994. *Coming on strong: Gender and sexuality in twentieth-century women's sport*. Cambridge, MA: Harvard University Press.

Carruthers, Susan L. 2000. *The media at war: Communication and conflict in the twentieth century*. New York: St. Martin's Press.

Cashman, R. 2002. Impact of the Games on Olympic host cities. *Barcelona: Centre d'Estudis Olimpics*. Retrieved from http:olympicstudies.uab.es/ lectures.

Caudwell, Jayne. 2003. Sporting gender: Women's footballing bodies as sites/sights for the (re)articulation of sex, gender, and desire. *Sociology of Sport Journal* 20(4): 371–86.

Coakley, Jay. 2008. *Sports in society: Issues and controversies*, 10th ed. New York: McGraw-Hill.

Coalter, Fred. 2010. The politics of sport-for-development: Limited focus programmes and broad gauge problems. *International Review for the Sociology of Sport* 45(3): 295–314.

Cox, Barbara and Shona Thompson. 2000. Multiple bodies: Sportswomen, soccer and sexuality. *International Review for the Sociology of Sport* 35(1): 5–20.

Crompton, John L. 2006. Economic impact studies: Instruments for political shenanigans. *Journal of Travel Research* 45(1): 67–82.

Cummings, David. 2009. Beijing's empty venues reveal heavy cost of Olympics. http://www.findingdulcinea.com/news/sports/2009/feb/Beijing-s-Empty-Venues-Reveal-Heavy-Cost-of-Olympics.html.

Darnell, Simon. 2010. Power, politics and "sport for development and peace": Investigating the utility of sport for international development. *Sociology of Sport Journal* 27(1): 54–75.

Farooq, Samaya and Andrew Parker. 2009. Sport, physical education, and Islam: Muslim independent schooling and the social construction of masculinities. *Sociology of Sport Journal* 26(2): 277–95.

Feezell, Randolf. 2006. *Sport, play and ethical reflection*. Champaign: University of Illinois Press.

Fisher, Eric and Tripp Mickle. 2010. NHL pushes digital syndication into overdrive. *Street & Smith's Sports Business Journal* 12(40): 8.

Gee, Sarah. 2009. Mediating sport, myth, and masculinity: The national hockey league's "inside the warrior" advertising campaign. *Sociology of Sport Journal* 26(4): 578–98.

Gibson, Owen. 2011. Golf suffers funding cut despite major magic of Rory McIlroy. http://www.guardian.co.uk/sport/2011/jun/22/golf-funding-cut-sport-england (accessed April 23, 2012).

Gill, Jr., Emmett L. 2011. The Rutgers women's basketball and Don Imus controversy (RUIMUS): White privilege, new racism, and the implications for college sport management. *Journal of Sport Management* 25(2): 118–30.

Giulianotti, Richard. 2011. Sport, transnational peacemaking, and global civil society: Exploring the reflective discourses of "Sport, Development, and Peace" project officials. *Journal of Sport and Social Issues* 35(1): 50–71.

Global Peace Support Group. 2011. Why a sports boycott is essential for justice. http://www.globalpeacesupport.com (accessed July 30, 2011).

Goig, Ramon Llopis. 2008. Learning and representation: The construction of masculinity in football. An analysis of the situation in Spain. *Sport in Society* 11(6): 685–95.

Guthrie, Sharon T., Michelle Magyar, Ann F. Maliszewski, and Alison Wrynn. 2006. *Women, sport, and physical activity: Challenges and triumphs.* Dubuque, IA: Kendall/Hunt Publishing.

Halliman, Chris and Barry Judd. 2009. Race relations, indigenous Australia and the social impact of professional Australian football. *Sport in Society* 12(9): 1220–35.

Harrison, Lisa A. and Ashley M. Secarea. 2010. College women's attitudes towards the sexualization of professional women athletes. *Journal of Sport Behavior* 33(4): 403–26.

Hemphill, Dennis. 2009. Performance enhancement and drug control in sport: Ethical considerations. *Sport in Society* 12(3): 313–26.

Hockey Dad Found Guilty. 2009. www.cbsnews.com/stories/2002/01/02/national/main322819.shtml (accessed August 14, 2011).

Houlihan, Barrie. 2007. Politics and sport. In *Handbook of sports studies,* ed. Jay Coakley and Eric Dunning, 213–27. Thousand Oaks, CA: Sage Publications, Inc.

Jiwani, Nisara and Geneviève Rail. 2010. Islam, Hijab and young Shia Muslim Canadian women's discursive constructions of physical activity. *Sociology of Sport Journal* 27(3): 251–67.

Jones, Luisa and Mac McCarthy. 2010. Mapping the landscape of gay men's football. *Leisure Studies* 29(2): 161–73.

Jonsson, Kutte. 2010. Sport beyond gender and the emergence of cyborg athletes. *Sport in Society* 13(2): 249–59.

Judge, Lawrence W., David Bellar, Bruce Craig, and Erin Gilreath. 2010. The attitudes of track and field throwers toward performance enhancing drug use and drug testing. *SD Journal of Research in Health, Physical Education, Recreation, Sport & Dance* 5(2): 54–61.

Kirkup, Naomi and Bridget Major. 2006. Doctoral foundation paper: The reliability of economic impact studies of the Olympic Games: A post-games study of Sydney 2000 and considerations for London 2012. *Journal of Sport and Tourism* 11(3–4): 275–96.

Kwak, Dae Hee, Yu Kyoum Kim, and Matthew H. Zimmerman. 2010. User-versus mainstream-media-generated content: Media source, message valence, and team identification and sport consumers' response. *International Journal of Sport Communication* 3(4):402–21.

Lanter, Jason R. 2011. Spectator identification with the team and participation in celebratory violence. *Journal of Sport Behavior* 34(3): 268–80.

Laurendeau, Jason and Carly Adams. 2010. "Jumping like a girl": Discursive silences, exclusionary practices and the controversy over women's ski jumping. *Sport in Society* 13(3): 431–47.

Lenskyj, Helen J. 2000. *Inside the Olympic industry: Power, politics, and activism.* Albany: State University of New York Press.

Lu, Chia-Chen, Yin-Hua Leaw, and Susan M. Barnd. 2004. Cultural and social factors affecting women's physical activity participation in Taiwan. *Sport, Education and Society* 9(3): 379–93.

MacDonald, Brent Douglas. 2009. Learning masculinity through Japanese university rowing. *Sociology of Sport Journal* 26(3): 425–42.

Markula, Pirkko. 2005. Firm but shapely, fit but sexy, strong but thin: The postmodern aerobicizing female body. *Sociology of Sport Journal* 12(4): 424–53.

Mathner, Robert P., Christina L. L. Martin, Shane A. Tatum, and Deepak Chouti. 2010. The effects of a sportsmanship education program on the behavior of college intramural sports participants. *Recreational Sports Journal* 34(2): 119–28.

Mazanov, Jason. 2008. Performance enhancing drugs in sport: The dark side of performance psychology. *InPsyche* (February). The Australian Psychological Society, Ltd. http://www.psychology.org.au/inpsych/ped/ (accessed Sept. 5 2011).

Messner, Michael. 2007. *Out of play: Critical essays on gender and sport.* Albany: State University of New York Press.

Messner, Michael A. and Cheryl Cooky. 2010. *Gender in televised sports: News and highlight shows, 1989–2009.* Los Angeles: Center for Feminist Research, 1–35.

MLB. 2011. The official site of major league baseball. http://mlb.mlb.com/index.jsp (accessed May 10, 2012).

Moesche, Karin, Daniel Birrer, and Roland Seiler. 2010. Differences between violent and non-violent adolescents in terms of sport background and sport-related psychological variables. *European Journal of Sport Science* 10(5): 319–28.

Morgan, William. 2009. Athletic perfection, performance-enhancing drugs, and the treatment-enhancement distinction. *Journal of the Philosophy of Sport* 36(2): 162–81.

Munthe, Christian. 2000. Selected champions: Making winners in the age of genetic technology. In Tamburrini, C.M. and T. Tännsjö, eds. *Values in sport: Elitism, nationalism, gender equality and the scientific manufacture of winners.* New York: E & FN SPON.

Nike CR report. 2008. Let me play. Retrieved from http://www. nikeresponsibility.com (accessed May 10, 2012).

Olympic Charter. 2011. Official Web site of the Olympic Movement. http://www.olympic.org/olympic-charter/documents-reports-studies-publications (accessed April 23, 2012).

Olympics and Television. 2012. The Museum of Broadcast Communications. http://www.museum.tv/eotvsection. php?entrycode=olympicsand (accessed May 10, 2012).

Opaszowski, Benedykt H. 2008. Doping: A dilemma of the modern sport. *Polish Journal of Sport Tourism* 15(3): 93–101.

Ourand. John. 2010. Pleased with ProFootballTalk.com's performance. NBC Sports looks to expand on concept. *Street & Smith's Sports Business Journal* 12(40): 29.

Outsports. 2011. Matthew Mitchum. http://outsports.com/ olympics2008/2008/08/24/matthew-mitcham-talks-with-partner-at-side/ (accessed July 10, 2011).

Pfister, Gertrud. 2010. Women in sport—gender relations and future perspectives. *Sport in Society* 13(2): 234–48.

Pieterse, Jan Nederveen. 2001. *Development theory: Deconstructions/ reconstructions.* London: Sage Publications.

Pringle, R. G. and C. Hickey. 2010. Negotiating masculinities via the moral problematization of sport. *Sociology of Sport Journal,* 27(2): 115–138.

Rudd, Andy and Brian S. Gordon. 2010. An exploratory investigation of sportsmanship attitudes among college student basketball fans. *Journal of Sport Behavior* 33(4): 466–88.

Sanderson, Jimmy. 2010. Framing Tiger's troubles: Comparing traditional and social media. *International Journal of Sport Communication* 3(4):438–53.

Schoenstedt, Linda J. and Jackie Reau. 2010. Running a social-media newsroom: A case study of the Cincinnati Flying Pig Marathon. *International Journal of Sport Communication* 3(3): 377–86.

Sheffer, Mary Lou and Brad Schultz. 2010. Paradigm shift or passing fad? Twitter and sports journalism. *International Journal of Sport Communication* 3(4): 472–84.

Silk, Michael, David Andrews and Cheryl L. Cole, eds. 2005. *Sport and corporate nationalisms*. New York: Berg.

Sport England. 2011. 2012 to make history as first gender equality Games http://www.sportengland.org/about_us/our_news/2012_to_make_history.aspx on (accessed August 6, 2011).

Spracklen, Karl. 2008. The holy blood and the holy grail: Myths of scientific racism and the pursuit of excellence in sport. *Leisure Studies* 27(2): 221–27.

Stephens, Thomas. 2011. Hooliganism ball kicked to clubs and cantons. http://www.swissinfo.ch/eng/swiss_news/Hooliganism_ball_kicked_to_clubs_and_cantons_.html?cid=31034498 (accessed September 10, 2011).

Suddath, Claire. 2010. Why can't women ski jump? www.time.com/time/nation/article/0,8599,1963447,00.html (accessed July 12, 2011).

Tannenbaum, Gershon, David N. Sacks, Jason W. Miller, Amy S. Golden, and Nora Doolin. 2000. Aggression and violence in sport: A reply to Kerr's rejoinder. *Sports Psychologist* 14(4): 315–26.

Thibault, Lucie. 2009. Globalization of sport: An inconvenient truth. *Journal of Sport Management* 23(1): 1–20.

Tucker, Ross and Jonathan Dugas. 2007. The science of sport. http://www.sportsscientists.com/2007/06/culture-of-doping-in-cycling-anything.html (accessed August 11, 2011).

Van Riemsdijk, Micheline. 2010. Variegated privileges of whiteness: Lived experiences of Polish nurses in Norway. *Social & Cultural Geography* 11(2): 117–31.

Vargas, A. 2004. The globalization of baseball: A Latin American perspective. In Scott R. Rosner & Kenneth L. Shropshire, eds., *The business of sports*, 718–24. Sudbury, MA: Jones and Bartlett Publishers, Inc.

Vellur, Nishad. 2011. And the Oscar goes to Olympics? http://zeenews.india.com/news/exclusive/and-the-oscar-goes-to-olympics_731742.html (accessed September 15, 2011).

WADA. 2011About WADA. http://www.wada-ama.org/en/About-WADA/ (accessed September 4, 2011).

Willis, Jeremy. 2009. Technology will always play role. http://sports.espn.go.com/ncaa/recruiting/football/news/story?id=4428912 (accessed September 3, 2011).

3

North American Sport

Bidding for and Hosting the Super Bowl

The Super Bowl is the world's most-watched sport event, drawing 80 to 90 million viewers each year (Mohr 2007). In many ways, this event has ceased to be a mega-sporting event and transformed into an American national holiday, in which people who do not normally follow football become fans for a day. While the screen version of the Super Bowl allows widespread viewership, hosting the event brings prestige and revenue to the host city. Similar to the Olympics, many host cities desire to host a Super Bowl because of its sentimental aspects. Proponents of hosting a Super Bowl often highlight the legacy it will leave for the host city and emphasize the idea the event is a way to reward fans of the host city (O'Reilly et al. 2008). According to Taylor (1987), however, the decision to award a city the Super Bowl depends less on these intangible aspects and more on the revenue potential. The host city can expect to earn hundreds of millions of dollars with the influx of 200,000 people needing accommodation, buses, limousines, taxis, rental cars, and places to eat (Heid 2010). One aim of host cities is to use government funds, usually in the form of taxes, to improve the region's infrastructure and build new stadiums. Host cities hope that improved infrastructure will bring more tourists and other events to the area. The National Football League (NFL) also benefits from a well-chosen host city. The home NFL team directly earns about 6 percent of ticket sales (Cimini 2010) while the majority of the earnings goes to the league. The league then passes on a generous share of these earnings to all league teams. Thus, a host city's earning potential is critical because all league owners benefit from a profitable Super Bowl.

The bidding process for a Super Bowl appears on paper to be fairly straightforward. It begins at least five to six years before the event and is decided upon four years prior to it. Potential host regions or cities prepare a Request for Proposal (RFP) according to NFL guidelines. The 32 league owners review the proposals. The final vote is cast by secret ballot at a meeting of all the owners, who listen to each host city's final 15-minute presentation (Heid 2010). Up to four rounds of voting occurs. A host city must be selected by at least three-fourths majority. If no city wins by three-fourths majority in the first three rounds, a fourth round ensues between the top two cities in previous votes. A simple majority wins in that case (Heid 2010).

An official bid committee writes the proposal, but the groundwork to write the bid is substantial (Heid 2010). RFPs are 200–300 pages and organized into approximately 13 chapters (Heid 2010). The background work is political, as hundreds of people need to be supportive of the event in order to show how well the region or city can deal with all the logistics of hosting a Super Bowl. The NFL's Special Events staff reviews all the information pertaining to stadium, tickets, security, accommodations, media center, transportation plan, venues for satellite events, relations with local governments, and a corporate social responsibility plan (Heid 2010). In the end, the relationships with local governments and businesses are key (Heid 2010). In particular, the contracts that ensure anti-gouging practices from all the service organizations are critical to a successful bid (Heid 2010).

While logistical and political factors contribute to the overall success of the bid, the weather and stadium stand out as major considerations. The weather is so critical that the NFL has a 50-degree rule. In other words, the average temperature needs to be 50 degrees or above to be considered. This rule restricts the number of cities that can engage in the bidding process. Yet, the stadiums themselves are perhaps more crucial than the weather. Stadiums with state-of-the-art technology, numerous luxury suites, and a high overall seating capacity are highly attractive Super Bowl sites (Cimini 2010). In fact, the renovated

MetLife Stadium at $1.6 billion was such an attractive stadium that it will be the site of the 2014 Super Bowl, making it the first Super Bowl to take place in an open stadium in the northern states and becoming an exception to the 50-degree rule. Between weather and stadium attractiveness, only a handful of sites can be considered, resulting in some cities or regions getting the Super Bowl multiple times. For instance, South Florida has hosted the Super Bowl 10 times, while New Orleans will host its 10th Super Bowl in 2013.

When analyzing the factors to a successful Super Bowl bid, history shows that the final decision has been influenced by revenue potential to a greater degree since the 1980s. Taylor (1987) argues that the 1984 meeting to award the 1987 Super Bowl was the turning point in which cities began emphasizing money over sentimentality. Philadelphia included almost $3 million in concessions and revenues to the NFL as part of its bid for the 1987 Super Bowl. Such an offer was astounding at the time and considerably higher than previous bids. Ultimately, the weather factor came into play, and Pasadena was awarded Super Bowl XXI instead of Philadelphia. Taylor points out that this was the very first time that the NFL had ever seriously considered an open winter stadium. The extent to which money came to the forefront in the 1984 bid process marked the beginning of a new era for Super Bowl bids. Taylor notes that the bid process in 1991 for the XXV Super Bowl felt like "an auction" with revenue potential in the form of incentives being raised to unprecedented levels. The bid cities vying for Super Bowl XXV were Tampa and San Diego. Tampa had the backing of an "old guard" owner, Culverhouse, who had developed many important relationships over the years. In contrast, a new owner, Alex Spanos, owned the San Diego chargers. San Diego decided that they would have to "buy" the Super Bowl. Their subsequent bid was one of the most aggressive bids in the history of the NFL (Taylor 1987). San Diego's package included more than $4 million in incentives such as concession revenue, novelty revenue, parking, and free use of the stadium. In addition, sales tax was waivered on tickets and game day costs along with free rooms for the NFL (Taylor 1987). To make the offer even better, Spanos offered $700,000 of revenues from the already awarded 1988 Super Bowl. Spanos's actions brought the issue of money to the forefront. NFL owners began calling Tampa asking for more incentives such as free hanger space for their private jets, free limousines, and free go-fers during their Super Bowl stay. Tampa kept adding more incentives in order to reduce costs to the NFL, which would result in higher revenues. In the end, Tampa won the bid. While Culverhouse was happy that Tampa was selected, he lamented the process, which he said simply became a high-stakes bidding war.

Today, Super Bowl bids far exceed these earlier numbers as the competition among potential host cities heightens. For instance, New Orleans's bid for the 2013 Super Bowl came to approximately $12 million (Baker 2009). Such special incentives as tax exemption remain key components of the bidding. For instance, Arizona's bid for the 2015 Super Bowl included the complex negotiation of these incentives. While Kansas City originally won the 2015 bid, local sales taxes were voted down, and local businesses felt they were giving up too much, so Kansas City withdrew. The 2015 Super Bowl was awarded to Arizona. Awarding host cities or regions for the Super Bowl has become much more about profits and less about prestige, legacy, or sentimental gestures.

Reviewing the decision to award the 2014 Super Bowl to MetLife Stadium, home of the Giants and the Jets, highlights the complexity of what makes a successful bid. As the first Super Bowl to be held in an open stadium in a northern city, this award is a notable exception to the 50-degree rule. Some argue that potential revenue was a defining factor because of stadium capacity, luxury suites, and technological advances. MetLife Stadium holds the greatest number of spectators in the NFL with a capacity of over 82,500. Others point out that there were symbolic reasons for the decision. One defining factor was the sense that playing in potentially harsh winter conditions is getting back to "what football is all about" (Cimini 2010). Resiliency and being able to deal with adverse conditions dominates the language regarding the selection. While fans have mixed feelings about the northern open-air venue, many NFL owners are counting on the resiliency theme resonating with the general public. The proximity to New York City could be an attempt by the NFL to show solidarity with those directly affected by 9/11. In addition, the economic times in 2010 when the bid process occurred were bleak. Perhaps, the NFL chose MetLife Stadium in order to stage a sport event that symbolizes American strength, perseverance, and resilience. It would not be the first time that sport served such a purpose.

Player Salary Debates among Professional Sports Teams

Despite professional sports being firmly planted in the entertainment industry, there is much debate about what is an appropriate salary for professional athletes. While the general public rarely questions the incomes of actors, actresses, or rock stars, they are quicker to be critical of athlete salaries. Perhaps the fact that the media has highlighted instances in which athletes complained that several million dollars for a year's salary was too low accounts for some of this criticism. Understandably, as professional athletes' salaries look relatively high compared to the majority, people begin to question whether or not professional athletes are overpaid. A closer look into how salaries are established for professional athletes in North America offers insights into the mechanisms that both increase as well as limit player salaries.

As an entertainment business, professional athletes' salaries are not set according to traditional business models; that is, with few exceptions, salaries are not based on position or rank within the organization. Instead, player salaries are determined by factors that are common among entertainment industries. Some of these factors include a player's public profile, specialized skills, or charismatic personality. Some players are compensated largely by their performance. In such sports as horse racing, NASCAR, golf, tennis, rodeo, and cycling, much of the income for these athletes comes from prize winnings, which are directly related to performance (Hilpert et al. 2007). Still, each of these sports is set up in unique ways that regulate the percentage of total revenue that athletes take home. For instance, in men's professional golf, players earn 100 percent of the prize money while jockeys earn only 7.5 percent of total earnings (Hilpert et al. 2007). In addition, superstar athletes often earn much more money based on sponsorship and endorsement contracts with companies who desire to associate their brand with professional sports. Many athletes' sponsorship and endorsement earnings depend largely on their performances as well as highly positive personal images (Harrow and Swatek 2011). Corporations are beginning to be more selective about athlete endorsements given the power of social media to quickly "catch" any questionable behaviors (Harrow and Swatek 2011). Should scandals come out about athletes, it can cost a company millions of potential profit. In the case of Nike, Reebok, and Adidas, endorsement of athletes amounts to billions of dollars. With respect to shoes, athlete endorsement seems to be working. For instance, 70 percent of basketball shoes bought by American men each year never touch the basketball court (Harrow and Swatek 2011).

Another primary determinant of player salaries is the relative bargaining power that players have with respect to owners. In early modern sport, leagues instituted a reserve clause that gave owners the right to renew athlete contracts at salaries determined solely by owners. Athletes were not free to switch teams unless a team released them first. Under this system, athletes' salaries remained relatively low, often forcing players to obtain other jobs in the off-season in order to make a living. In addition, players stayed with teams for their athletic lifetime, rarely moving between teams unless they were traded based on owner negotiations. Some scholars (e.g., Kahn 2000) point out that under this system, franchises were able to set salaries lower than the marginal revenue product (MRP) because athletes had no choice, and leagues operated more or less as a monopoly. In response to not wanting to be traded without his consent, an MLB player fought for his right to become a free agent in the case of *Flood v. Kuhn* in 1967. Although the case was decided against Flood, his court case raised players' awareness of the power held by owners. While the history is complex, it was ultimately the repeal of the reserve clause, the advent of collective bargaining agreements, and the emergence of the free agent that gave more negotiating power to athletes. Under these conditions player salaries began to rise.

Such high-profile professional sports as the NFL, MLB, NBA, and the NHL have collective bargaining agreements (CBAs), which control player salaries through a variety of mechanisms. The purpose of CBAs is to balance the tensions between franchise profitability, league profitability and stability, player compensation, winning teams, and competitive balance. To achieve balance among these variables, CBAs attend to the following five major areas: drug testing, salary cap, luxury tax, rookie salaries, and revenue sharing. Salary caps, luxury taxes, and rookie salary rules determine basic pay for athletes.

Although drug testing does not directly impact player salaries, at some level leagues are concerned about public image and competitive balance in order to ensure profitability. At the very least, this form of drug testing as part of the CBAs publically announces a concern for fairness, which theoretically produces a positive image. Yet, leagues vary considerably on their emphasis in this area. For instance, the NFL is more proactive by regularly testing players for performance enhancing drugs (PEDs) while the MLB tests each player only once each season (Harrow and Swatek 2011).

Prior to the 1970s, salary caps did not exist; but with the rise of the free agent and CBAs, salary caps, luxury taxes, and rookie salary limits have emerged. Salary caps came into being as a way to preserve competitive balance. The concept is simple. Limit the amount a team can spend on payroll, and no single team can hire all the very best players, which would lead to predictable dominance. A specific share of revenue determines the salary cap in most CBAs. For instance, in the NHL, the salary cap increases as the revenue increases. In this way, players benefit from the success of the franchise and league. In addition, competitive balance is maintained under the salary cap system given the variable of related party revenues. For instance, some teams may receive millions in related party revenue while other teams do not. Teams that have this increased revenue possess the ability to bid for free agents, sometimes to the extent that teams without this benefit are priced out of good players. In these instances, a salary cap can help mitigate the impact related party revenue. The luxury tax was initiated to penalize teams that went over the salary cap. In most instances, there was a penalty of one dollar for every dollar over the salary cap. Yet, some teams are willing to incur such penalties because they desire a talented roster in hopes of boosting overall team revenue. Finally, rookie salary determinants vary among the leagues, but the intent is to reduce the risk that franchises incur with players who have an unproven record in the professional leagues. Such limits promote the financial stability of franchises, especially those with poor past performances.

However, salary caps are controversial with respect to ensuring competitive balance as well as player compensation. At the time of this writing, the NFL has a hard cap, the NBA has a soft cap, and the MLB has no cap. With respect to the NFL, Leeds and Kowaleski (1999) found that salary caps along with free agency amplified the revenue discrepancies among teams within the league. The very fact that payroll ranges are narrow in a salary cap system means that higher-revenue teams will generate significantly more revenue than others. In other words, the salary cap benefits higher-revenue teams more than it benefits low-revenue teams. In addition, Zimbalist (2010) points out that under the salary cap system, teams may feel more pressure to underestimate their revenue by adjusting related party revenue that may be counted in the revenue sharing contracts, effectively reducing player salaries. Such accounting practices also radically change the total revenue that teams report, which complicates and affects player compensation. Ideally, related party revenue accountability is delineated in the collective bargaining agreement. Zimbalist (2010) points out that under the no cap system of MLB, related party revenues are more likely to be reported as team income so that they can lure talented players with larger salaries. In this instance, players may be receiving more share of total revenue, but wealthier teams are still in a position to sign the more talented players. There is also evidence of related party income being underestimated in MLB in order to increase profit. Major League Baseball has very complex revenue sharing clauses, which accounts for hundreds of millions of dollars being transferred from high-revenue teams to low-revenue teams in the name of preserving competitive balance (Zimbalist 2010). Yet, some low-revenue teams do not use these transferred funds to hire more talented players in order to maintain competitive balance. Instead, they low-ball payroll in order to increase profits for the franchise.

While the issues of player compensation essentially revolve around the tensions between employer and employee, the details and nuances of these negotiations are far from simple in professional sports. Whether part of a sport with CBAs or not, sports agents have become essential for athletes. Given the complexities of CBAs, opportunities for bonuses, sponsorships, and endorsements, players look to professionals to help them negotiate in order to earn the most money they can at the time of signing (Harrow and Swatek 2011). A major incentive for these negotiations is that professional athletes' careers are short relative to other professions, so their earning potential is limited. Harrow and Swatek (2011) report that for the four major league sports (NFL, MLB, NBA, NHL), player salaries are set between 52 percent and 62 percent of total revenue. As shown above, many of the rules are set up to promote league and franchise profitability, not to increase player salaries per se. It can be argued that despite the seemingly high salaries of professional athletes, their take home pay is relatively small given the fact that they are the central figures in this entertainment industry.

The Commercialism of Intercollegiate Athletics

Universities in the United States are the only higher education institutions in the world that include competitive sports as an integral part of their programs. More than half a million women and men play collegiate sports every year (Branch 2011). A much smaller number of those athletes are responsible for bringing millions of fans to the stadiums or courts. For example, March Madness, the annual men's collegiate basketball tournament, generates a viewership of over 80 million (Branch 2011). Through ticket sales, concessions, merchandising, and the sale of media rights, billions of dollars flow through the National Collegiate Athletic Association (NCAA) and universities every year (Branch 2011). In his detailed account of the NCAA and university practices, Taylor Branch (2011), a leading civil rights historian, points out the harmful effects of the commercialization of intercollegiate athletics. He argues that the NCAA and universities rely on a sentimental attitude toward amateurism to maintain their control over athletes' labor, making millions in the process. Branch admits that most people have a visceral negative reaction to the thought of openly paying college athletes. But Branch's investigation into the corruption and politics of intercollegiate athletics reveals that the highly successful, high-profile athletic programs do not simply make money through the labor of "unpaid" athletes; they make millions. While Branch's assessment of intercollegiate athletics is cynical, his insights raise important issues in intercollegiate sport.

The revenue that the NCAA and universities earn through successful athletics programs, which rely primarily on basketball and football, is noteworthy. Media contracts are significant sources of revenue. Most sports are not allowed to negotiate media contracts on their own. They depend on the NCAA to negotiate media contracts on their behalf. The NCAA redistributes a portion of revenue back to participating universities but also retains a portion. While actual sharing percentages are unavailable, the NCAA seems to be an extremely profitable enterprise, especially for a nonprofit organization whose purpose is to ensure the "fairness" of intercollegiate competition and "to integrate intercollegiate athletics into higher education so that the educational experience of the student-athlete is paramount"

(NCAA 2012). When the NCAA moved its headquarters to Indianapolis just prior to 2001, the space cost $50 million that year for 116,000 square feet. By 2010, the NCAA expanded another 130,000 square feet. In addition, NCAA officials fly in private jets, a luxury most nonprofit organizations cannot afford. Football is the only sport that has managed to collectively free itself from NCAA rules regarding media negotiations. Conferences and universities with highly successful or admired football programs are negotiating media contracts and benefiting from fan loyalty in profound ways. For example, in 2010, the Southeastern Conference earned over $1 billion in athletic sales (Branch 2011). Some such larger football programs as Texas, Florida, Michigan, and Penn State bring in between $40 million and $80 million in profits each year, even after paying coaches six figure salaries (Branch 2011).

Although the NCAA and the universities presumably work to uphold the amateur code and support student-athletes, they also work relentlessly at trying to bring in more money. In an effort to look for more revenue streams, the NCAA sells DVDs with footage of famous games as well as selling likenesses rights to video game companies. All the proceeds go the NCAA. In contrast, when NFL players' likenesses are in films or video games, the profits go to the players. These monies are significant as Electronic Arts Entertainment paid over $30 million in royalties to NFL players while former college players received nothing. Universities are using similar strategies to garner as much money as they can from their high-revenue sports. As a result, head football coaches' salaries have grown 750 percent since 1984, rising to an average of $2 million. Head basketball coaches now earn on average $4 million per year. To put this in perspective, Branch remarks that this number is 20 times the cumulative 32 percent raise of most college professors. A look at the NCAA budget gives a clear picture of where they put their energies. While claiming to uphold amateurism and the care of the student-athlete, the NCAA's 2010 budget reveals that they spent less than 1 percent on enforcement. In the meantime, millions of dollars were spent on NCAA overhead and large sums given back to 1,200 universities. Such aggressive approaches to revenue streams and the creation of arguably "professional" teams calls into question whether or not universities and the NCAA really have student-athletes' best interests in mind.

Branch asserts that while universities and the NCAA appear to have the same "noble" goals of keeping intercollegiate athletics "pure," their hidden agendas of making money keeps them loosely bound in an unspoken agreement. That agreement has the NCAA shirking responsibilities with respect to regulations, creating scapegoats when there are easy targets, and disregarding students' best interests when it comes to education. Recently, issues relating to the NCAA's refusal to enforce regulations are surfacing. In particular, the NCAA did not look into calls made about illegal postseason football practices at the University of Iowa in which 41 out of 56 athletes collapsed, and 13 were sent to the hospital for kidney failure after a grueling workout. Also, the NCAA finds relatively public and accessible violations to investigate in order to appear to be keeping intercollegiate sports free from "rampant commercialism." For example, Cam Newton of Auburn University was under investigation for allegedly receiving money during the recruitment process at another university. But while the NCAA investigated Cam Newton, they had no objections to him wearing at least 15 corporate logos as part of Auburn's $10.6 million clothing deal with Under Armour. Such a scenario begs the question about who is being corrupt. Finally, a case that calls into question the NCAA's overt purpose of helping student-athletes in their educational endeavors is the story of Jan Kemp, an English professor who refused to change athletes' grades so that they could remain eligible. Although the NCAA officially supports the educational goals of universities, they failed to come to Jan Kemp's side when she was fired and could not get a job at any other university. Kemp filed a lawsuit asking for $100,000 in damages. The jury awarded her $2.6 million, later reduced to a little over $1 million.

The NCAA defends its position by shifting people's attention to what they do to make sure athletes remain "amateur" by adhering to recruiting rules, scholarship regulations, and eligibility requirements. Universities focus on the fact that they are giving student-athletes an education in exchange for their athletic talents. The reality is that in most instances, if an athlete on scholarship gets hurt, her/his scholarship is withdrawn, and athletes receive little assistance in trying to figure out how they might still meet their educational goals. In other words, universities are committed to the athlete but not necessarily the student. Some individuals are beginning to question the efforts of the NCAA and universities to capitalize on a few talented athletes in order to make money. These people are filing lawsuits against universities and the NCAA and basing their cases on the hypocrisy of the term "amateur." First, Branch (2011) notes that there is no legal definition of the word amateur. Second, even so, "amateur" was eliminated from the Olympic Charter after the Amateur Sports Acts. Athletes played a key role in this ruling and now can earn money outside of Olympic competition and still remain Olympics eligible. Branch's point is that if the premiere "amateur" event in the world can handle the shift to overt commercialism, then collegiate athletics just might be able to as well. Third, the NCAA claims that student-athletes have no rights, but the NCAA makes every college athlete sign a waiver relinquishing his or her rights to proceeds from any sales based on their athletic accomplishments. The obvious question is finally being asked by lawyers defending athletes: "What right is it that they're waiving? [. . .] You can't waive something you don't have. So they had a right that they gave up in consideration to the principle of amateurism, if there be such" (Branch 2011, ¶95). Finally, there is differential treatment of student-athletes compared to other students (Anderson 2010). For instance, a drama major is allowed to pursue outside revenue with no consequences. If a drama major wants to earn money from being in commercials based on her/his talents, he or she is allowed to do so. An athlete is not allowed to earn any money based on his or her talents. The university is the only entity that can earn money from an athlete's talents.

The business of intercollegiate athletics is complex. Most university athletic programs do not make money, but for those few programs that do, Branch raises some ethical and philosophical questions. In the case of the NCAA, Branch suggests that their primary function appears to have shifted from oversight to profitability. It remains to be seen whether the NCAA's recent efforts to return to "integrity" (NCAA 2011) mark a significant change in intercollegiate athletics.

Racial Diversity and Racism in Collegiate and Professional Sports

On the surface, it appears as though racial diversity has been achieved in collegiate and professional sports. A closer look reveals the reality that collegiate and professional sports remain white dominated. Looking at the diversity of players offers some insight into the uneven ways in which various groups are represented in collegiate sports. According to the 2011 Racial and Gender Report Card produced by The Institute for Diversity and Ethics in Sports, African American football players account for 45.8 percent of Division I football players while the percentage of white players remains close at 45.1 percent. In basketball, the percentages are fairly even for women's basketball with African Americans making up 51 percent of the total. For men's basketball, African Americans represent 60.9 percent of the total number of players, and whites make up 30.5 percent. Besides these two sports, whites comprise the majority of collegiate athletes. The percentage of whites combined for Division I, II, and III is 70.4 percent for male student-athletes and 77.2 percent for female student-athletes. As of 2010, the percentages of minority players in professional sports are a little higher than in collegiate sports. For instance, the MLS consists of 46 percent minority players, the NFL is at 67 percent, the WNBA is 65 percent with no Latina representation at all, the NBA is 82 percent minority, and MLB stands at 39.6 percent with 27 percent of that being Latino. For these high-profile professional sports, nonwhite athletes represent approximately 60 percent of the total. Yet, numbers from the NHL are omitted as well as tennis, golf, triathlon, cycling, and a myriad of other professional sports. At the very least, these numbers illustrate the degree to which minority athletes are overrepresented in a few professional sports, but remain largely underrepresented in North American collegiate and professional sport in general.

The overrepresentation of minorities, especially African Americans, in high-revenue sports serves as a draw for many young African American males (Upthegrove, Roscigno, and Zubrinsky 1999). The large number of African Americans in these high-profile sports encourages other African American young men to believe that sports will provide upward mobility. African American families are four times more likely to encourage their sons to pursue sport than their white counterparts. Many scholars argue that the academic-athletic tension for these student-athletes is the highest for any other student-athlete population. The desire of universities to produce athletically winning teams forces a rift between serving the student-athletes as athletes versus serving them as students. For years, the lowest graduation rates occur among African American student-athletes. To begin with, they are often not well prepared for college level academics and get relatively little support for academic development while in college. Such patterns highlight the tensions these high-profile, mostly African American student-athletes experience as a result of universities placing emphasis on sports programs as revenue generating enterprises. Furthermore, it challenges universities to consider their missions more seriously, especially with respect to student-athletes in general and minority student-athletes in high-profile sports in particular.

Despite overrepresentation of minority athletes in some sports, leadership positions at both the collegiate and professional levels remain predominately filled by white males (Armstrong 2011). For instance, whites hold an average of 90 percent of collegiate head coaching jobs, and approximately 93 percent of athletic director positions with Latinos and Asians making up only a combined 1 percent of the minority total. In 2011, efforts by the Black Coaches and Administrators (BCA) association to put consistent pressure on universities to increase the number of black coaches in the applicant pool appear to have paid off. In addition, the BCA focused on ensuring that more search committees had people of color on them. Many scholars (e.g., Smith and Hattery 2011) feel that these two initiatives resulted in 18 coaches of color beginning the 2011 season in FBS (Football Bowl Subdivision) schools. This is the highest percentage of minority coaches ever in the history of university athletics. Lapchick, director of the Institute for Diversity and Ethics in Sports, agrees with the focus of the BCA. It appears as though increasing the number of minorities in the applicant pool and developing policies that require people of color to be on hiring committees will help diversify leadership positions in sport.

While people of color have some opportunities to play professional sports, becoming a majority owner of a professional sports team has been elusive until recently (Armstrong 2011). Reggie Fowler, an African American businessman, put forth a bid for an NFL franchise in the early 2000s. Despite a strong investment group, his bid was not even looked at by the other owners (Armstrong 2011). After becoming involved in some controversy over the facts on his résumé, Fowler did not continue to pursue majority ownership. In 2011, Fowler eventually became a minority owner of the Minnesota Vikings. While other African American investors have attained minority ownership of football teams, as of this writing 100 percent of NFL franchise majority owners are white. In contrast, the NBA made history in 2003 when Robert L. Johnson became the first African American majority owner of an NBA franchise, the Charlotte Bobcats. After losing money, Michael Jordan bought the franchise from Johnson in 2010 and became the second African American to have majority ownership of a professional sports team.

Although majority ownership for people of color has been extremely slow to emerge in professional sports, part ownership is becoming more available to minority investors. Some investors see the move into sports ownership not only as economically sound, but also socially important. Martin Luther King III's reason for seeking part ownership of the New York Mets was to set an example for others. King III's interest in minority ownership of a professional sports team was to show others that it is possible for people of color to be sport leaders. Other minority leaders have advanced this vision as well. Bertram Lee and Peter Bynoe bought 37.5 percent share of the Denver Nuggets in 1989, becoming the first black managing general partners of a major professional sports franchise. Sheila Johnson has part ownership in NHL and WNBA franchises. In addition, Venus and Serena Williams have invested in the Miami Dolphins. Many of these black owners see their investments as ways of giving back to sport and of promoting diversity efforts at this leadership level. Certainly, it remains to be seen whether these pioneers are an anomaly or part of a trend.

Recently, professional sports are feeling compelled to promote diversity at several different levels (Kim and Cheong 2011). NASCAR's Drive for Diversity program provides support at the developmental level for minority drivers. Despite these efforts, no driver from this group has successfully jumped into the mainstream racing circuit, primarily due to a substantial increase in funding necessary to make the leap. Also, Major League Baseball has begun a "Diverse Partners Program" that aims to increase racial diversity among baseball affiliates. Specifically, it aims to increase the applicant pool of vendors who get the opportunity to sell their goods at games. Major League Baseball sees this move as improving both their efficiency and profitability while helping minorities benefit from the baseball industry. For many franchises, this move is framed in terms of economics. They view the diversity of vendors from which to choose as a smart business move because they can then select the best from a greater variety of vendors. The National Hockey League's efforts are more directed at player participation with their "Hockey is for Everyone" initiative in which they promote hockey in minority neighborhoods. The program garners support from NHL players, clubs, and fans to raise funds for nonprofit youth hockey organizations across North America who can access a diverse population. The NHL Web site claims to have introduced hockey to over 45,000 minority children since its inception.

One explanation of these recent efforts at diversification in high-profile sports at both the collegiate and professional levels can be found in Bell's interest-convergence principle (Singer, Harrison, and Bukstein 2010 and Nadeau et al. 2011). According to sport scholars, one reason that whites are willing to integrate minorities into what has traditionally been their domain is due to either an economic or social benefit in doing so. Specifically, the goal of winning in intercollegiate athletics and professional sports promotes diversity in that these institutions are most interested in having the best players possible, thus willing to expand the applicant pool in order to attain the best players. In addition, the willingness to expand vendor opportunities to more diverse groups is largely seen as an economic advantage. Furthermore, athlete-endorsed advertising has found advantages in matching the ethnicity of the athlete with the target audience (Kim and Cheong 2011). The likelihood of the target consumer purchasing commodities is greater when they can relate ethnically to the players. Finally, social capital can be gained as well. As collegiate and professional sport organizations diversify their athletes, the more they find themselves able to compete in a more global and diverse marketplace.

While the previous information provide insights into the landscape of racial diversity among players as well as leadership in sport, it is important to try to understand the processes at work that sustain white majority. A rather simple theoretical explanation may serve as solid grounding for understanding the social forces at work despite civil rights legislation. In 1947, Emory Bogardus (see Smith and Hattery 2011) proposed the theory of "social distance." Within this theory, the assumptions are that people like to be with people most like themselves. As a result they develop all kinds of strategies to distance themselves from people unlike themselves. During the 1970s, researchers began asking questions of both whites and African Americans about their attitudes toward each other. While they generally held positive attitudes about each other, there were subtle ways in which they would distance themselves from each other. For instance, although whites stated they would feel comfortable working with people of color, most said they would not be comfortable living in the same neighborhood or socializing in other ways. Extending this rationale to sports management and leadership positions, many scholars have noted the "good ole boys network" is typical of the sport management world. As such, entry into this white, fraternal group has been difficult for people of color since it operates much more on the familial level. Given the paucity of people of color in sport leadership positions, it appears that the economic imperative has not yet been felt.

Furthermore, it is important to look at how racism continues in subtle ways, contributing to sports remaining white dominated. Symbolic Racism or New Racism is a term used to describe the subtle ways in which racism manifests in the 21st century (Armstrong 2011). The three tenets of this type of racism are (1) the assumption that racism does not exist anymore, (2) the idea that people of color are entirely to blame for their position in society, and (3) the use of the concept of "fit" with organizations. These assumptions promote a new language in terms of racial discrimination. For instance, whites often state they are color blind and that decisions involving people of color are based on "merit" or "fit." As such, the belief that there is a "level playing field" removes them from any personal responsibility for racism. The simple example of "select" sports teams shows how racism continues in different ways than in the past. While parents do not overtly say that sports should be segregated, they enroll their children in "select" teams, which are presumably about playing ability. In reality, the cost of these programs is prohibitive for many people of color. Yet, the belief that only skilled athletes make the teams allows whites to feel as though the selection process is free from racism. In addition, when final decisions are made about hiring coaches or administrators, whites often talk about the right "fit" for the organization. Language about how a person of color might not feel comfortable in such certain settings as alumni brunches and sponsor banquets keep people of color from being hired.

The media continues to be a site in which racism manifests in both subtle and overt ways, reinforcing limited and stereotypical views of athletes of color. A 2011 study (Eagleman 2011) analyzing MLB news stories revealed that whites, blacks, Latinos, and Asians were represented in consistently stereotypical ways. Whites were often depicted in the sports media as having a strong work ethic and an "all-American" background. In contrast, stories about blacks emphasized the adversity they faced as young players, the tattoos they had on their bodies, or the "gangsta" clothing they wore. Success was attributed to natural ability. There were consistently references to children born out of wedlock or divorces of athletes, alluding to questionable moral character. If a black player did not fit this mold, then descriptions about how he was neither tattooed nor from a rough background were the focus. In other words, the emphasis was on how these black players fit or did not fit according to the social norms of whites. Latino players were depicted in various ways depending on whether or not they were U.S. born. U.S.-born Latino players were described as working hard, having family values, and being good looking, similar to white players. Non-U.S.-born Latino players were described very similarly to the black athletes. These depictions differentially value "American" over foreign. Asians were consistently framed as the "other." Ethnicity differences were highlighted through a focus on anything reporters could find that contrasted American players. For instance, Asians were described as having different warm-up routines or techniques, liking different foods, having a different physique, and not knowing English well. The fact that consistent categorizations occurred across time and various news stories points to racism operating at the subconscious level. While depictions are not always derogatory, regular stereotyping reinforces very narrow views of capabilities, moral character, and personalities along racial and ethnic lines.

Overt racism in sport is rarer, but there are instances in which this issue arises. One recent example is the overt racism expressed by Don Imus in 2007 on his radio talk show (Gill 2011). After the Tennessee versus Rutgers women's basketball game, Imus and a guest on his radio talk show referred to the primarily African American team from Rutgers as having tattoos and being "nappy headed hos." Such language was offensive to the players, who were surprised and shocked to be considered in this manner. Furthermore, they said the white girls from Tennessee "all looked cute." More important, the responses to Don Imus's overt racism highlight the phenomenon of white privilege. White privilege refers to the idea that all kinds of privileges go along with being white. The sense of "normal" attached to whiteness places expectations on others based on what white people can do, and it obscures the ways in which white people benefit everyday from being white. Rutgers's response was negligible, and counseling for the team distraught by the controversy that lasted 13 days was never given. White privilege accounted for little help going out to the players because university administrators did not consider the comments to be serious. They also felt that recovery from the comments would be easy since it was a matter of recognizing that the comments were not "intended" to be harmful. Players were expected to be able to "deal" with the insults. Fortunately, the media was willing to view the comments as serious. Within those 13 days, Don Imus was fired, and MSNBC and WFAN lost just over $6 million in revenue from advertising dollars. While this seemed a step in the right direction in order to make a public statement that overt racism is not accepted, white privilege meant that Don Imus had avenues for full recovery from his transgressions. Imus was back on the air with an ABC affiliate within eight months at an annual salary of $8 million.

These insights show that racial diversity in collegiate and professional sports is an ongoing issue. Sports remain predominantly white. Other than player representation in select sports, most collegiate athletes and professional players are white. In addition, sport leadership positions remain overwhelmingly white, and minority ownership in professional sports is rare. The notions of social distance, new racism, and white privilege offer some explanations about the mechanisms that drive the status quo, showing how difficult it is for people of color to gain access to the same sport opportunities as whites. The media remains a powerful structure through which these mechanisms operate. Yet, raising awareness allows for more critical and informed perspectives to emerge around the issues of racial diversity and racism in sport.

Gender (In)equity in Sport Leadership

Despite significant increases in women's sport participation, women hold relatively few sport leadership positions. Coaching appears to be the area in which women have the best access to leadership positions. Women make up 42.6 percent of head coaches for female sports in intercollegiate athletics even though this is a drop since 1972 when women held approximately 90 percent of the coaching positions for female sports (Burton, Grappendort, and Henderson 2011). In positions of higher rank, men far outnumber women (Pfister 2010). Including all divisions in NCAA sports, women make up approximately 19 percent of athletic director positions. Moreover, at the Division I level, there were only 30 women (9%) who were athletic directors in 2010 (Burton, Grappendort, and Henderson 2011). This trend is even observed at the international level. For instance, only 9.5 percent of the total membership of the International Olympic Committee is female (Pfister 2010). Thus, the higher the prestige of the sport leadership position, the less likely it is for women to be represented. While several strategies have historically focused on acquiring skills, seeing women's strengths as leadership strengths, and removing structural barriers, sport scholars argue that gender ideology remains a significant barrier for women in sport leadership.

Assumptions about women's strengths and commonly held views of leadership qualities do not coincide, resulting in few women becoming and remaining sport leaders. Burton, Grappendort, and Henderson (2011) suggest that role congruency theory helps frame why women are vastly underrepresented in sport leadership positions even though female sports participation is increasing. Burton suggests that gender expectations for women and gendered beliefs about leaders in sport partially explain why women find it difficult to get jobs. Gender ideology currently frames women as being supportive, emotional, and relational (Burton, Grappendort, and Henderson 2011 and Sibson 2010). In contrast, such attributes most often associated with sport leadership as independent, charismatic, rational, and able to make decisions are considered masculine qualities. Regardless of whether or not women and men can cross gender ideological boundaries, in reality, is a mute point. What seems to matter is the *perception* of men's and women's strengths and liabilities with respect to commonly held beliefs about leadership. Burton, Grappendort, and Henderson (2011) found that men were much more likely to obtain a sport leadership position despite the fact that female applicants had exceptional professional experience and that most men felt that women would be equally successful. In other words, despite being qualified and perceived as capable, the overriding factor regarding not hiring women was "lack of fit" between perceived ideal leadership qualities (masculine) and women's strengths (feminine). Similarly, men were also less likely to be considered for a position perceived more as a supportive role. Instead, they were hired into leadership roles more frequently despite showing interest and skills in supportive positions. The actual hiring of women in sport leadership positions was found to be even more complex and paradoxical. For instance, if women acted more masculine or focused on their "masculine" attributes during the hiring process, they were less likely to be considered for the position because they did not fit societal expectations of females in general (Burton, Grappendort, and Henderson 2011). Alternately, if they focused on their more "feminine" traits such as being supportive or collaborative, they were not likely to be hired for the reasons stated above (Burton, Grappendort, and Henderson 2011). For women, attaining sport leadership positions appears to be filled with tensions created by gender ideology.

Other scholars have explored the internal ideological constraints regarding women being hired for sport leadership positions. Some sport scholars argue that women internalize dominant gender ideology to such an extent that they do not actively seek higher positions (see Sartore and Cunningham 2007). For example, these researchers found that female assistant coaches frequently have little intention of becoming head coaches. Explanations for such curbed desire for higher positions are thought to result from internal identity conflicts. These scholars suggest that women in support roles are more likely to remain there because the personal and public feedback they receive aligns with their own sense of self. They suggest that this internal sense of self results from dominant gender ideology, which sustains specific ideas about how women should behave. Judith Butler (2006) explains this idea through her concept of gender performance. As an example, femininity is a performance, not a natural way of being. But femininity can feel like a natural way of being once the requisite feminine behaviors are internalized. While the process is complex, this internalization results in real actions. Sartore and Cunningham (2007) propose that as long as women feel that assistant coaching aligns well with their own self-perceptions, they are unlikely to seek higher positions because they may perceive the leadership skill set to be different from their self-concept. When women do switch roles, they are likely to experience incongruence among feedback and self-perceptions. In these instances, women will alter their behaviors, alter self-perceptions, or resist the new identity and seek a new situation.

While theoretical explanations for women's struggles regarding sport leadership are useful, understanding the various ways in which the struggle takes place is insightful. Policies such as gender quota requirements in order to receive funding or accreditation have helped women attain sport leadership positions. The Senior Woman Administrator (SWA) in intercollegiate athletics is one good example. Language changes from "chairman" to "chair" have symbolically encouraged a sense of opportunity for women. However, significant tensions exist in subtle ways that extend from the highly masculinized culture of sport. Sibson (2010) found that women who were hired in order to meet a quota often felt excluded. Sibson's case study of women hired to the board of an Australian sport organization illustrates the ways in which exclusion can occur. When the women were hired, they were not given any specific position with specific duties. Only men held these positions, leaving the women with very little positional power. With no specific title or duties, the men did not feel they needed to consult the women. For instance, when a major renovation was approved, not one of the women was consulted. The men felt that the approval was only needed from the man officially assigned to facilities. Paradoxically, the facility was for women's sports, and the facilities director unilaterally agreed that women's sports would pay for the renovation. In this case, women were not consulted although the decision had a major impact on women's sports and their financial commitments. In addition, the three women on the board kept bringing up important issues such as inefficiencies in the canteen or evening maintenance crews. In both instances, the men gave very little attention to these agenda items, often suggesting that these issues were not important, and quickly moved onto the agenda item that most interested them. In this particular case study, at least one female quit because she felt unheard and underutilized. While she felt she had skills that could move the organization forward, she was never given the chance to use them.

Some strategies that have been shown to work for women sport leaders are mentoring and mainstreaming. Having a mentor has been crucial for women in sport leadership. A focused support system is critical because the larger social support system is culturally masculine (Oglesby 2001). In addition, a newer form of tackling gender equity—mainstreaming—is emerging in a select few European sport organizations (Pfister 2010). Mainstreaming is the idea that both genders are required in any organization in order to move it forward in the 21st century. Such an idea seems obvious, but it has not necessarily been a widely held assumption. Mainstreaming seeks to "call out" the obvious through gender training for women and men. The goal of this training is to show how exclusionary practices hurt both women and men. The core of these arguments is that as organizations become more diverse, a wider variety of ideas emerge. While few scholars are not suggesting that antidiscrimination initiatives be abandoned at the moment, they do call for deeper cultural changes.

NASCAR: Hanging onto "Local" Roots While Going "Global"

NASCAR is the acronym for the National Association for Stock Car Auto Racing. The growth of NASCAR in the past two decades has positioned it as the second most watched professional sport, just behind professional football (Levinson 2001 and NASCAR 2010). Stock car racing has grown from its grassroots beginnings to capture a global audience. Today, NASCAR has more than 75 million fans in over 150 countries. NASCAR events hold 17 of the top 20 single-day sporting events attendance records in the world. In addition, fans spend more than $3 billion every year on merchandise purchases. NASCAR's history shows how the powerful intersections of culture, politics, and economics affect growth. NASCAR's recent negotiation between the economic pull to reach a global audience and the cultural, local grounding of the South exemplifies the issues that arise in the process of sport globalization.

Stock car racing was born out of people who transported moonshine, an illegal whiskey made from distilling potatoes or corn. These moonshine drivers improved their personal car engines so that they could outrun the federal agents when delivering this illegal beverage. As a way to extend their passion for driving fast and attain "bragging rights," drivers began testing their limits through informal races called stock car races (Levinson 2001). Eventually, running moonshine was no longer a needed service, but stock car racing continued to grow in the southern United States. Substantial growth occurred post World War II, but the races were all local phenomena. While racetracks were being built all over the South, rules, regulations, and venues were radically different. Some tracks were simple dirt ovals at county fairs. These races were meant to capitalize on the crowds that were already attending a local event. Other tracks catered to the cars with paved ovals and banked turns but could not always accommodate crowds very well. In short, stock car racing was growing in popularity, but there was very little standardization and consistency in what spectators saw.

In December 1947, Bill France Sr. organized a meeting in Daytona Beach, Florida, to address the issues of inconsistency facing stock car racing (NASCAR 2010). He proposed establishing a governing body for stock car racing in order to standardize the rules and launch a series of racing to enhance winners' prestige and prize money. With this vision, NASCAR was born. Two months after organizing, NASCAR held its first sanctioned race. Then, in 1949, NASCAR hosted its inaugural series, now known as the Cup series, America's premiere racing circuit. Under France's direction, NASCAR operated in an autocratic manner. Unlike other professional sport governing bodies, in which owners of different teams made decisions together about how the sport was to be administered and shared in profits equally, NASCAR held full authority over decisions and benefited from all the profits. NASCAR controlled how much money went to the organization itself or was distributed to the drivers in the form of prize money.

During the post–civil rights movement, NASCAR saw considerable growth. This growth was largely due to the intersections of politics and culture. Politically, the South was being forced to change its ways through various social movements, civil rights being the most acutely felt. As desegregation spread throughout the South, stock car racing remained an event through which whiteness and the values associated with whiteness could be celebrated. NASCAR's strong cultural connection to the deep South was reinforced as white male southerners flocked to NASCAR races. For these people, stock car racing represented the blue collar worker who embraced such "traditional" American values as heteronormativity and patriarchial mindsets, conservative politics, and an underlying ethos of entrepreneurialism (Newman and Beissel 2009). NASCAR events were exclusive to whites, and as Newman and Beissel (2009) suggest, "created symbolic value out of that exclusivity" (523). As a result, it was the local character of NASCAR events and symbolic attachments to conservative politics that accounted for its economic growth post–civil rights.

By the 1990s, NASCAR's intersections with politics helped further promote its popularity. The phrase "NASCAR nation" became synonymous with conservative politics throughout George W. Bush's administration (Newman and Beissel 2009). Political supporters of conservative, Republican politics found symbolic meaning in the term. NASCAR nation simultaneously represented local, rural, mostly white Southern culture, a return to "traditional" America, and the American conservative nationalism of the Bush years. Through this unique combination of local grounding and widespread political appeal among supporters of Bush, NASCAR moved in the national spotlight. Leaders of NASCAR during this time capitalized on media contracts in order to broadcast events to a much wider range of people. In turn, corporate sponsors were seeing the economic potential of being linked to this growing sport. With the combination of politics, media exposure, and corporate sponsorship, NASCAR's growth as a professional sport was exponential through the 1990s.

Moving into the 21st century, political ties to George W. Bush's agenda inherently allied NASCAR to a market-oriented mentality (Newman and Beissel 2009). It became the economic imperative of NASCAR to broaden its appeal to consumers beyond its "traditional" market segment. Using tactics of media exposure, corporate sponsorship, and the lure of competition, NASCAR grew to be the second largest viewed sport in the world. NASCAR capitalized on deregulation of the media industry in 2001 and signed contracts with Fox and NBC/TNT to the tune of $2.4 billion. Such an influx of money meant that more race series could be offered with more prize money, which resulted in the increased competition that spectators desired. In 2007, NASCAR made its most significant move with respect to the media by adding partnerships with ABC and ESPN. It was the relationship with ESPN that really brought widespread exposure to NASCAR given that ESPN could help NASCAR reach a more global audience through magazines; Web sites; and, more significantly, ESPN *Deportes*, the Spanish speaking ESPN TV and radio broadcasts. In addition, the ESPN affiliation helped legitimize stock car racing to a much broader audience, making it no longer the exclusive sport of the Southern white male.

Not only were media connections important in the rise of NASCAR as a more globally recognized sport, but also corporate sponsorships from more such global companies as McDonald's, Coca-Cola, Nextel, AT&T, Home Depot, and Fedex helped bring

NASCAR to consumers worldwide. With an influx of new monies, NASCAR then decided to enter new markets by appealing to a more international audience. While still maintaining its local Southern flavor, NASCAR wanted to capture these untapped markets. In rebranding itself, NASCAR entered the ambiguous territory of hybridization as it was pulled forward into these new markets by the significant economic gains to be had.

Scholars Newman and Beissel (2009) point out three ways in which NASCAR decided to enter a broader, more global market. First, NASCAR focused efforts on what Newman and Beissel call the "Latinization of NSACAR Nation." Second, NASCAR pursued a more diverse driver population by bringing in "celebrity drivers" from other types of racing. Third, NASCAR decided to allow non-U.S.-made cars into their races, namely Toyota. The intent of these moves was for NASCAR to appeal to the broader markets they were now reaching through new media channels and corporate sponsorship affiliations.

Yet, these moves into a wider market segment have proved tumultuous because the "local good ole boy" audience has not fully embraced these changes. In the attempt to grow, NASCAR tried to connect with a growing Latin U.S. population as well as international Spanish speaking nations, primarily South America. Two notable actions represent the impetus of this movement. First, NASCAR lured and promoted one of South America's most famous drivers, Juan Pablo Montoya, from Columbia. Formerly a Formula One race car driver, Montoya became one of the first Latino drivers to compete in the NEXTEL Cup race series. In addition, advertising campaigns included the famous South American singer, Juanes. Such efforts not only contributed to the hybridization of NASCAR but also to the hybridization of Montoya himself. For instance, Montoya has simultaneously been asked to host a series of educational sessions about NASCAR racing in Spanish as well as take English immersion language courses. Thus, while being asked to connect directly to the new market, Montoya is also expected to be more "American." Despite these efforts to please different consumers, Montoya has been subject to insults and discontent from the white, "local" spectator, emerging as the embodiment of "otherness." As Newman and Beissel (2009) suggest, Montoya represents the "immigrant" whose citizenship rests clearly outside of U.S. soil. For the traditional, white Southern male NASCAR fan, Montoya symbolizes a threat to the "homeland security" ethos. Despite this backlash,

NASCAR continues to support Montoya because of the growth they see in this particular market segment.

In the attempt to internationalize stock car racing, NASCAR has also focused on making their events more international in general. One way in which NASCAR has sought to increase revenue along with international appeal is by luring celebrity drivers from such other countries as Scotland, Australia, and French-speaking Canada. The cost of acquiring these celebrities is substantial, but NASCAR hopes to increase brand equity by featuring some of the best drivers in the world. The influx of international celebrity race car drivers has subsequently resulted in the displacement of "All-American" drivers on many teams. The increased presence of famous international drivers has met with resistance from NASCAR traditionalists primarily based on personal disconnect. The working class consumer has traditionally represented the majority of NASCAR consumers, yet in light of more foreign-born, well-paid race car drivers, the blue collar worker has little in common with this new demographic. Similarly, the introduction of Toyota into NASCAR events heightens the discontent of traditional, American consumers. In many ways, the decision to incorporate Toyota into the NASCAR family made financial sense. When American car companies were struggling, being supported by taxes and government subsidies, Toyota was thriving. Teams sponsored by American car manufacturers were carrying more of the cost of racing due to lower sponsorship dollars. On the other hand, Toyota was able to support teams at a greater percentage of sponsorship, as a result of their financial stability.

While Toyota was hoping to edge into the "local" scene and appear more American through their presence in NASCAR, the "local" consumer felt disenfranchised more than ever. For the NASCAR traditionalists, stock car racing had moved too far from its "Southern" roots. As Newman and Beissel (2009) point out, NASCAR became "too global for the local" (531). Just as their drivers were becoming less American, so too were the cars. As such, the economic advantages of repackaging the brand came into conflict with cultural and political sensibilities. The consumer upon which the brand was built resisted in a formidable fashion. They started not attending NASCAR events. For the past several years, many fans have expressed a desire for NASCAR to "return to its roots." In an attempt to respond to this demographic, NASCAR has tried to connect more locally by refurbishing several racetracks and launching advertising campaigns that focus on getting back to basics by promoting NASCAR's heritage as well as enlisting country music singers in their ads to create the ambience of the "good ole South."

What remains to be seen is whether or not NASCAR can successfully engage and sustain a hybrid image. To do so may require substantial reinventions of the social and cultural norms of stock car racing. For instance, the international component of NASCAR may lead to a greater acceptance of this demographic by the conservative, white Southerner and, in turn, fulfill the aims of the current rebranding efforts. On the other hand, resistance may become more vehement, forcing NASCAR to make a choice between going "global" as is the tendency for large companies to do in search of greater profits or reverting to the "local" by aligning itself exclusively with conservative, white, patriarchal, heteronormative consumer sensibilities, thereby firmly attaching themselves to the politics and culture of this insular demographic. While the historical conditions place NASCAR in a unique situation with respect to local-global tensions, the tensions NASCAR feels epitomizes the dilemma that large sport organizations face when they try to brand a "local" image in the "global" arena.

Concussions and Brain Trauma: Growing Concerns, Growing Knowledge

Concussion and brain trauma injuries are perhaps the most controversial injuries in professional and youth sports today. Given that sport is a place of high stakes, there is more pressure to keep good players playing. In addition, sport culture encourages acceptance of pain and injury as part of what is valued (Malcolm 2009 and Messner 1992). As a result, there are numerous instances of letting players play through pain and injury despite the fact that physicians know more about when it is advisable for athletes not to play. Sports medicine has developed to the point that protocols for most injuries are fairly standard. Athletes can be made aware of specific timelines and protocols for healing. Yet, the nature of concussion and brain trauma is different because so little is known about them, and the symptoms vary. As such, concussion and brain trauma remain the most serious sports injuries.

While the number of concussions and brain injuries reported each year in the United States is rising dramatically, that number may be only a fraction of the number that actually occur given the complexity and ambiguity of diagnosis. Concussion and brain injuries are estimated to occur in 1.6 to 3.8 million athletes each year in the United States (Crisco and Greenwald 2011). Sports reporting the greatest number of incidents are American football, ice hockey, lacrosse, and women's ice hockey (Crisco and Greenwald 2011). There is some evidence that many athletes are asymptomatic upon trauma to the head. In these cases, concussion is not officially diagnosed right away, but athletes report brain impairment 24 to 48 hours post head trauma impact (Crisco and Greenwald 2011). Typically caused by rapid deceleration or rotation of the head, concussion may or may not be accompanied by loss of consciousness. Such other symptoms as burred vision, disorientation, and vomiting are often taken as indicators of concussion (Crisco and Greenwald 2011 and Malcolm 2009). Beyond the sure signs of concussion, there are many degrees of mild concussion that are much harder to determine (Crisco and Greenwald 2011 and Malcolm 2009).

The gray area with respect to diagnosis of a concussion is partly a result of medical uncertainty (Malcolm 2009 and Tator 2011). The medical world is not in agreement about what constitutes a concussion and much misinformation abounds. For instance, while many believe that loss of consciousness is the key determinant of concussion, recent research suggests that 95 percent of concussions are not associated with loss of consciousness (Malcolm 2009). Also, the physicality of sport complicates diagnoses because dehydration, athlete feedback while physically exhausted, and other physical stressors can interfere with proper diagnoses. More important, common knowledge about concussion holds more weight in sport culture than clinical or medical knowledge. Tator (2011) suggests that most sport participants do not know that "seeing stars" are most often concussions. Furthermore, Tator says that many participants do not recognize concussion as a brain injury. Malcolm's (2009) research into general knowledge about concussion within professional Australian rugby confirms such incomplete knowledge. He found that most players and coaches adhere to the "loss of consciousness" signifier as the determining factor for diagnosis of concussion.

Malcolm (2009) suggests that the gray area of medical analysis results in players and coaches creating a culture of denial with respect to concussions. With such other types of injuries such muscle, tendon, or ligament, there are visible signs of trauma and persistent pain that athletes are not likely to ignore. In addition, with advancements in physical therapy and medical care, the prognosis and treatment protocol is well defined and predictable. While never ideal, players employ many tactics for negotiating these types of injuries so that they can increase the likelihood of keeping their jobs. For concussion, however, Malcolm points out that there is an automatic three-week hiatus from sport imposed on players as soon as concussion is diagnosed. This protocol is difficult for many players and coaches to handle because there are often no other symptoms. Players feel ready to play again even though they intellectually know that they may be at risk for severe head trauma should a subsequent blow to the head re-occur soon after the first. Malcolm shows how this uncertainty forces players, coaches, and even medical practitioners to avoid concussion diagnoses. In his case study of rugby medical advisors, Malcolm demonstrates how they tended to accept "loss of consciousness" as the defining symptom of concussion, avoiding any gray area in order to maintain their relationships with the players and coaches, keeping their jobs in the process. In other words, "where athletes tolerate injuries to maintain their athletic self" (Pike and Maguire 2003), clinicians tolerate "compromised" diagnoses to maintain their medical self" (Malcolm 2009: 206).

Despite the tendency for people to focus on the immediate issue of keeping valuable players in the game and the long-term issue of keeping their jobs, there is a strong movement to change rules, improve safety equipment, and improve coaches' education. Crisco and Greenwald (2011) suggest that rule changes regarding intentional head impacts or using protective gear as an offensive "weapon" be explicitly illegal. So far the NFL and the NHL have new policies making intentional head butting illegal, imposing significant fines to those who break the rules (Crisco and Greenwald 2011). Additionally, Crisco and Greenwald note that technology is helping practitioners gain valuable information regarding brain injuries. For instance, helmets are so advanced that they can record the severity of impact, location of impact, and number of impacts a player receives in any given season and over their career. This information can help shape policy with respect to game rules and decisions about post-trauma playing. Some data suggests that a player can receive over 1,400 impacts over a season (Crisco and Greenwald 2011). This information can be used to detect patterns within the currently ambiguous mild concussion category to improve diagnoses and determine better protocols for treatment. Tator (2011) holds the view that coaches are critical components to reducing head trauma because they hold most of the power. He argues that coaches should be required to take concussion education courses so that they are better informed about the serious aspects of concussion and brain trauma. His assumption is that once coaches understand the severity of brain injuries, they might decide to take a more conservative approach. Indeed, with more widespread education, the general public, as well as athletes, might also demand more conservative approaches. As Malcolm (2009) suggests, a cultural shift must occur for concussion to be diagnosed differently. Hard data may be the impetus for change.

The Culture of Skateboarding and the Commodification of "Cool"

In 2002, a teen poll conducted by a marketing firm found that Tony Hawk, arguably the best male skateboarder in the world at that time, was the "coolest big time athlete" (Beal and Wilson 2004). This distinction placed Hawk ahead of such sport celebrities as Tiger Woods and Michael Jordan. The popularity of skateboarding has experienced ups and downs, but since the 1960s, skateboarding has ultimately experienced steady growth. While skateboarding began as an antiestablishment experience, grounded in surfing's culture of freedom and individualism, it has grown into a sport intricately linked to commercialism and corporate culture (Beal 1995, 1996, and Beal and Wilson 2004). Today, skateboarding is not a homogeneous culture. Instead, the growth and commercialization have expanded the range of subcultures within skateboarding. Subcultures have emerged because corporations and participants constantly negotiate the production and meanings of cultural symbols and values in skateboarding.

Much like surfing, skateboarding began as a grassroots effort to define itself differently from mainstream sport. While football, baseball, and basketball were well entrenched in the American psyche as being representative of mainstream culture, skateboarding took off as a counterculture. It was shaped by the desire to avoid extrinsic rewards, obedience to authority, and competition (Beal 1995). Skateboarding took place on the street in unsupervised spaces, had no rules, was not formally organized, and was based on cooperation in its early forms. The appeal of skateboarding was that participants were free to challenge their own limits in individual ways. They practiced techniques and created new ones as a self-directed activity. Young skaters shaped the culture by overtly expressing the positive feelings that accompanied freedom of choice, creativity, and self-expression (Beal 1996). Furthermore, participants reveled in the anticompetitive aspects of their physical activity, eschewing competition and embracing a "lifestyle."

Although this form of sport counters the mainstream sporting ethos, there are aspects about skateboarding's dominant culture that reproduce several aspects of mainstream sport culture (Beal 1996 and Beal and Wilson 2004). The two most prominent aspects are embracing risk and the marginalization of women. Mainstream sport is defined by masculinity. In other words, mainstream sport helps reproduce masculine values, through which risk is encouraged and women are subordinated. In skateboarding media, images of injuries and stories about being injured are valorized. Pain is the currency with which skaters gain acceptance and establish cultural capital. Female skaters are not viewed as risk takers, nor willing to get hurt. This assumption translates to female skaters having less cultural capital and being marginalized. In addition, male skaters view women as wanting to be associated with skateboarding just to "hook up" with guys. This latter aspect is also part of skateboarding media. Highly sexualized images of female skaters as well as nonskaters appear throughout magazines and Internet sources. In this way, skateboarding maintains a culture that opposes mainstream sport on one level but reproduces specific forms of masculinity in alignment with mainstream sport on another one. The paradoxical positioning of skateboarding as a counterculture, although it maintains many aspects of mainstream culture, becomes more pronounced when viewing it from the perspective of commercial growth.

Each time skateboarding has experienced periods of growth, corporations have taken notice. Corporate attention has been facilitated by the creation and development of the National Skateboard Association (NSA) in 1981 (Beal and Wilson 2004). The NSA was developed to legitimize skateboarding by offering competitions. To help this progress, several CEOs of skateboarding companies have served on the board of the NSA over the years. This relationship has hastened the commercialization of skateboarding, bringing it to new levels of popularity and increasing the forms through which it is practiced. The NSA supports both amateur and professional events throughout the United States in terms of sponsoring events, obtaining corporate sponsorships, and securing media coverage for them. Skateboarding has been a key component of the X Games since its inception in 1995. Once the X Games demonstrated their ability to raise sport and brand awareness, the media companies Primedia (owner of nine action sport magazines), Octagon (sport event marketing agency), and NBC created the Gravity Games in 1999 through a strategic partnership. In essence, it is the "extreme" component and the association with risk that sells.

The significant commercialization of skateboarding during the 1990s and into the 21st century has brought skateboarding into the mainstream and the mainstream into skateboarding (Beal and Wilson 2004). For instance, *Transworld Skateboarding*, *Thrasher*, and *Skateboard* magazines and Web sites with around 500,000 viewership help shape the "authentic" skater in powerful ways. Their representations of competition along with the marginalization of women, high-risk activity, images of injuries, and individualistic values are reproduced and sold as a culture. Skateboarding is now recognized by more youth as a legitimate sport. The younger skaters now relate to both a competitive form of skateboarding and a counterculture attitude (Beal 1995). Ironically, it is the branding of skateboarding's core values of risk, freedom, masculinity, and countercultural attitudes that helps skateboarding become symbiotically reliant on corporate culture. Media contributes to skateboarding's popularity and brings competition into the range of legitimate skating forms. The effects of the media's involvement are seen in the younger skaters' desires to wear the clothes of famous skaters and become professional skaters. As such, these skaters are much more accepting of corporate culture as they embrace organized competition and are willing to be aligned overtly with skateboarding brands.

In addition, the mainstream form of skating has helped create a more comfortable space for female skaters (Beal 1995 and 1996). In an attempt to capitalize on a perceived unrealized market, corporations have targeted young females as well. While supporting magazines that reproduce mainstream masculinity, they simultaneously have appealed to female skaters by creating organized competitions such as the All-Girls-Skate-Jam. During these events, female skaters say that they feel empowered and comfortable. They remark that typically they are the only females in the local parks or spaces where they skate. These local spaces are male dominated and governed by a masculine culture that subordinates women and their abilities. As a result, female skaters rarely feel accepted, which results in a greater amount of pressure for them to prove themselves. Beal, a sport sociologist specializing in skateboarding culture, explains that female skaters often talk about needing to be tough in the skating space but then more feminine outside of that space. Skating events for female skaters eliminates that tension but still allows them to participate in a sport that is viewed as embracing freedom, creativity, and anti-authority attitudes. It appears as though these competitions have opened up skateboarding to women in ways that other skateboarding sites have not been able. Events such as the All-Girls-Skate-Jam helped legitimize female skaters and their presence in this sport. Yet, other tensions exist. Corporations have tried to promote a fairly traditional representation of female, which is heterosexual, family oriented, and middle class. Many of the female skaters at these events have tried to resist these portrayals by smoking, swearing, and walking hand in hand with their female partners. Thus, while supported by mainstream corporate America, fluid forms of female identity are constructed in these corporate spaces. Certainly commercialization of female skating has contributed to the rise in numbers of female skaters. In 2001, women comprised 7.5 percent of skaters. A year later, in 2002, that number had grown to 26 percent (Beal and Wilson 2004). Recognition of and branding directed toward this niche market has benefitted both female skaters and corporations.

The merging of skateboarding culture and the corporate world has created multiple forms of skateboarding that are now recognized and encompass a broader range of participants. The commercialization of risk, counterculture, as well as a "cool" lifestyle and attitude has provided space for a multiplicity of skaters. Although they do so carefully, skaters who express disdain for competition and corporatization of skating still buy boards and clothes from companies (Beal and Wilson 2004). For example, they often decorate their skateboards themselves with poetry or other individualized symbols. Simultaneously, there are those who openly display brand logos and stickers, who video tape themselves to send to corporations in hopes of getting "sponsored," and who openly aspire to be a professional. There are female skaters, who are finding spaces in which they are accepted more readily. There are many other participants who define skateboarding as a complex mix of all the above. Indeed, skateboarding's appeal to a wider range of participants can partly be attributed to its corporate ties, paradoxically growing as a result of the commodification of 'cool.'

The Lure of "Lifestyle" Sports: A Case Study in Ultrarunning

In *Understanding Lifestyle Sports: Consumption, Identity and Difference* (2004), Belinda Wheaton points out the myriad ways that lifestyle sports emerge and flourish. She suggests that such lifestyle sports as skateboarding, snowboarding, surfing, B.A.S.E. jumping, and windsurfing have two major facets. One aspect centers on the commercialized version of lifestyle sports as seen in the above discussion of skateboarding. The other aspect deals with understanding the intricate ways that lifestyle sport subcultures are produced, challenged, and reproduced, especially noting how people's identities are shaped through engagement in a particular sport. Lifestyle sports are often synonymous with "alternative" or "extreme" sports. While they vary widely in form, they have several common characteristics. First, they are primarily grass roots individual sports with a strong sense of community that emphasizes fun, participation, and self-actualization. Second, participants tend to spend large amounts of time, money, and emotional energy being involved such that general attitudes and social identities are intimately tied to the subculture. Finally, they involve a certain amount of risk, focus on intrinsic motivation, and emphasize the aesthetic. This section focuses on a case study of ultrarunning, exemplifying some of the key aspects of lifestyle sports that lure people into participation.

Ultrarunning is defined by running any distance longer than a marathon. Participation varies widely, but unlike other lifestyle sports, which eschew competitive forms, ultrarunning embraces racing. The standard racing distances are 50 kilometers, 50 miles, 100 kilometers, and 100 miles although longer multiday stage races and longer single day races exist. The sport has undergone tremendous growth since the early 1980s. In 1981, there were a total of 56 races listed in *Ultrarunning* magazine (Hanold 2008) as compared to over 650 races listed on their Web site for 2011. Before the 1980s, most ultra races took place on roads or tracks. Eighty-seven percent of the total number of races were on tracks or roads in 1981 (Massa 2006). However, since the early 1980s, more ultra races have occurred on forest or mountain trails (Brannen 2006). In 2011, only 10–15 percent of ultras occurred on roads, track, or smooth trails. This is significant because in road ultras competitors can compare times over specific distances more easily (Massa 2006). With the onset of more trail ultras and vastly varied terrain, comparisons over distances are much more difficult (Brannen 2006 and Massa 2006). Brannen laments that such a shift has made ultra racing less "competitive" because there are fewer races in which the top competitors go head to head. On the other hand, Massa argues that these changes "have made the sport more enjoyable" (14).

Participants note that one of the most enjoyable aspects of ultrarunning is not the competition, but the challenge of completing the distance over varied terrain. Ultras take place on terrain that varies from paved roads over gentle rolling hills to technical, single track trails up and over mountain passes. For example, in a 100-mile race the elevation gain and loss might be less than 1000 feet while runners may gain and lose more than 33,000 feet in another race. Elevations of races range from sea level to as much as 11,000 feet. Also, ultra races are held in all climates and weather conditions. Extreme conditions include deserts where temperatures might rise to 120 degrees Fahrenheit and the arctic where temperatures might drop 20 degrees below zero. Runners are typically on a course from 4 to 48 hours. Facing these challenges is framed as both intimidating and fun (Hanold 2008). The challenge is to overcome all obstacles, terrain, and weather, in order to finish. Participation is valued over winning. It is not uncommon for winners at the most prestigious races to stay around the finish line and cheer on others finishing after them. The faster runners frequently remark that they admire the slower runners because of the "will" and determination it requires to be out there for so long. From this shared sense of challenge and accomplishment, a strong sense of community results. Hanold (2010) notes that this sense of accomplishment reproduces the middle-class value of achieving goals through perseverance, making it a comfortable sporting site for white, middle to upper class participants. In this way, ultrarunning reproduces values found in mainstream sport.

On another level, ultrarunning counters some dominant ideologies with respect to distance running bodies and female running bodies. In contrast to marathon, Hanold (2010) found that successful ultrarunning bodies varied widely. Whereas successful marathon bodies are lean and toned, ulrarunning bodies ranged from thin to overweight. Given that ultrarunning as a subculture values finishing over being fast, any "body" that finishes is valued. While one may see various body types in marathons today, the marathon subculture values fast bodies over finishing bodies (Chase 2008). In this way, ultrarunning is a distance running subculture that is inclusive of many different body types. The effect of inclusivity is significant, especially for women. Specifically, female distance runners have historically experienced pressures to become an accepted distance running body by being extremely thin, often resulting in the female athlete triad. In contrast, women experience less conflict with their bodies in ultrarunning (Hanold 2010). Hanold found that women felt good about their strong, muscular, and resilient bodies. For some women this was a significant change from how they felt prior to ultrarunning. As a result, participants of all different body types are able to shape new identities and self-perceptions around the "finishing" cultural value.

Yet, perhaps the most significant cultural values that lure participants into ultrarunning are risk, intrinsic motivation, and aesthetic pleasures. Running any ultra distance is risky. Participants report that they love the fact that they never know what is going to happen. In some instances, the desire to be an ultrarunner, to persevere and endure physical and mental pain, has resulted in hospitalization, near-death experiences, and injuries. Nevertheless, the unknowns of both physical and mental challenges continue to draw more and more participants each year. With the emphasis on the challenge of the course, direct competition with others is less valued. Instead, ultrarunning fits the construct of lifestyle sport with a focus on intrinsic motivation. In turn, intrinsic motivation becomes a common bond among competitors, resulting in race practices unique to ultrarunning. For instance, it is a regular ultrarunning practice to encourage each other during races, help those in need of gear or food, run with each other for emotional support, and even cross the finish line together in solidarity. Finally, the overwhelming lure of ultrarunning appears to be a sense of connection with nature and wilderness surroundings. Perhaps one of the reasons for the shift from road ultras to forest and mountain trails reflects this value.

Ultrarunners talk about how the beauty around them inspires them, makes them feel alive, and puts their lives in perspective. During the process of being in nature, ultrarunners frequently allude to the joy of running through the woods as reasons they are drawn to this lifestyle sport. For example, high performance female ultrarunners said that during races they would frequently run fast not because they wanted to maintain a certain pace but because it simply felt good. This race strategy is unheard of in marathon running, which is first and foremost framed as grueling and tough. In contrast, ultrarunning's embracing of both pain and joy seems to be an appealing aspect of the sport. Participants have room to create their own personal reasons for competing in ultrarunning. With a wider array of subjectivities that are valued, ultrarunning is attracting participants at a rapid rate.

In sum, lifestyle sports are constructed around dominant themes in sport, such as the normalization of pain and overcoming adversity. Lifestyle sports also reproduce many racial and ethnic ideologies. On another level, however, lifestyle sports are examples of how sports can be re-conceptualized in ways that are different from mainstream sports. For ultrarunners, such reconceptualization comes through overt acceptance and valuing of the "pleasure and participation" model of sport (Coakley 2008), which is in opposition to the "power and performance" model of sport. The inclusive attitudes toward body types creates a more welcoming place for all types of distance running bodies, as long they are bodies that finish. Furthermore, such aesthetic pleasures as appreciating the environment and overtly expressing that joyful running can be a competitive strategy is unique. As Coakley points out, sports are often symbols whose meaning and purposes are constantly contested. Participants have the power to shape those meanings and purposes in unique ways, creating sporting environments that "fit" many different people. The lure of ultrarunning appears to be due to the multiple ways that participants can experience running, which are much broader than in the marathon (Hanold 2008).

References

Anderson, Eric. 2010. *Sport, theory and social problems: A critical introduction*. New York: Routledge.

Armstrong, K. L. 2011. Lifting the veils and illuminating the shadows: Furthering the explorations of race and ethnicity in sport management. *Journal of Sport Management* 25(2): 95–106.

Baker, Bill. 2009. Super Bowl bidding process challenges creativity. *The Times-Picayune*. http://blog.nola.com/saintsbeat/2009/05/super_bowl_bidding_process_cha.html (accessed September 10, 2011).

Beal, Becky B. 1995. Disqualifying the official: An exploration of social resistance through the subculture of skateboarding. *Sociology of Sport Journal* 12(3): 252–67.

Beal, Becky B. 1996. Alternative masculinity and its effects on gender relations in the subculture of skateboarding. *Journal of Sport Behavior* 19(3): 204–20.

Beal, Becky and Charlene Wilson. 2004. "Chicks dig scars": Commercialization and the transformations of skateboarders' identities. In *Understanding lifestyle sports: Consumption, identity and difference,* ed. B. Wheaton, 31–54. New York: Routledge.

Branch, Taylor. 2011. The shame of college sports. *Atlantic Magazine*. http://www.theatlantic.com/magazine/archive/2011/10/the-shame-of-college-sports/8643/2/ (accessed April 23, 2012).

Brannen, D. 2006. Opinion: State of the sport. *Ultrarunning*. May: 28–29.

Burton, Laura J., Heidi Grappendort, and Angela Henderson. 2011. Perceptions of gender in athletic administration: Utilizing role congruity to examine (potential) prejudice against women. *Journal of Sport Management* 25(1): 36.

Butler, Judith. 2006. *Gender trouble: Feminism and the subversion of identity*. New York: Routledge Classics.

Chase, Laura F. 2008. Running big: Clydesdale runners and technologies of the bodies. *Sociology of Sport Journal* 25(1): 130–47.

Cimini, Rich. 2010. NY/NJ has it down cold as XLVIII host. http://sports.espn.go.com/new-york/nfl/news/story?id=5219486 (accessed September 12, 2011).

Coakley, Jay. 2008. *Sports in society: Issues and controversies,* 10th ed. New York: McGraw-Hill.

Crisco, Joseph J. and Richard M. Greenwald. (Jan/Feb 2011). Management of sport-related brain injuries: Preventing poor outcomes and minimizing the risk for legal liabilities. *Current Sports Medicine Reports* 10(1): 7–9.

Eagleman, Andrea M. 2011. Stereotypes of race and nationality: A qualitative analysis of sport magazine coverage of MLB players. *The Journal of Sport Management* 25(2): 156–68.

Gill, Jr., Emmett L. 2011. The Rutgers women's basketball and Don Imus controversy (RUIMUS): White privilege, new racism, and the implications for college sport management. *Journal of Sport Management* 25(2): 118–30.

Hanold, Maylon. 2008. *Ultrarunning: A Foucauldian analysis of high-performance female ultrarunners.* EdD diss., Seattle University, 2008.

Hanold, Maylon. 2010. Beyond the marathon: (De)constructing female ultrarunning bodies, *Sociology of Sport Journal* 27(2): 160–77.

Harrow, Rick and Karla Swatek. 2011. *Beyond the scoreboard: An insider's guide to the business of sport.* Human Kinetics: Adobe Digital Editions.

Heid, Jason. 2010. "How the Bid was Won." D—Dallas/Fort Worth, 30–30. http://search.proquest.com/docview/193907214?accountid=28598 (accessed September 12, 2011).

Hilpirt, Rod, Scott Wysong, Sheila Hartley, Mike Latino, and Andrea Zabkar. 2007. Show Me the Money! A Cross-Sport Comparative Study of Compensation for Independent Contractor Professional Athletes. *Sport Journal* 10(4): 8–15.

Kahn, Lawrence M. 2000. The sports business as a labor market laboratory. *Journal of Economic Perspectives* 14(3): 75–94.

Kim, Kihan and Yunjae Cheong. 2011. The effects of athlete-endorsed advertising: The moderating role of the athlete-audience ethnicity match. *Journal of Sport Management* 25(2): 143–55.

Leeds, M. and S. Kowalewski. 1999. Winner takes all in the NFL: The effect of the salary cap and free agency on the compensation of skill position players. *Journal of Sports Economics* 2(3): 244–56.

Levinson, Meridith. 2001. CIO News. A brief history of NASCAR: From moonshine runners to Dale Earnhardt Jr. http://www.cio.com/article/17142/ (accessed April 14, 2011).

Malcolm, Dominic. 2009. Medical uncertainty and clinician-athlete relations: The management of concussion injuries in rugby union. *Sociology of Sport Journal* 26(2): 191–210.

Massa, T. 2006. 1981 to 2006: A look inside the numbers. *Ultrarunning.* May: 14–15.

Messner, Michael. 1992. *Power at play: Sports and the problem of masculinity.* Boston: Beacon Press.

Mohr, Iris. 2007. Super Bowl: A case study of buzz marketing. *International Journal of Sports Marketing & Sponsorship* (October): 33–39.

Nadeau, John, Floyd D. Jones, Ann Pegoraro, Norm O'Reilly, and Paulo Carvalho. 2011. Racial-ethnic team-market congruency in professional sport. *Journal of Sport Management* 25(2): 169–80.

NASCAR. 2010. The history of NASCAR. http://www.nascar.com/news/features/history/ (accessed April 10, 2011).

NCAA. Where does the money go? http://www.ncaa.org/wps/wcm/connect/public/NCAA/Answers/Eye+on+the+Money (accessed May 30, 2012).

Newman, Joshua I. and Adam S. Beissel. 2009. The limit to "NASCAR Nation": Sport and the "Recovery Movement" in disjunctural times. *Sociology of Sport Journal* 26(4): 517–39.

Oglesby, Carol. 2001. Intersections: Women's sport leadership and feminist praxis. In *Women on power: Leadership redefined*, ed. Sue J. M. Freeman, Susan C. Bourque, and Christine Shelton, 290–311. Boston: Northeastern University Press.

O'Reilly, Norm, Mark Lyberger, Larry McCarthy, Benoît Séguin, and John Nadeau. 2008. Mega-special-event promotions and intent to purchase: A longitudinal analysis of the super bowl. *Journal of Sport Management* 22(4): 392–409.

Pfister, Gertrud. 2010. Women in sport—gender relations and future perspectives. *Sport in Society* 13(2): 234–48.

Pike, E. J. and J.A. Maguire. 2003. Injury in women's sport: Classifying key elements of "risk encounters." *Sociology of Sport Journal*, 20(3): 232–251.

Sartore, Melanie L. and George B. Cunningham. 2007. Explaining the under-representation of women in leadership positions of sport organizations: A symbolic interactionist perspective. *Quest* 59(2): 244–65.

Sibson, Ruth. 2010. "I was banging my head against a brick wall": Exclusionary power and the gendering of sport organizations. *Journal of Sport Management* 24(4): 379–99.

Singer, John, N., C. Keith Harrison, and Scott J. Bukstein. 2010. A critical race analysis of the hiring process for head coaches in NCAA college football. *Journal of Intercollegiate Sport* 3(2): 270–96.

Smith, Earl and Angela Hattery. 2011. Race relations theories: Implications for sport management. *Journal of Sport Management* 25(2): 107–17.

Tator, Charles H. 2011. The coach is the most important person. *Coaches Plan/Plan du Coach* 18(1): 36–38.

Taylor, John. 1987. The NFL's best moves aren't always on the field. *Florida Trend* 30(4): 50. http://search.proquest.com/docview/212285749? accountid=28598 (accessed September 8, 2011).

Upthegrove, Tanya R., Vincent J. Roscigno, and Camille Zubrinsky Charles. 1999. Big money collegiate sports: Racial concentration, contradictory pressures, and academic performance. *Social Science Quarterly* 8(4): 718–37.

Zimbalist, Andrew. 2010. Reflections on salary shares and salary caps. *Journal of Sports Economics* 11(1): 17–28 doi: 10.1177/1527002509354890, Retrieved from Sport Discus.

4

Chronology

This book examines sport from a variety of perspectives, including its modern growth resulting in widespread popularity, the business of sport, issues regarding sport performance, and sport as a political and social enterprise. This chapter focuses on key events both worldwide and in North America that are significant from these perspectives. The events covered emerge from both professional and amateur sport in order to show the pervasiveness of sport. Significant events come from a variety of sports, sport industry developments, and political and social concerns in order to illustrate how sport is embedded in North American and global cultures.

Both sport participation rates and spectatorship have grown since the late 1800s, making sport one of the most dominant forms of social activities globally. This growth throughout the 20th century has given rise to a whole industry that either supports participation or enhances fan experiences. In conjunction with sport industry growth, such specific professions as trainers, sports medicine doctors, physiologists, and coaches have flourished. These developments show how sport is moving away from a local leisure activity to a highly organized, regulated, and veritable industry. Given the passion that people have for sports, many governmental agencies and international organizations have used sport as a means toward improved international relationships and betterment of less-developed countries. Finally, as sports have become more desired, many groups have found themselves marginalized in the process. Highlighting some of these events and actions taken to ameliorate participant experiences in sport is key to moving sport forward in the 21st century. The events mentioned in this section inform the reader about the origins of modern sport and youth organizations, such sports industry developments as sporting goods, sport agencies, sports marketing and sponsorship, important research into human performance, and significant political and social developments in sport.

The Rise of Modern Sport

1800s   Forms of American football take shape during the early 1800s. Primarily, such Ivy League schools as Yale, Harvard, and Princeton participate in these early versions of football. Rules are not uniform but rather unique to each school. Rivalries between freshman and sophomore classes are common. The game is extremely bloody and brutal with little regard for score. Spectators focus on which team incurs fewer seriously injured bodies. These games often lead to more widespread destruction, which ultimately causes university administrators to ban football.

1806   The first official 24-hour ultrarunning event takes places in England. Runners are called pedestrians during this period. Two of England's most famous pedestrians compete with each other in this event, but another pedestrian, Glanville, ends up winning the event by running and brisk walking. Glanville completes 117 miles within 24 hours to become the official winner.

1844   The first Young Men's Christian Association (YMCA) is founded in London. The purpose is to provide young men a place to go for physical activity when not working in the factories. The YMCA concept is inspired by the idea that sport can promote good sportsmanship, spiritual development, mental fortitude, and physical strength. It is during this time that the term "muscular Christian" emerges. This Victorian expression highlights the idea that spiritual development is enhanced through the pursuit of sports and physical strength.

1863   In England, football (soccer) finally organizes into its own game, distinct from rugby. Rules are codified, and such limitations are set as no shin kicking and no tripping. Proponents of the "football" version propose limited use of the hands. This suggestion is highly controversial and forces the rugby supporters to separate from the football enthusiasts. This separation cements the establishment of football (soccer) as a unique sport. Within a few years, football is being played internationally within the United Kingdom. The next countries to form football associations before the founding of the Federation International de Football Association (FIFA) are the Netherlands, Denmark (both in 1989), New Zealand (1891), Argentina (1893), Chile (1895), Switzerland, Belgium (both in1895), Italy (1898), Germany, Uruguay (both in 1900), Hungary (1901), and Finland (1907).

1871   The first sport professional league in North America is founded. It is the National Association of Professional Base Ball Players (NA). Although this league is home to the highest caliber play in the United States at the time, today, the Baseball Hall of Fame does not recognize its existence. The National League replaces the NA in 1876.

1892   The first professional football player emerges out of the rivalry between two Pittsburg football teams. In order to secure an advantage, the Allegheny Athletic Association pays former Yale All-America guard William (Pudge) Heffelfinger $500 to play in a game against the Pittsburgh Athletic Club. Heffelfinger wins the game for the Allegheny Athletic Association when he picks up a fumble and runs 35 yards for a touchdown.

1896   The first modern Olympic Games are held in the Panathenaic Stadium in Athens. These Games are organized by the International Olympic Committee. They include participation from 14 nations and 241 athletes. Athletes compete in 43 different events including pole vaulting, sprints, shot put, weight lifting, swimming, cycling, target shooting, tennis, men's marathon, and gymnastics. Athletes pay their own way to compete at these first Games, wearing their

1896
(cont.)
local club uniforms instead of national team uniforms because the idea of competing as a national representative is not developed and instituted until 1908.

1904
FIFA is founded with seven countries as members: France, Belgium, Denmark, the Netherlands, Spain, Sweden, and Switzerland. Notably absent is the federation from the United Kingdom, who is not ready to join an overarching umbrella organization. Germany joins just as FIFA gets underway.

1924
The first Winter Olympic Games is held in Chamonix, France. The sports in which athletes participate include alpine and cross-country skiing, figure skating, ice hockey, Nordic combined, ski jumping, and speed skating.

1949
The National Basketball Association is formed through a merger of two preceding basketball leagues. This league starts with 17 franchises in both small and large cities, playing in both arenas and local gymnasiums.

1970s
Skateboarding gains ground with participants in California as surfers experiment with ways to still "surf" when the waves are flat. Attaching clay wheels to square boards transforms into more sophisticated "skateboards." Polyurethane wheels make the ride smoother, and boards shaped like surfboards become the norm.

1993
Major League Soccer (MLS) becomes the premier men's soccer league in North America. MLS begins with 10 teams divided into two conferences. Play does not begin until 1996. Showing moderate success in the first year, the MLS struggles to attract spectators on a regular basis, especially after poor showings in the 1998 World Cup.

2003
One of the most prestigious ultrarunning races in the world, the Ultra Trail du Mont Blanc (UTMB), makes its debut. This race circumnavigates Mont Blanc. The route is a 166 km loop including 9,400 meters total elevation gain. The North Face, a large outdoor company, is the primary sponsor. The race draws more than 700 competitors, of which only 67 finish. UTMB

continues to grow, and in 2008, over 2,000 competitors register online for UTMB within seven minutes.

Sport as a Business

1912   For the Indianapolis 500, Carl Fisher increases the total prize money to $50,000 and first prize to $20,000. This substantial purse makes the Indy 500 the highest paying sporting event in the world at the time.

1928   Coca-Cola begins its involvement with the Olympic Games by sending 1,000 cases of Coca-Cola along with the United States Olympic team on a freighter to the Amsterdam Summer Olympics. Coca-Cola remains the longest continuous sponsor of the Olympic Games and is continuing its support through the 2020 Summer Olympics, for a record 92 years of uninterrupted sponsorship.

1936   Adi Dassler, the founder of Adidas, makes a pair of shoes for Jesse Owens. Owens wears those shoes in the 1936 Olympic Games. Owens becomes the first American in Olympic track and field history to win four gold medals in a single Olympiad. He wins gold in the 100-meter dash in 10.3 seconds (tying the world record), the long jump with a jump of 26 feet 5 and one-fourth inches (Olympic record), the 200-meter dash in 20.7 seconds (Olympic record), and the 400-meter relay (first leg) in 39.8 seconds (Olympic and world record). This exposure positions Adidas as the forerunner of sport shoes and launches its growth though the 1964 Olympics when over 80 percent of the athletes are wearing Adidas.

1939   The men's Division I end-of-year basketball tournament known as "March Madness" is established. It is a single elimination tournament featuring 68 teams from all conferences. Games take place by region in the initial stages and are played all over the United States. The final games, known as the "Final Four" include the winners from each region, from which a champion emerges. Today, March Madness is televised

1939 (*cont.*)	on CBS, TBS, TNT, and truTV and remains a major sporting event followed by millions of fans each year.
1947	NBC broadcasts the World Series, heavyweight fights, and the Army-Navy football game. As a result, the sales of television sets soars. At this point, NBC is in the business of manufacturing television sets, and their goal is to increase television sales through broadcasting sporting events. The tactic works. Later on, the idea of selling advertising becomes the primary revenue stream for major television networks.
1956	Horst Dassler brings on the era of corporate sponsorship by being the exclusive (or almost) shoe supplier to athletes during the Melbourne Olympic Games. His tactic is simple. He hands out free shoes to as many athletes as he can. From this moment forward, corporate connections with the Olympics are solidified.
1960	Mark McCormack shakes hands with Arnold Palmer, agreeing to be his business advisor and protector. There are no contracts ever signed, but through this one gesture, McCormack initiates the sports agency industry.
1967	The first Super Bowl is played in Los Angeles between the Green Bay Packers and the Kansas City Chiefs. Under the direction of Vince Lombardi, the Green Bay Packers win the game. Bart Starr, the Packers' quarterback, completes 16 of 23 passes for 250 yards. With two touchdowns scored on these passes, Starr earns most valuable player. The Green Bay Packers earn $15,000 per player while the Kansas City Chiefs earn $7,500 per player. This is the largest single-game share distribution in the history of team sports. The Super Bowl proves a success and continues as the most watched sporting event in North America.
1973	The NCAA divides colleges and universities into the three major divisions that exist today: Division I, II, and III. Along with this decision are important implications for pursuing advertising and sponsorship dollars. The larger schools are now free to pursue their own relationships with television, and the smaller

schools no longer benefit as much from NCAA revenue along these lines. It is at this point that the complexity of commercialism in college sports grows significantly.

1974   Jim "Catfish" Hunter becomes baseball's first free agent when owner of the Oakland A's, Charles Finley, breaches Hunter's contract. A court rules that the breach of contract invalidates the reserve clause, and Hunter is no longer required to return to the Oakland A's. Such a ruling opens the gateway for other players to become free agents. Baseball retains full power of the reserve clause until 1975, when it becomes limited to a single season, not the lifetime of a player. Major League Baseball is the only league to still have a reserve clause.

1978   Snowboarding moves from idea to major business. Jake Burton in Vermont and Tom Sims in California are the first people to mass produce what is later known as the snowboard. Burton's business acumen places Burton Snowboards as the preeminent snowboard manufacturer. Burton remains a good example of how a simple innovation gives rise to whole new sporting opportunities and businesses.

1982   The Olympic Program (TOP) is created to offer billion-dollar companies exclusive rights to the Olympic rings in their advertising efforts. TOP is the highest level of sponsorship for the Olympic Games, also offering category exclusivity and various marketing rights in different regions worldwide.

1987   Hammer Nutrition opens as a source for endurance specific nutrition and fuel. Gaining ground as ultra endurance racing becomes more popular through the 1990s, Hammer Nutrition emerges as one of the leaders in this niche market.

1988   The Portland, Oregon, advertising agency Wieden+ Kennedy continues its work with Nike. The agency cofounder Dan Weiden coins the phrase "Just Do It." The ad campaign is so successful that "Just Do It" is chosen by *Advertising Age* as one of the top five ad

1988 (*cont.*)	slogans of the 20th century. It also becomes part of the Smithsonian.
1991	TOP is providing 50 percent of the International Olympic Committee's income while the other 50 percent remains connected to the selling of television rights.
1992	Professional skateboarders Tony Hawk and Powell Peralta create Birdhouse Skateboards while skateboarding is in a lull. As street skating takes off in the mid- to late 1990s, Birdhouse Skateboards experiences success.
1995	The Extreme Games, now known as the X Games, debuts in Rhode Island and Vermont. The X Games is an event created by ESPN in order to showcase action sports. The first X Games features 27 events in nine sport categories: Bungy Jumping, Eco-Challenge, Inline Skating, Skateboarding, Skysurfing, Sport Climbing, Street Luge, Biking, and Water Sports. There are over 190,000 spectators who attend and seven major sponsors: Advil, Mountain Dew, Taco Bell, Chevy Trucks, AT&T, Nike, and Miller Lite Ice. The event is so successful that ESPN decides to host it annually instead of the proposed every two years. The X Games remains a quintessential example of how media can control the way sports are organized and marketed to the general public.
1996	Adidas sponsors over 6,000 Olympic athletes from 33 countries for the Atlanta Olympic Games. Athletes wearing Adidas win 220 medals, of which 70 are gold. Adidas sees its apparel sales increase by 50 percent.
1999	Tony Hawk works with Activision to create the *Tony Hawk's Pro Skater* video game franchise. In this same year, Tony Hawk becomes the first skateboarder to perform and land a 900, two and one-half revolutions in the air. This accomplishment is captured on television. The convergence of video game success and physical prowess positions Hawk as the most recognized action-sports figure in the world.
2000	In an attempt to move into the global market, the Indianapolis Motor Speedway prepares for the inaugural

United States Grand Prix, which is held on September 24, 2000. The construction includes the new Bombardier Learjet Pagoda control tower, which is modeled after the original towers at the speedway. Thirty-six new pit-side garages that can accommodate Formula I cars are constructed. In addition, a new 2.605-mile road course is constructed. Drivers race the course in the traditional counterclockwise direction. It is the most ambitious construction project in speedway history.

2006 MLS in the United States decides to sign superstars in order to boost their popularity and increase ticket sales. The MLS begins this new approach with the signing of David Beckham to the L.A. Galaxy on a five-year contract for $250 million. This celebrity effect continues with the signing of other such talented and famous players as Juan Pablo Ángel, Marcelo Gallardo, Cuauhtémoc Blanco, Denílson, Claudio Reyna, Guillermo Barros Schelotto, Ronald Waterreus, and Abel Xavier. This movement of players across international boundaries confirms soccer as a globalized sport.

2009 Tiger Woods becomes the first professional athlete to make over $1 billion. Woods earns his money through tournament winnings, but the most lucrative revenue stems from new sponsorship deals with Gillette and Gatorade.

2010 While professional and competitive sports increase in popularity, bowling is the United States' number one participatory sport for the fourth consecutive year. This year marks an increase of 4.6 percent over 70 million bowling participants in 2009. Bowling as an industry continues to have a significant impact on the U.S. economy, generating more than $10 billion in a single year.

2010 The Dallas Cowboys open their newly built stadium, which costs $1.25 billion. As the second most valuable sports team in the world, the Cowboys are valued at $1.81 billion. The stadium represents the latest in technology and luxury. It hosts a 152-foot wide

2010   HD TV screen for showing close-up shots of the ac-
(*cont.*) tion to spectators on site. There are 320 luxury suites
          and 15,000 club seats. These premium seats generate
          more than $100 million annually.

2011   Manchester United, the British Premier League soccer
          team, ranks as the top sport franchise in the world.
          The team is worth $1.86 billion. This year marks the
          first year with the new sponsor, Aon, an insurance
          company. This sponsorship is worth $32 million an-
          nually over four years, a 50 percent increase over
          Manchester United's previous sponsorship deal with
          AIG. In addition, Manchester United expects close to
          a 50 percent increase in sponsorship dollars with Nike
          before their 13-year contract valued at $40 million
          annually expires in 2015.

The Growth of Sport Professionals

1898   Dr. Norman Triplett publishes first documented schol-
          arly article on sport psychology in the United States
          in the *American Journal of Psychology*. His article, "Dy-
          namogenic Factors in Pacemaking and Competition,"
          shows how and why cyclists perform better when
          riding in pairs or groups.

1930s   Exercise physiology is born in Sweden under the direc-
          tion of researchers Christensen, Hansen, Astrand, and
          Saltin. They examine human performance from nutri-
          tional, exercise, and muscle metabolism perspectives.

1972   Dr. Kennedy becomes the first chief medical officer of
          the first official medical team at the Summer Olympic
          Games in Munich, Germany. Kennedy is instrumental
          in bringing sports medical care to Olympic athletes
          at a more comprehensive level. This move is based
          on a precedence of doctor representation since the
          1928 Olympics in St. Moritz where the term "sports
          medicine" originates.

1974   Dr. Frank Jobe performs surgery on pitcher Tommy
          John. The surgery repairs an injury to the ulnar col-
          lateral ligament of the elbow joint. In this surgery,

a ligament from another part of the body is used to replace the damaged elbow ligament. After this surgery and a year of rehabilitation, Tommy John returns to professional baseball. Today this surgery is now known as the Tommy John surgery and gives a player an 80 percent chance of returning to former playing standards.

1986   The Association for Applied Sport Psychology is founded in order to provide sport psychology professionals with a means to share information and latest research with respect to health psychology, performance enhancement, and social psychology.

1989   The American medical professional organization, the American Board of Medical Specialties (ABMS), officially recognizes sports medicine as a distinct subspecialty of medicine. This move helps sports medicine grow into a sizable industry. Individuals can now specialize in sports medicine at a variety of medical schools.

1990   The American Medical Association decides to include athletic trainers as fellow allied health professionals. Such recognition helps establish athletic trainers as competent health care providers. Their work is categorized as health care providers who support physically active people and serious athletes with the prevention, recognition, and rehabilitation of athletic injuries.

2001   United Kingdom Association of Doctors in Sport is established to help sport physicians gain respect, certification, and specialized training within the United Kingdom. Looking forward to the London Olympics in 2012, this organization remains focused on serving physically active people and high-performing athletes.

2002   Engineers at the University of Nebraska–Lincoln finish development of the Steel and Foam Energy Reduction (SAFER) barrier, and the barrier is installed on the first raceway in the United States. The SAFER barrier is installed just in time for the Indianapolis 500. The technology behind the barrier allows it to absorb more kinetic energy than concrete walls. The

2002
(*cont.*)

result is less impact for the driver, less chance the car will bounce back into other cars, and less damage incurred by the crashing car. In 2010, the SAFER barrier is installed in its first international location, Brazil, just in time for the Brazilian Grand Prix.

2011

Boston University, along with the Center for the Study of Traumatic Encephalopathy at BU's School of Medicine, launches the first study dedicated to testing living patients for Chronic Traumatic Encephalopathy (CTE). The study, named DETECT, is a three-year one designed to learn more about the early onset of CTE. The NFL contacts retired players for the study. Response is positive, as former players are interested in helping current and future athletes learn about the signs of CTE and reduce the risks—by being proactive about concussion and brain trauma care.

Sport: Politics, Social Issues, and Developments

1870s

Women participate in long distance walking events of which the most popular form is the six-day walking contests. They are called pedestriennes and attract thousands of spectators to their events as they walk around sawdust tracks. It is not uncommon for these women to walk between 300 and 400 miles during the six-day period. Some sports writers suggest that these feats dispel ideas that women are fragile and frail, noting how they complain much less than their male counterparts. Others disapprove of these events and begin limiting the number of miles women are allowed to walk in a day to 12 miles. At this point, the six-day events lose their appeal and decline significantly in number. Such control by men over how women get to participate in sport is typical of women's struggles to become legitimate sports participants throughout history.

1912

Jim Thorpe wins two gold medals and sets world records in both the pentathlon and decathlon in the

Summer Olympic Games in Stockholm, Sweden. Sweden's king tells Thorpe that he is "the greatest athlete in the world." Thorpe's medals and world records are revoked in 1913 when officials find him guilty of receiving money from his participation in semiprofessional baseball. His medals are reinstated posthumously.

1945   Jackie Robinson signs a contract to play in the all-white baseball league. Under the guidance of Branch Rickey, Robinson becomes the first black baseball player to move from the Negro Leagues to Major League Baseball. Robinson joins the Montreal Royals, a farm team for the Brooklyn Dodgers. With this signing, Major League Baseball becomes racially integrated. Robinson helps pave the way for other athletes of color to become integrated into professional sports. Robinson works toward racial equality the remainder of his life.

1960   The first Olympic athlete involved in drug use dies. Knut Jensen, a Danish cyclist, dies on August 26 at the Summer Olympics in Rome. While competing in the 100-km team time trial race, Jensen collapses. Authorities think that he fell due to heat exhaustion. During his autopsy, traces of an amphetamine called Ronicol are found.

1963   The first prohibited substance list is published under the direction of the International Olympic Committee.

1964   South Africa is banned by the International Olympic Committee from competing in the Olympics because of their apartheid practices. This is a clear example of how politics and sport are interconnected. South Africa remains barred from the Olympics until 1992.

1968   The first drug testing at the Olympics begins. Hans-Gunnar Liljenwall, a Swedish pentathlete, is the first Olympic athlete to be banned from competition and loses a bronze medal for testing positive for use of an illegal substance—alcohol.

1969   Jody Conrad becomes the women's head coach at Sam Houston State University. As a physical education teacher, Conrad is not paid to coach. She establishes

1969 **(cont.)**	herself as a competent coach, eventually joining the coaching staff at the University of Texas. She has a successful career, becoming the second most winning coach in the NCAA at the University of Texas. When she retires in 2007, she is earning just over $500,000 annually.
1972	Arab terrorists break into the Olympic Village in Munich, Germany. They invade the rooms of Israeli athletes and coaches. Two Israelis are killed onsite. Nine Israeli athletes and coaches are taken hostage. The Arabs announce they are Palestinians and demand the release of 200 Arab prisoners to be let go and freed. The plan involves carrying the Palestinians and hostages by helicopter to a German airbase from where they are to catch a plane to Cairo, Egypt. The Germans plan to send marksmen to shoot the terrorists, but instead of five Palestinians, there are nine. Germans do not have enough marksmen to shoot all nine, firefight ensues, and a second round of fighting leaves all remaining Israeli athletes and coaches dead. In one of the most controversial decisions, Avery Brundage holds a memorial for the fallen athletes but insists that in such a time of political despair, the Games must go on. He insists that the international cooperation and goodwill of the Olympic Games should not be destroyed at such a moment in time.
1972	Title IX passes as a law as part of the larger Education Amendments to the Civil Rights Act. Title IX is a small section of the amendments, which states that federal funds can be withdrawn from any university that engages in intentional discrimination with respect to curriculum, counseling, academic support, or general educational opportunities—which includes interscholastic or school sports.
1973	Billie Jean King defeats Bobby Riggs in a tennis match known as "The Battle of the Sexes" in Houston, Texas, on September 20. Riggs thinks he can easily defeat King, and the media sensationalizes the match. Riggs appears on the television program, *60 Minutes*, to promote the event and hype the importance of the match.

ABC televises the event. King wins the best three out of five sets with scores of 6–4, 6–3, and 6–3.

1974   The International Olympic Committee removes the word "amateurism" from the Olympic Charter. There is no immediate impact, but this significant shift in attitude toward amateurism establishes new directions for athletes, sponsors, and Olympic participation for future years.

1982   The first Gay Games take place in San Francisco. The purpose is to offer a safe sporting event for athletes of all sexual orientations. The intent is to raise awareness, support inclusivity, and enhance self-respect.

1995   Nelson Mandela's efforts to unite South Africa after the shift in power and abolition of apartheid involve rallying the country around rugby. Mandela specifically encourages the national rugby team, the Springboks, to reach out to the black community to gain support for rugby and to try to unite the country around the very sport that had represented oppression for decades. Mandela uses the political and emotional impact of sport to convince other black leaders to embrace the Springboks. South Africa hosts the Rugby World Cup in which the Springboks emerge victorious, uniting a historically divided country for the first time.

2000   The Millennium Development Goals are established by the United Nations. These goals include a commitment to using sport as a vehicle for promoting peace, eradicating poverty, and bring struggling nations into the world economy.

2004   At the Summer Olympics in Athens, 44 percent of all athletes are women. This is a historic moment for women's participation in this prestigious event. The number of countries sending female athletes sets a record with only five nations not sending women. Even Afghanistan, a country previously banned from the games because of its cruel gender apartheid, brings three women runners to compete. One of the women carries the Afghan flag in the opening ceremonies.

2004 Betsey Stevenson, a public policy professor at the Wharton School of Business, provides new research about women's participation in sport and the correlations to education and employment opportunities. Her paper, "Beyond the Classroom: Using Title IX to Measure the Return to High School Sports," sums up her findings. Stevenson empirically shows that women who play sports are more likely to stay in school, attend higher education institutions, and gain employment.

2005 Lance Armstrong makes cyclist history by winning the Tour de France for an unprecedented seventh consecutive time. With this win, Armstrong breaks the previous record of five wins, shared by Miguel Indurain, Bernard Hinault, Eddy Merckx, and Jacques Anquetil. Armstrong recovers from a 1996 diagnosis of testicular cancer that had metastasized to his brain and lungs. He defies the poor odds of recovery, undergoing brain and testicular surgery as well as extensive chemotherapy. He is suspected of drug use but never tests positive for it.

2005 Victor Conte, founder of BALCO, is officially sentenced to four months in prison and four months of house arrest. He is found guilty of distributing undetectable performance enhancing drugs to professional athletes. BALCO's vice president, James Valente, receives probation after pleading guilty to providing professional athletes with steroids. Greg Anderson, Barry Bonds's trainer, also pleads guilty to steroid distribution, which he obtained from BALCO.

2006 Pat Summitt becomes the first female coach in the NCAA to earn over $1 million. Summitt's increase in pay is a landmark event, coming from a $250 per month stipend in 1969. It only takes five more years for Summitt to break the $2 million mark, which she does in the summer of 2011.

2007 The Women's National Basketball Association (WNBA) creates the Inspiring Coach Award. Its purpose is to honor those coaches whose achievements have left a lasting, positive impact on the world of sport and who have been positive role models and mentors for the athletes they coach.

2007   Wimbledon, the famous tennis tournament held in the United Kingdom each year, announces they will pay women players the same as men. Wimbledon continues as the world's most prestigious lawn tennis tournament in the world.

2009   Pat Summitt, women's head coach at the University of Tennessee, becomes the only female to make the list of the 50 greatest coaches of all time in all sports. Summitt is ranked number 11 on this list because of her superior win-loss record. She earns the recognition of never having a losing season in 36 years of coaching. She remains the all-time winningest coach in NCAA history, including both men's and women's sports.

2011   Eight North Korean soccer players test positive for steroids at the Women's World Cup in Germany. The North Korean officials state that steroids had accidently been taken when players took a traditional Chinese medicine made from musk deer glands. Players take this medication to alleviate symptoms associated with being hit by lightning during training for the World Cup. North Korea is eliminated from the tournament because they do not score any points in their first three games.

2011   During the collective bargaining agreement, the NFL revises its antidiscrimination policy to include homosexuality. This agreement will remain in effect until 2021. This inclusion is acknowledged by many constituents to be a significant step toward ending homophobia and acknowledging the rights of the lesbian, bisexual, gay, transsexual and queer/questioning (LBGTQ) community on the football field. Concurrently, a handful of players—Michael Strahan, Steve Nash, and Sean Avery—step up to support the Marriage Equality Act in the state of New York in order to raise awareness and bring support to the rights of the LBGTQ community.

5

Biographical Sketches

Kate Ackerman, MD

Dr. Kate Ackerman specializes in female athlete injuries, stresses, and the female athlete triad, which is a combination of disordered eating, low bone mass, and menstrual irregularities. As a former national team rower, Dr. Ackerman practices at Children's Hospital Boston and Massachusetts General Hospital and teaches at Harvard Medical School. Dr. Ackerman examines current medical issues in young female athletes from medical as well as sociological and historical perspectives. Her research interests focus on understanding the relationship among pressures to perform, overuse injuries, and the female athlete triad. Her approach is holistic, advocating for the prevention of overuse injuries through proper training and proper technique. Such an approach counters the "no pain, no gain" mentality that is prevalent in sport. Also, her approach to helping women recover from the female athlete triad emphasizes all aspects of the person. She stresses the idea that it takes a team of such people as parents, family, friends, teammates, support groups, coaches, medical professionals, nutritionists, and sports psychologists to help female athletes in this condition. Dr. Ackerman serves as a team physician for USRowing and other rowing groups local to the Boston area. She is also a consultant to other sport organizations and the Boston Ballet.

John Uzoma Ekwugha Amaechi (November 26, 1970–)

John Amaechi is a U.S.-born British retired NBA player who now devotes his life helping others. Focusing on several unique aspects of his life, Amaechi inspires through true stories of determination and caring. Amaechi began his basketball career late in life at the age of 17 and was considered "not athletic enough." Within six years, however, he was a starter for the Cleveland Cavaliers in the National Basketball Association (NBA). In 2007, John Amaechi broke ground again by being the first NBA player to come out and speak openly about his experiences as a closeted gay basketball player in his memoir *Man in the Middle*. He currently works as a motivational speaker, helping business, educational, and philanthropic organizations understand and develop human potential. Amaechi is also involved in a number of charitable projects primarily directed at helping youth. He works with the National Literacy Trust, the NSPCC, which works to stop cruelty to children; and the ABC foundation, which encourages children to become involved in sport. Through his own charity, Amaechi Basketball, he works with local and national governments in the United Kingdom to create support networks for urban children to become physically active. In 2008, Amaechi took his desire to promote human rights to the international level by becoming a sport ambassador for Amnesty International. He continues to parlay his athletic achievements and personal story into activism.

Eric Anderson (January 18, 1968–)

In 1993, Eric Anderson became the first openly gay high school coach at the age of 25 in one of California's most conservative counties. Anderson's personal journey of coming out and the hardships that his cross country team endured are highlighted in his autobiography *Trailblazing: America's First Openly Gay High School Coach*. Anderson recounts how his team became a victim of homophobia. During the early years of his coming out, a football player beat up one of his runners, leaving him with a broken jaw. His team was subject to such high levels of verbal and physical harassment that Anderson advised his runners to practice in groups. He even personally learned martial arts for self-protection. As a result of these hardships, Anderson went on to pursue a PhD in sociology, focusing on the experiences of gay athletes. Currently, Anderson is a professor of sport studies at the University of Winchester. His research focuses on issues of sexuality, including homophobia, in sport. His groundbreaking theoretical framework of inclusive masculinity is based on his empirical studies in which he found that 89 percent of 145 college males in Britain had kissed another male (Anderson 2010). Notably, *none* of them considered kissing to be a sexual act. Along with his research on bisexuality, Anderson has evidence of diminishing homophobia and increasing acceptance of a "softer" masculinity among heterosexual men. His research demonstrates a significant positive shift in how gay male athletes experience sport. Anderson is cautious and admits that such changes are not revolutionizing sport overnight, but he is surprised by the rate at which attitudes toward homosexuality and bisexuality are currently changing. As he admits, the world of sport is no longer what it was when he came out in 1993.

Roone Pickney Arledge Jr. (July 8, 1931–December 5, 2002)

Roone Arledge had the most impact on the development of sports broadcasting than any other individual in the 20th century. He is among the top 40 individuals who have had the greatest impact on the world of sports in the last four decades and ranks in the top 100 of the "Most Important Americans of the 20th Century." Arledge pioneered ABC's *Wide World of Sports* in 1961, which became the most popular sports series of its time. It was from this series that the phrase "the joy of victory and the agony of defeat" by Jim McKay became a household expression. In addition, sensing something special about what football meant to the American public, Arledge created *Monday Night Football*. In 1968, Arledge became president of ABC Sports, covering 10 Olympics during his tenure. He shaped Olympic broadcasting by expanding coverage to include personal stories of athletes. Arledge also oversaw significant changes that enhanced the drama of televised sport. Under his direction, ABC Sports developed such techniques such as slow motion, freeze frame, instant replay, end-zone camera angles, underwater camera shots, and strategic microphone placement, all of which brought viewers into sport competition more effectively than in prior years. Some say that Arledge's genius was knowing exactly what viewers would like and then relentlessly going after it.

Sir Roger Gilbert Bannister (March 23, 1929–)

Roger Bannister is known for being the first person to break the four-minute mile barrier. His entry into running began in 1946 at Oxford University. By 1947, Bannister ran a mile in 4:24.6 based on only three weekly half-hour training sessions. Bannister was one of the first athletes to embrace both the scientific and aesthetic aspects of running. Feeling defeated after the 1952 Olympic Games in Helsinki in which he placed fourth in the 1500 meters but established a new British record, Bannister committed himself to a new goal. He decided that he wanted to break four minutes for the mile distance. As a premed student, Bannister used what he was learning in physiology to inform his training. In many ways, Bannister was an experiment of one. Yet, he paved the way for more scientific training by experimenting with interval training and focused intensity. On May 2, 1953, Bannister ran 4:03.6. This achievement was a confidence boost for him. Then, on May 6, 1954, during a meet between British AAA and Oxford University at Iffley Road Track in Oxford, Bannister ran 3:59.4. Bannister's collapse at the end of his historical sport moment gave support to the idea that sport is about pushing the limits. Simultaneously, Bannister openly talked about the aesthetic dimensions of running. He said, "I discovered a new unity with nature. I had found a new source of power and beauty, a source I never dreamt existed." Certainly, Bannister's reflections illustrate the complexity and almost paradoxical experience of sport participation. Bannister went on to become a successful neurologist.

Charles Wade Barkley
(February 20, 1963–)

Charles Barkley, an NBA player from 1982 to 2000, remains one of the most successful and controversial players in professional basketball history. He played for the Philadelphia 76ers, Phoenix Suns, and the Houston Rockets. His talent for rebounding, along with the fact that he struggled with weight issues, eventually earned him the moniker "The Round Mound of Rebound." His tattoos and dramatic behavior made him popular with fans. His on- and off-court fighting as well as controversial comments kept him in the media. Barkley's famous declaration that professional athletes should not be role models resulted in public criticism. Barkley publically resented the pressure to be a role model. Nike even created a commercial around the slogan, "I am not a role model." Barkley criticized parents for not being better role models themselves, commenting on the fact that most young black kids would never become basketball players like himself and Michael Jordan. What they needed, he argued, were more realistic role models close to them in their lives. Upon retirement, Barkley said he had no regrets except for when he spit on a young girl. In a reaction to a male spectator yelling racial epithets, Barkley tried to spit on the man, but missed and hit a young girl instead. The media highlighted this incident, being highly critical of Barkley's angry reaction. Later on, Barkley apologized to the young girl, became friends with the family, and sent them numerous free tickets to subsequent games. Charles Barkley remains a reminder of the power of sport to provide drama both on and off the court or field and of the power of media to promote sport celebrity.

Avery Brundage
(September 28, 1887–May 8, 1975)

Avery Brundage was perhaps the most controversial president of the International Olympic Committee. Serving from 1952 until 1972, Brundage oversaw the IOC during some of the most politically turbulent times. Most notably, Brundage was known for his supremely autocratic leadership style, through which he often made unilateral decisions that offended people. During his tenure as president of the United States Olympic Committee, Brundage made some controversial decisions at the 1936 Olympic Games in Berlin. Brundage was a firm believer in keeping politics out of sport, yet he often failed to realize that politics were already part of it. Brundage was highly criticized for a decision made during the 1936 Olympics during which he removed the only two Jews on the U.S. team from the 400-meter race because he did not want to upset the Nazi regime. Ironically, he did not equate Aryan supremacy with racial ideology and consider Jesse Owens's participation in a similar manner. Furthermore, Brundage overtly opposed female participation in the Olympics in certain sports. His extremely sexist comments did not win friends, but his power position meant that few would stand up to him. He is known to have criticized female track and field athletes as grotesque while praising female swimmers and divers as elegant, charming, and pleasing to the eye. Brundage also opposed professionalism at the Olympics, but his views were hypocritical. While he approved of the Eastern countries' system of employing athletes as soldiers, which allowed them to train as a full-time job, he was relentless in dismissing any athlete in a Western country that received even the smallest amount of money for his athletic prowess. Other instances of hypocrisy include openly accepting Nazi salutes while dismissing John Carlos and Tommie Smith from the 1968 Olympics in which they raised black fists in support of the Black Power movement during the medal ceremony. The one political decision that Brundage is perhaps most famous for involves the Israeli massacre during the 1972 Summer Olympic Games. He suspended Olympic competition for one day then resumed the Games with a special memorial service consisting of 80,000 spectators and 3,000 athletes. In his memorial speech, Brundage acknowledged that the Olympic Games would intersect with commercialism, nationalism, and global politics in more nuanced and complex ways. While the Olympics had always been implicated in politics and commercialism, this was the first time a president had acknowledged this connection.

John Wesley Carlos (June 5, 1945–)

Carlos was a sprinter in the 1968 Olympics in Mexico City who became renowned for his political activism. Carlos formed the

Olympic Project for Human Rights (OPHR) prior to the 1968 Olympics. As a founding member, Carlos was initially thinking of boycotting the 1968 Olympic Games. Instead, he decided to attend them. After placing third in the 200-meter dash, Carlos and his teammate, first-place Tommie Smith, raised their black-gloved fists at the medal award ceremony in order to represent African American power in the face of racial oppression. IOC president Avery Brundage disapproved of the Olympics being a stage for political protest. He immediately dismissed Carlos and Smith from the U.S. Team and the Olympic village. Post-protest life was difficult for Carlos, who often had to endure harassment and even death threats. Carlos briefly played in the NFL and Canadian Football League. Eventually, he worked for Puma, the United States Olympic Committee, and the organizing committee for the 1984 Olympic Games in Los Angeles. Despite the negative attention from the general public for his and Smith's political statement on the podium, Carlos was elected to the National Track & Field Hall of Fame in 2003. More significantly, a statue of Carlos and Smith with their hands raised on the podium in 1968 resides on the San Jose State University campus, where the two athletes had been students, and was dedicated in 2005. In 2008, Carlos continued his activism for human rights as a torch bearer for the Human Rights Torch, which was intended to bring attention to human rights issues in China.

Bill Colson (1951–)

Bill Colson was editor-in-chief of *Sports Illustrated* from 1996 to 2002. Having joined as a research/reporter in 1978, Colson worked for *Sports Illustrated* for 24 years before retiring. Under Colson's leadership, *Sports Illustrated* changed the way sports were covered. In his years as top editor, Colson moved the magazine from information focused to dramatic storytelling. Notable stories include a cover story about the number of children born out of wedlock to athletes, a special story on rampant gambling in sport, and a detailed account of domestic violence committed by professional athletes. Desiring to capitalize on being the first magazine to present interesting stories, Colson would alter print dates or approve second editions within the week in order to catch the drama at its height. When Mark McGuire broke the single-season home run record, Colson called for a second edition to be printed that week, the first time ever in the history of the magazine. On another occasion, Colson delayed the printing of *Sports Illustrated* for three days in order to capture the latest news of the Bowl Championship Series final game. During Colson's term, *Sport Illustrated* became known for glossy photos, with the creation of "Leading Off," the opening photo spread. For these stories and innovations, *Sports Illustrated* won three National Magazine Awards (NMA) as well as received three NMA nominations for General Excellence. While some sports critics feel as though *Sports Illustrated* currently presents few stories that are newsworthy, Colson is known for moving the magazine into new directions. Critics argue that such a change is needed now.

Bob Costas (March 22, 1952–)

Bob Costas began his sports commentating career with the minor hockey team, the Syracuse Blazers. Costas has become one of the most recognized voices of sport. He has worked for NBC sports, covering a multitude of sports events associated with the NFL, NBA, NHL, and Olympics. He hosted such shows as *The NFL on NBC*, *The NBA on NBC*, *The 2010 Winter NHL Classic*, and the Summer Olympics from 1992–2008 and the Winter Olympics in 2006 and 2010. In addition, Costas has made several guest appearances as a host on such talk shows as *Late Night with David Letterman*. Costas is an intelligent sportscaster, known as someone who prepares, is not afraid to include politics, and possesses excellent interviewing skills. During the 1996 Olympics, Costas talked about possible drug use among the Chinese swimmers. He was vilified by Chinese Americans for making such comments, but later on, evidence surfaced that Costas made his comments after the Chinese coach had been suspended due to seven of his swimmers testing positive for drug use. Costas would stand up for political rights in other ways as well. He is known for saying, "Were there better baseball players than Jackie Robinson? Yes. Were there more important baseball players than Jackie Robinson? Who?" (IMDb.com). The talk shows have given Costas an opportunity to go in-depth with people. He has been known to conduct two-to-three day interviews of 45 minutes to an hour. The editors have to reduce these interviews to 22 minutes, but they have plenty of engaging material with which to work because of Costas's skills. The National Sportswriters and Sportscasters

Association has awarded Costas with Sportscaster of the Year a record eight times.

David Costill (1936–)

Dr. David Costill is one of North America's most renowned sports physiologists, having been one of the first to apply scientific principles to the study of sport and exercise. He asked such questions as what does it take to maximize one's performance? Are there different physiological body types that make people better at one sport than another? How does athletic development differ between younger and older athletes? Early in his career, he received a grant from Gatorade to study the effects of sports drinks on marathon runners. Yet, as a scientist of integrity, throughout his entire career, he has never endorsed specific products. He was the first chair of the Human Performance Laboratory at Ball State University, serving from 1966 to 1998. Some of his most interesting findings include understanding that high-performing distance runners had hearts that efficiently emptied, refilled, and distributed oxygen-rich blood back to the muscles. His research determined that these runners had hearts one and one-half to two times the size of normal adults. Other research that he conducted had definitive implications to training. Discovering fast-twitch and slow-twitch muscle fibers in sprinters and distance runners, respectively, led to training techniques that emphasized the development of one over the other. Dr. Costill discovered that slow-twitch fibers can be developed more easily the older one gets, although they are still trying to figure out why. Such scientific findings helped pave the way for more focused training efforts for elite performers as well as older recreational athletes, making better performances accessible to more people.

Mihaly Csikszentmihalyi (September 29, 1934–)

Csikszentmihalyi is a psychologist who originated the concept of "flow" and contributed to the emergence of positive psychology. Flow describes a state of complete focus and concentration such that happiness and pleasure result. Technically, flow occurs when people are presented with a challenge that lies within their skill level. It often manifests in sport through the language of being "in the zone." Not only are these states equated with happiness and pleasure, but also high performance. Csikszentmihalyi noted that when athletes are in the state of flow, they are able to respond to the moment quickly and efficiently. Although sports psychologists have employed the concepts of total focus and full concentration, it is rarely acknowledged as a key component of happiness and joy, two important factors for children when they talk about why they play sport.

Horst Dassler (1936–April 9, 1987)

Horst Dassler is the son of Adolf "Adi" Dassler, the founder of the German company, Adidas. While Horst Dassler founded Adidas France, competing against his father's company, he became most well known as the father of sport sponsorship. Seeing the potential of a global market, Horst Dassler brought Adidas into the spotlight during the 1956 Olympic Games in Melbourne, Australia. His strategy involved giving shoes to athletes in return for Olympic sponsorship rights. By the 1960 Olympics in Rome, 75 percent of all athletes wore Adidas. This dominance in the market continued through the 1964 Olympics when 80 percent of all athletes were wearing the Adidas brand. Horst Dassler was the first to see the potential in selling media rights to sporting events, especially when the world's best athletes were wearing Adidas. In the 1970s, Horst Dassler created the sports marketing company called International Sport and Leisure (ISL). Through this organization, Horst Dassler made billions of dollars negotiating exclusive media rights for such major sports events as the Olympics, the football (soccer) World Cups, and the World Championships in athletics. Horst Dassler was extraordinary in developing relationships and convincing people to come on board with his new ideas. These relationships resulted in a very successful enterprise for many years. Unfortunately, ISL began to run into cash flow issues, and there were rumors of questionable accounting practices during the late 1990s. In 2001, ISL declared bankruptcy. Yet, the legacy of linking sport sponsorship, professional sport, and media (the "Golden Triangle") remains as powerful today as ever.

Pierre de Coubertin
(January 1, 1863–September 2, 1937)

Pierre de Coubertin was born into an aristocratic family and is considered the founder of the modern Olympic Games. As a young man, de Coubertin was most interested in education, especially the role that athletics might play in developing character. He pursued these ideas relentlessly, studying education and sport. Eventually, he became an advocate for the inclusion of athletics in educational settings. In the early 1880s, de Coubertin was successful in persuading a noted English educator to incorporate athletics into regular education. As a result, playing fields and sports programs developed quickly in England. His view of athletics not only included a concern for character development, but also for creating healthy, strong men suitable for going to war and for encouraging an idealized belief in the ancient Greeks' aesthetic view of competition. Beginning in 1889, de Coubertin worked hard to bring the modern Olympics from dream to reality. In his mind, such a sporting event as the Olympic Games was valuable in that it would promote amateur sport versus professional sport, world understanding and peace through interaction, and the idea that the struggle for excellence was more important than winning. One challenge he faced was the fact that most sport organizations were set up to serve a single sport; thus, while they generally approved of the idea, they had little interest in actually creating a sporting event on such a grand scale. De Coubertin persisted despite lack of engagement. Finally, at an international sport congress in Paris in 1894, a commission on the Olympics was created. In the summer of 1896, the first modern Olympics was held in Athens, Greece, from April 6 to April 15.

Richard Giulianotti

Giulianotti is a professor at Durham University in the United Kingdom, specializing in globalization in sport, popular culture, crime and deviance, and social theory. He recently published *Football and Globalization* in 2009 with coauthor Roland Robertson. Their analysis of football (soccer) examines the effects of globalization on the social worlds of football across the globe. Giulianotti is expert in contextualizing football so that the current cultural, economic, political, and social dimensions of football are revealed. They explore transnational identities, Americanization, and the various ways that globalization processes impact local sport communities. Additionally, Giulianotti has written extensively about the Sport for Development movement. In this research, he seeks to understand the intricate relationships among governments, grassroots efforts, nationalism, and social identities. Giulianotti is often invited to be the keynote speaker at prestigious sport conferences around the globe.

Pat Griffin (1946–)

Pat Griffin was one of the first activists and scholars in addressing LGBT issues in sport. After attending the 1979 March on Washington for Lesbian and Gay Rights, Griffin decided to take her personal life and make it political. Having a passion for sport, Griffin decided to focus her energies on speaking out against homophobia and heterosexism in athletics. Her own athletic accomplishments continue to make her credible to sport enthusiasts. She was on the 1971 U.S. Field Hockey team, coached swimming and diving at the University of Massachusetts, won a bronze medal at the Gay Games IV in 1994 in triathlon, and won a gold medal at Gay Games V in 1998 in the hammer throw. Griffin has had numerous articles published, but her book in 1998 entitled *Strong Women, Deep Closets: Lesbian and Homophobia in Sports*, remains the most widely read account of the effects of homophobia and heterosexism on lesbians in sport. In it she recounts the myriad of ways that homophobia has prevented many women from participating either fully or at all in sport. Her historical account of the struggles that lesbians in sport have faced provides a solid perspective from which to understand how homophobia affects all women in sport. Griffin has been a consultant to many educational institutions that are working toward inclusion of people with various sexual orientations. In January 2011, Griffin became program director of "Changing the Game: Sports Project," a Gay, Lesbian, Straight Education Network (GLSN) sport project that is designed to help K–12 schools specifically create and maintain safe physically active spaces for all students and coaches regardless of gender identity, gender expression, and sexual orientation. In addition,

Griffin continues to be an activist for the LGBT community in sports via her blog, *LGBT Sports Blog*.

Benjamin Sinclair "Ben" Johnson (December 30, 1961–)

Johnson was a Canadian Olympic sprinter, who was highly successful in the 100-meter sprint during the 1980s. Originally from Jamaica, Johnson immigrated to Canada in 1976. He began to be noticed by the sport world when he won two silver medals at the 1982 Commonwealth Games in Brisbane, Australia. Through the mid- to late 1980s, Johnson had a highly publicized rivalry with Carl Lewis, the famous American sprinter who was also vying to break the world record. In 1987, at the World Championships, Johnson solidified his place as the best sprinter by beating Lewis and setting a new world record of 9.83 seconds. At this point in his career, Johnson had very lucrative corporate endorsements. He had several injuries leading into the 1988 Olympics in Seoul, Korea, and suffered some losses to Lewis. Yet, on September 24, 1988, Johnson defeated Lewis with a new world record of 9.79 seconds. Three days later, the world was shocked as Johnson tested positive for steroid use. His medal and world record were revoked. After more investigation, Johnson admitted to using steroids in 1987 at the Rom World Championships. His medal was revoked for that win as well. Since Johnson's highly public disqualification at the 1988 Olympic Games, he is the most well-known athlete to have used performance enhancing drugs to win and then be stripped of his winning. The press coverage of the drug scandal made news for weeks following the disqualification. Canadian media framed Johnson as the tragic fallen hero. In a span of four days, Johnson brought the reality and controversy of PED usage in high performance sport to the world's attention. Later on, through several other drug tests, five of the finalists of the 1988 Olympic100-meter race either tested positive for or were implicated in PED use.

Billie Jean King (November 22, 1943–)

Billie Jean King is a former professional tennis player who pioneered efforts to fight sexism in sports. While King won 39 Grand

Slam singles, doubles, and mixed doubles tennis titles, including a record 20 titles at Wimbledon, she is most well known for her tennis match in 1973 with Bobby Riggs called "The Battle of the Sexes." This tennis match was a public demonstration meant to highlight the sexist language and assumptions that society in general had about women in sport. Winning the match, King inspired many women to feel good about sport participation and helped change society's views toward women in sport. Her personal experiences throughout the 1960s and 1970s in which she noticed the discrepancy between what professional male tennis players made versus what professional female tennis players made sparked her interest in becoming a promoter of women's rights in sport. In her efforts to counter sexism, King founded the Women's Tennis Association and the Women's Sports Foundation, both of which function as advocates for women in sport today. Additionally, she cofounded the World Team Tennis in 1974, a landmark move to bring professional female and male tennis players into the same league. Following this, she founded the World Team Tennis Recreational League, one of the most popular recreational tennis formats in the United States. For her efforts in women's rights in sport, *Life* magazine named King as one of the top 100 most important Americans in 1990. Today, she serves on the board of the Women's Sports Foundation and speaks at numerous sport events.

Össur Kristinsson

Össur Kristinsson, an amputee from complications at birth, invented the first-ever silicone liner for prosthetic limbs in the late 1960s. Kristinsson had the idea for using silicone for prostheses liners because it was much more comfortable than any other liner at the time. After significant research, Kristinsson founded Össur in 1971. Headquartered in Iceland, Össur is dedicated to making high-quality prosthetics. The company now operates five research and development operations in four different countries and has acquired 15 other companies devoted to restoring biological function to those who have been compromised. The basic products consist of bracing and support, compression therapy, and prosthetics. Kristinsson believes that the company's vision "Life without Limitations" provides a positive and uplifting view of those who need help to move in ways that other people take for granted. Kristinsson has been creative and adamant about bringing passionate and talented people into his company, giving them freedom to invent. The Cheetah Flex-Foot is the company's noteworthy prosthetic foot used by high-performance athletes. It was designed by Van Phillips, one of the company's notable inventors. Össur is the world's leader in high-performance prosthetics. Paralympians and other high-performing athletes in running, triathlon, swimming, and cycling use prosthetics by Össur. Some say that Össur's future may be solid given that the world is suffering from such conditions as obesity and diabetes, which account for more than 40 percent of amputees while fewer than 10 percent are caused by accidents.

Donna Lopiano (1946–)

Donna Lopiano is a creative and intelligent advocate for women's sports. Serving as director for Intercollegiate Athletics for Women at the University of Texas (UT) from 1975 to 1992, Lopiano brought success, integrity, and money to women's sports. She was adamant about producing quality sports programs for women at UT. She went through 16 coaches in 10 years in order to find the right fit. She demanded that her teams win and put pressure on coaches to make sure students were doing well in academics and graduating. To make this happen, Lopiano was able to increase the budget for women's sports at UT from $57,000 in 1975 to almost $3 million in 1987. The results are unequivocal. During her tenure, women Longhorns graduated at a rate of 95 percent, won 18 National Championships and 62 Southwest Conference Championships, and produced over a dozen Olympians. In 1992, Lopiano continued her advocacy for women's sports by becoming the executive director of the Women's Sports Foundation. During her 15 years in this position, Lopiano enlightened both the public and corporations about the importance of physical activity and sport for girls and women. Through the Women's Sports Foundation, she promoted health, advocated gender equality in sport, and secured funding for girls' and women's sport programs. In 2007, Lopiano retired from the Women's Sport Foundation and founded her own company titled Sports Management Resources (SMR) in 2008. SMR is dedicated to helping academic organizations negotiate the complexity of gender and race inequalities in scholastic and collegiate programs. SMR is a group of consultants who have worked in educational sport environments and offer expertise in practical solutions to raising money in order to open up more opportunities for athletes so that race and gender equity is achieved.

Rainer Martens (1942–)

Rainer Martens, a kinesiology professor at the University of Illinois, is president and founder of Human Kinetics. Founded in 1974, Human Kinetics is the world's largest publishing company that specializes in physical activity and sport. Today, they employ 320 people and are dedicated to publishing textbooks, journals, software, and consumer books. Through Human Kinetics, Martens's aims have been to help more athletes enjoy sport, improve performance, and engage in sport in safe ways. Dr. Martens wrote a highly accessible book about coaching methods, titled *Successful Coaching 3rd edition*, in 2004. He also founded the American Sport Education Program, the largest coaching education program in the United States. There have been over one million coaches who have gone through these programs. Dr. Martens is a pioneer in sport research at the university level during a period of time when physical education was being attacked by academics. With the guidance and support of Earle Ziegler, Martens was able to pursue his doctorate in sports psychology. His achievements grew out of a love for sport and a desire to help coaches and physical educators create positive sport environments for children and young athletes. Still active in his 60s, Dr. Martens plays on a senior softball league for those aged 65 and over. In 2009, Dr. Martens was inducted into the Senior Softball Hall of Fame based on his dedication, work ethic, and positive team attitude.

Mark McCormack
(November 6, 1930–May 16, 2003)

Mark McCormack began his career as a lawyer but soon saw the earning potential that televised sport could bring to professional athletes. McCormack became the first "sports agent" and founded the International Management Group (IMG) in the

1960s. His first three clients were Arnold Palmer, Jack Nicklaus, and Gary Player for whom he significantly raised incomes, making IMG profitable from the start. McCormack realized that the connection between athletes, media, and corporate sponsorships was going to be very lucrative. Today, there is hardly an aspect of sport of which IMG is not a part. They are the world's largest distributor and producer of televised sports, managing a library of more than 150,000 hours (IMG.com). They are involved in an average of 11 major sporting events worldwide each year, producing original programming in over 200 countries covering over 200 sports. They also manage arts and entertainment groups, play host to several sports academies, consult on management and sponsorship strategies for intercollegiate athletics, and act as a liaison between stadium and arena owners and franchise owners. McCormack chronicled every moment of his life. He pursued connections and never forgot one. Because of attention to detail and personalized consideration, IMG became known for treating clients very well. McCormack died in 2003, and his family sold the company in 2004. Today, IMG is the largest, oldest, and most respected sports agency and sports industry consulting firm in the world.

Jeremy McGhee (1977–)

Jeremy McGhee is an avid outdoor athlete, whose motorcycle accident in 2001 left him paralyzed. Coming from a background in bordercross, a snowboard event with head-to-head competition over extreme obstacles, McGhee was determined to get back to all the activities he had done before the accident. While he is not the first disabled athlete to sitski because it is a Paralympic event, McGhee is the first to push the boundaries of what paralyzed athletes can do beyond the ski area boundary. He first developed his skills such that he could ride *any* terrain within a ski area. Mammoth, California is his home and served as an excellent location for his passion. McGhee's desire to head out into the backcountry on a sitski has required technological advances. McGhee worked closely with a ski company to create the first "powder" sitski. Currently, he is working closely with another company to work out the details of a sitski in which he can actually go up mountains in order to ski back down them. When the backcountry sitski is perfected, McGhee plans to be the first disabled athlete to climb a major peak and descend under his own power. McGhee serves as a role model for athletes involved in extreme sports and believes that his limitations are merely challenges to overcome.

Andy Miah

Andy Miah is an ethicist who writes and speaks about philosophical and ethical issues that technology raises in the 21st century. He writes in the areas of cyberculture, medicine, technology, and the Olympics. He has studied genetic modification and continues to speak about the possibilities of what genetic modification might provide for future generations. While his interests are broad, and he currently is chair of the Ethics and Emerging Technologies in the Faculty of Business & Creative Industries at the University of West Scotland, Dr. Miah has maintained an interest in high-performance sport. He is author of *Genetically Modified Athletes* (2004), the first book to be published on gene doping in sport. In addition, he is coeditor of the online serial, *Culture at the Olympics*, which hosts discussions about "transhuman" athletes. Miah insists that technology is outpacing methods for testing by authorities, giving room for athletes to not simply enhance but optimize their own biology for high performance. The Web site deals with debates over what constitutes innovation or cheating in elite sport. As Miah indicates, questions about what constitutes legitimate high performance in sport are currently facing the sport world. Since 2000, Dr. Miah has been researching the cultural, political, and media structures of the Olympic movement. His investigates nonaccredited media at the Olympics with an eye toward the ways in which their coverage of the Olympics intersects with current cultural and political trends.

William Morgan

Dr. Morgan's broad research interests include ethics, critical theory, and political theory. In particular, he has been especially prolific with respect to the study of popular culture, contemporary sport, and the Olympics. Dr. Morgan is a significant scholar as one of the early thinkers about sport and ethics. Today, Dr. Morgan remains an active scholar and is invited to sport conferences as a distinguished scholar and keynote speaker. His 2006 book, *Why Sports Morally Matter*, was runner up for the best book award from the North American Society for the Sociology of Sport. In it, he argues for a return to the progressive era way of thinking in order to determine ethical boundaries in sport. Also, his textbook, *Ethics in Sport*, was revised in 2007. In it, Dr. Morgan defines key terms in philosophy, then situates sport within that context. Key sections of the book include exploring such themes as competition and fair play, ethical dilemmas with respect to genetic modification and performance enhancing drugs, social issues related to gender and sexuality in sport, and such social ethical topics as violence, exploitation, spectatorship, and disability.

Fred Northrup

In 1998, Fred Northrup founded Athletes for a Better World (ABW) in response to a growing list of stories about violent behavior, inappropriate actions, greed, and scandals. The mission of ABW is to promote development of character and leadership. ABW works toward providing a means for athletes and coaches to make measurable and identifiable positive differences in sport. ABW's Code of Living provides guidelines for behaviors that promote the values of discipline, integrity, respect, cooperation, and compassion. ABW recognizes individuals and teams for being good role models through the Coach Wooden Citizenship Cup, an award given annually to one collegiate and one professional athlete whose actions have made the greatest positive influence on the lives of others. More locally, the Vincent J. Dooley Award and Scholarship is given to one male and one female senior athlete from Georgia high schools. The purpose of the award is to honor those athletes whose commitment to sportsmanship, hard work, and positive community involvement are recognized and rewarded. At its most basic level, ABW is proactive about changing the culture of sports in order to develop character.

Christopher Nowinski
(September 24, 1978–)

Chris Nowinski was a successful college football player and professional wrestler in World Wrestling Entertainment, whose career ended because of post-concussion syndrome. Before

concussion forced Nowinski to retire in 2004, he was the young-
est Hardcore Champion (2002) in the history of the sport. After
consulting with Dr. Robert Cantu, Nowinski understood that
his career ended because of lack of knowledge about concussion. Realizing that coaches, trainers, and sport physicians know
very little about concussion, Nowinski became active in promoting education and research about concussion. In 2006, Nowinski published *Head Games: Football's Concussion Crisis* in
order to educate parents, coaches, and sports medical special-
ists. Simultaneously, new medical research was emerging that
showed the relationship between repetitive concussions and
permanent brain tissue damage. Categorized as a disease, this
condition was identified as Chronic Traumatic Encephalopathy
(CTE). As a response to this research and the growing number
of athletes suffering post-repetitive concussion, Nowinski and
Dr. Cantu founded the Sports Legacy Institute (SLI) in 2007.
The SLI is dedicated to raising awareness about concussion
and continued research about brain injury by partnering with
the Center for the Study of Traumatic Encephalopathy (CSTE)
at Boston University. Nowinski has been highly successful at
conveying the issues of brain injury and how sports professionals should manage concussion. Through the SLI, Nowinski
has developed seven steps for brain safety, including manda-
tory education of coaches, athletes, and parents, easy access to
list of common concussive signs and symptoms, an action plan
when concussion is suspected, and a neck strengthening program. Since 2006, Nowinski has been invited to speak at over
100 corporations, medical institutions, schools, and sport organizations. Currently, he is president of the SLI, consults with
organizations, and serves on the board of the National Football
League Players Association, on the Mackey/White TBI Research
Committee, and on the board of directors of the Brain Injury
Association of America.

Oscar Leonard Carl Pistorius (November 22, 1986–)

Pistorius, known as "the fastest man with no legs," is a double amputee sprinter from South Africa. He is the world record holder in the 100, 200, and 400 meters for Paralympians.

Pistorius's prosthetic is the Cheetah Flex-Foot made by Össur. In 2007, Pistorius was allowed to compete with able-bodied athletes. Yet, his performances caused sport officials to question whether or not his artificial limbs were an advantage over able-bodied sprinters. When sports biomechanical experts performed tests that reportedly showed that Pistorius uses 25 percent less energy than an athlete with natural ankles and feet, Pistoruis was banned from the 2008 Summer Olympics. However, on May 16, 2008, the Court of Arbitration, an international court for amateur athletes and athletic disputes, ruled that there was no clear evidence that Pistorius's prosthetic gave him an advantage. The only way experts tested Pistorius was running in a straight line. They did not conduct any tests with him rounding curves, nor did they consider the disadvantages Pistorius encounters at the start and during acceleration phases. In the summer of 2011, Pistorius achieved an "A" qualifying time of 45.07 for the 2011 World Championships as well as the 2012 Summer Olympics. At the World Championships, he ran with the able-bodied relay team, becoming the first amputee to win a world medal as part of an able-bodied track team.

Katherine Redmond

A rape victim of a University of Nebraska football player, Redmond set course on a lawsuit against the University of Nebraska based on Title IX. In 1997, Redmond's case against the university and perpetuators was settled. Through this experience, Redmond became acutely aware of how the system protects athletes who commit rape or are involved in domestic violence while it denigrates victims. Wanting to help other victims of athlete violence as well as raise awareness of the systematic ways athletes are rarely held accountable for their actions, Redmond became an expert in athlete violence and the cultural and organizational responses to this violence. In 1997, Redmond founded the National Coalition Against Violent Athletes (NCAAVA). Redmond's organization is based on the premise that athletes should be held accountable to the same laws as others. The goals of the NCAAVA are to educate the public, coaches, and administrators about athlete violence; provide steps toward prevention and assessment; serve as a support and advocate for victims of athlete violence; and put pressure on sport organizations to take proactive steps toward prevention and accountability. Redmond's ultimate goal is to eliminate violence by athletes by reconsidering the privileged position these athletes have in society. She engages audiences and has had many television appearances, including being a guest on such shows as *Good Morning America*, *The Today Show*, *Dateline NBC*, *Fox News*, *HBO Real Sports*, *Fox Sports*, *ABC World News Tonight*, and the following cable stations: A&E, Court TV, CNN, MSNBC, and ESPN. Currently, Redmond is working on a book titled *Asking for It*, which reveals the issues of athlete violence and offers recommendations for action.

Jackie Robinson
(January 31, 1919–October 24, 1972)

Jackie Robinson was the first African American Major League Baseball player in the modern era. While there were black baseball players in the major leagues in the 1880s, Robinson's signing with the Brooklyn Dodgers in 1947 signaled an end to segregated professional sports. Prior to Robinson's entry into the major leagues, African American players were only allowed to play in the Negro Leagues. Robinson's signing with the Dodgers was not without controversy. Robinson had been known as an athlete who argued with officials or military officers. Branch Rickey, the Dodger's manager who signed Robinson, anticipated that there would be significant issues associated with racism. As a consequence, Rickey made Robinson agree to a "turn the other cheek" policy in the face of certain hostility and verbal abuse. Robinson agreed and signed a contract for $600 a month. Robinson endured racism in many forms, but the American public also loved him because he displayed a calm demeanor and physical prowess. Robinson kept his promise to abide by the "turn the other cheek" agreement. In 1947, Robinson won the inaugural Rookie of the Year Award. In 1949, he was the first black player to receive the Most Valuable Player Award. Through his athletic accomplishments, Robinson developed into an activist for African American rights. He became the league's first black television analyst as well as the first black president of a major U.S. corporation.

Juan Antonio Samaranch
(July 17, 1920–April 21, 2010)

Samaranch was president of the International Olympic Committee (IOC) from 1980 to 2001. He is best known for leading the
Olympic Games into the modern era, by embracing commercialism, professionalism, and consumerism as part of global sport. He
openly admitted that the Olympics had always been professional,
political, and commercialized on some level. Samaranch decided
that it was time the IOC took these developments seriously. In the
process, he transformed the IOC from an organization with barely
$200,000 in cash reserves to an organization now worth billions in
U.S. dollars. Under his 20-year leadership, the popularity of the
Olympics has grown tremendously. In turn, the deals between the
IOC and the media and corporate sponsors have proven highly
profitable. Samaranch was often criticized for bringing professionalism and money to the Olympic Games and compromising
the values on which it was based. He maintained that capitalizing on profitability of the Olympics has helped sport grow in
underdeveloped countries and brought the competition among
nations to a more level playing field. For example, with more revenue he was able to restructure Olympic Solidarity in 1981 and
provide assistance to National Olympic Committees in difficulty.
In addition, he felt that taking the concept of amateurism out of
the Olympic Charter raised the level of competition, providing
for a more exciting Olympics. He believes that the inclusion of
Western professional athletes into the Olympics counters professional athletes produced by Eastern block sport systems, which
in turn maintains a competitive balance. Samaranch was the first
IOC president to take on the responsibilities full time, advocating
change where he felt it was necessary. One significant result of
more revenue and full-time attention was the push to expand the
Paralympics to a winter version in Sarajevo in 1984.

Robert Edward "Ted" Turner III
(November 19, 1938–)

Ted Turner is founder of CNN, the first-ever 24-hour news program. Known as a businessman and media mogul, Turner led

the way in sports media and its intersections with sport team ownership. Turner purchased the Atlanta Braves in 1976. In 1977, he tried to become the manager of the team, but Major League Baseball declared that a manager could not have a financial interest in a team. While Turner relinquished his managerial dreams, he was a very "hands on" owner. Part of the lure to buy the team was to help keep his television superstation, WTBS, in Atlanta. The Braves became the major reason people tuned into WTBS. As a result, the Braves were the first team to have a nationwide audience. Both WTBS and the Braves benefited from the arrangement. Turner changed the name of WTBS to simply TBS, which is widely known as Turner Broadcasting System, Inc. In 1996, Time Warner purchased TBS. Turner saw another opportunity to merge media ownership with sports events and created the first Goodwill Games in 1986. These games were televised by Time Warner, of which Turner Broadcasting is an executive member. The Goodwill Games raised millions of dollars for various charities but no longer exists today due to the expense of hosting large multiday and multisport events. Additionally, Turner turned World Championship Wrestling (WCW) into a profitable media enterprise in the mid- to late 1990s. WCW was a Monday night show that became one of the highest rated programs on cable. In turn, the success of this show encouraged viewers to explore Turner's other such channels as TNT and WTBS.

6

Data and Documents

This chapter highlights facts, data, and documents that will help readers gain a deeper understanding of the current status, significant events, and issues as well as the historical context of modern sport. This detailed information sheds light on the phenomenon that is sport, the business of sport, politics and ethics, and social issues. Data regarding widespread sport participation illustrates the global reach of sport. Facts about the money flowing through sport also signify that not only is sport a passion of the world but also a global business. A few documents help readers understand when and how sport becomes political. Other information focuses on the high-performance ideology in sport that leads to ethical issues. Finally, issues related to gender, race, and ethnicity are more easily understood through the charts, tables, and graphs presented. The aim of this chapter is to bring tangible evidence to the concepts discussed in the remainder of the book.

The Phenomenon of Sport: Global Participation and North American Trends

Since the 19th century, sport has experienced tremendous growth. Once organized by local leagues and volunteers, sport has moved solidly into the global scene, becoming more business-like and professional on every level. The Olympics stands as the largest multisport event in the world. The International Olympic

Committee organizes the Winter and Summer Games held on alternating even years in conjunction with national governing organizations and local organizing committees. In other words, the efforts toward staging the Olympics are indeed global. Other worldwide sport events showcase the best athletes in such professional sports as soccer and baseball. The Fédération Internationale de Football Association's (FIFA) World Cup and the International Baseball Federation's (IBAF) World Cup are examples of international sporting events that have experienced consistent growth. Beyond these mainstream international sporting events, sporting events that celebrate different abilities and are aimed at creating a more inclusive sport world have also taken hold. The Paralympics and Gay Games have paved the way for all kinds of athletes, and in the process these events make strong social statements about who counts as athletes. Finally, North America remains the only country in the world offering athletic programs as part of higher educational institutions. Growth in intercollegiate athletic participation continues. Other trends include the steadily growing participation rates in various outdoor sports. In short, sports participation is global and continually being experienced in new forms.

The Olympics is a prime example of how sport has become a global phenomenon. The first Olympic Games held in Athens, Greece, in 1896 featured 241 athletes from 14 different countries. The next Olympic Games were held in Paris, France, in conjunction with the 1900 World's Fair. Such an association meant that the competitions lasted from May until October, the same length of time as the fair. Athletes grew to almost 1,000 competitors from 24 nations for the second Olympics. The third Olympic Games coincided with the 1904 St. Louis World's Fair in the United States. Over half of the competitors were from the United States, bringing the total to 651 competitors from 12 countries. Only 55 athletes were from outside North America, however. In 1924, the first Winter Olympic Games were held in Chamonix, France. A total of 16 nations with 258 athletes competed over a 10-day period. Despite this modest start, the modern Olympics survived and has grown into the world's largest multisporting event with more countries participating than there are United Nations members. Nearly all National Governing Bodies (NGBs) for Olympic sports are funded by national governments. The United States Olympic Committee (USOC) is the only NGB that is entirely privately funded. Whether publicly or privately funded, supporting Olympic athletes makes up a significant part of national pride. Nearly 84 percent of the world's recognized nations, colonies, territories, or sovereign states participate in the Olympic Games.

The Summer Olympics hosts more than 10,000 athletes from over 200 nations every four years. The 2008 Olympics in Beijing had the most number of countries participating with 204 nations sending athletes. The International Olympic Committee (IOC) has a limit of 205 nations. London anticipates that 204 nation-states will participate in the Summer 2012 Olympic Games with close to 10,500 athletes, 26 sports, and 39 disciplines. Disciplines refer to the subcategories of a sport. For instance, canoe-kayak is a sport with two disciplines: sprint and whitewater slalom. The Winter Olympics is much smaller. At the Vancouver 2010 Winter Games, 82 nations competed with almost 2,600 athletes. Still, such participation represents almost half of the world's nations. The United States and Canada sent the most athletes—215 and 206 respectively. Previously, the Winter Olympics occurred in the same year as the summer games, but since 1994 the Winter Olympics have been held on a separate four-year cycle. Now the Winter Olympics occurs on even years in between the Summer Olympics. Figure 6.1 is a visual map of Olympic participation in the most recent Olympic Games, the Vancouver 2010 Winter Olympic Games, while Table 6.1 lists the participating countries.

The Olympic movement continues to gain momentum as an important international sport event. Expansion of the Olympic ideals and traditions continues in various forms. The most recent iteration of the Olympic movement is the Youth Olympic Games. The first Summer Youth Olympic Games (YOG) took place in Singapore in 2010 while the first Winter YOG took place in Innsbruck in 2012. The YOG is an international sport event that focuses on the values of excellence, friendship, and respect. Athletes aged 14–18 years compete in sporting events and take part in a Culture and Education Programme in order to learn about people, customs, and values from around the world.

Not only are the Olympics a sporting event of worldwide appeal and participation, but many professional sports also have a global reach. Soccer (football) is one of the most popular sports in the world in terms of both participation and its ability to hold worldwide attention through annual tournaments and the World Cup held every four years. Founded in 1904 in Paris, the FIFA had

FIGURE 6.1
Map of Participating Countries in 2010 Winter Olympic Games

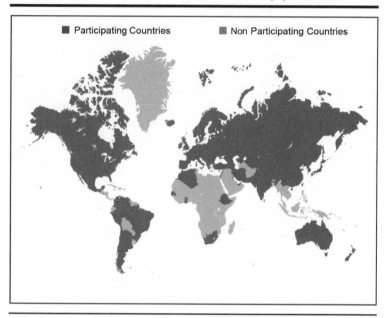

TABLE 6.1
The 82 Participating Countries of the 2010 Winter Olympic Games

Albania	Algeria	Andorra	Argentina	Armenia
Australia	Austria	Azerbaijan	Belarus	Belgium
Bermuda	Bosnia and Herzegovina	Brazil	Bulgaria	Canada
Cayman Islands	Chile	China	Colombia	Croatia
Cyprus	Czech Republic	Denmark	Estonia	Ethiopia
Finland	France	Georgia	Germany	Ghana
Great Britain	Greece	Hong Kong	Hungary	Iceland
India	Iran	Ireland	Israel	Italy
Jamaica	Japan	Kazakhstan	North Korea	South Korea
Kyrgyzstan	Latvia	Lebanon	Liechtenstein	Lithuania
Macedonia	Mexico	Moldova	Monaco	Mongolia
Montenegro	Morocco	Nepal	Netherlands	New Zealand
Norway	Pakistan	Peru	Poland	Portugal
Romania	Russia	San Marino	Senegal	Serbia
Slovakia	Slovenia	South Africa	Spain	Sweden
Switzerland	Chinese Taipei	Tajikistan	Turkey	Ukraine
United States	Uzbekistan			

Source: List created by author from data on the following Web sites: http://www.olympic.org/vancouver-2010-winter-olympics; http://en.wikipedia.org/wiki/2010_Winter_Olympics.

eight official members with one accepting membership through telegram. Today, FIFA has 208 national associations for men's teams and 129 women's national teams. There are only nine sovereign states that do not belong to FIFA. FIFA functions as it was originally intended, overseeing all international competition and the development of soccer worldwide. Given the scope of this task, FIFA oversees six confederations that deal with development of soccer on their continent or in their region. The six confederations are (1) the Asian Football Confederation (AFC), which includes Asia and Australia; (2) the Confédération Africaine de Football (CAF), which includes all of Africa except Western Sahara; (3) the Confederation of North, Central American and Caribbean Association Football (CONCACAF), which includes North America, Central America, and Guyana, Suriname, and French Guiana in South America; (4) the Confederación Sudamericana de Fútbol (CONMEBOL), which includes the remaining South American countries; (5) the Oceania Football Confederation (OFC), which includes New Zealand and Papua New Guinea; and (6) the Union of European Football Associations (UEFA), which includes Europe and Northern Asia. Figure 6.2 shows the confederations across the world.

Baseball holds a similar stronghold on the world. Although the World Series is strictly a North American championship, there are numerous international baseball events that establish baseball as a global sport. In addition to Olympic Baseball, the World Baseball Classic was the first international tournament to organize players from professional leagues into teams representing countries. The first two World Baseball Classics were held in 2005 and 2009 with the next one to be played on a four-year cycle in 2013. Japan won the first two World Baseball Classics. Held in the same years but initiated in 2001 is the IBAF World Cup. The 2009 IBAF World Cup hosted 22 teams in 7 different European countries. International development and promotion of baseball is a major function of the IBAF. Currently, there are three youth World Championships for athletes aged 12 and under, 16 and under, and 18 and under. The growth in European baseball is reflected in the fact that in 2011, approximately 40 players from 9 different European countries were playing in the major and minor leagues in North America. This is the highest number ever. Today, the IBAF has 125 member nations among five world federations. Figure 6.3 shows the world baseball leagues from the five federations of Africa, Americas, Asia, Europe, and Oceania.

FIGURE 6.2
FIFA Confederations

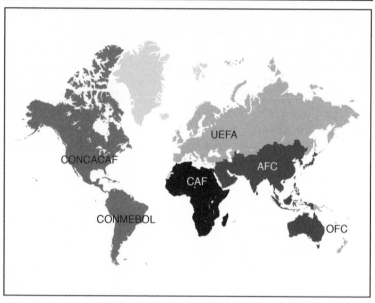

Even such nonmainstream sporting events as the Paralympics and the Gay Games have experienced global support and growth. The Paralympics occurs in the same year as the Olympics approximately two–four weeks after. The number of athletes participating in Summer Paralympic Games has increased significantly. The first Summer Paralympics in Rome in 1960 hosted 400 athletes from 23 countries. In Beijing in 2008, almost 4,000 athletes from 146 countries competed in the Paralympics. In London 2012, the number of Paralympians is expected to be similar to Beijing. The Winter Paralympic Games was instituted in 1976 in Sweden with 168 athletes from 16 countries. At the Vancouver 2010 Paralympic Games a total of 502 athletes from 44 countries participated. The International Paralympic Committee has 165 national members in four disability categories. Figures 6.4 and 6.5 show the growth of the Summer and Winter Paralympics, respectively.

The Gay Games are one of the newest international multisporting events held every four years similar to the Olympics

FIGURE 6.3
Map of the Five Baseball Federations

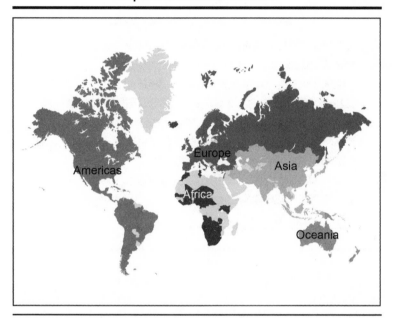

FIGURE 6.4
Growth of Summer Paralympic Games

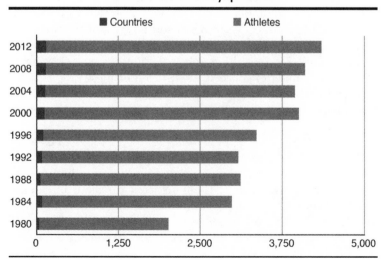

FIGURE 6.5
Growth of Winter Paralympic Games

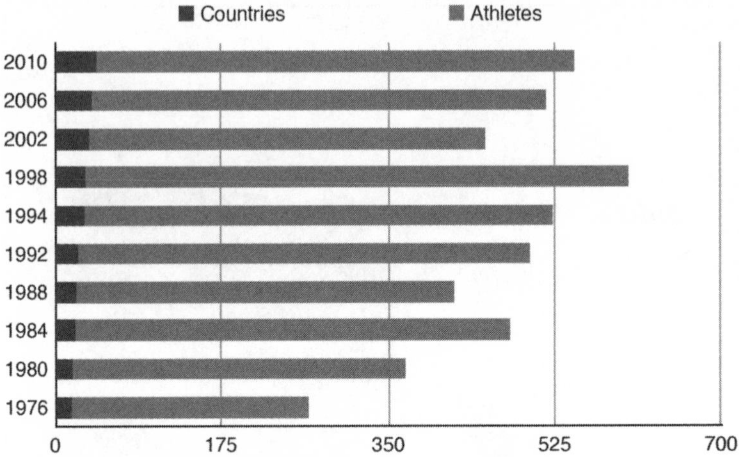

and World Cup. The Gay Games I took place in San Francisco in 1982, featuring 1,350 athletes in 11 sports. Overall growth and the number of participating countries more than doubled in each subsequent Gay Games. The Gay Games II in San Francisco in 1986 drew 3,500 competitors from 17 countries participating in 17 different sports. By the time of Gay Games III held in Vancouver, British Columbia, participation had grown to 7,300 athletes from 39 countries featuring 27 sports. Figure 6.6 depicts the solid growth and consistent participation rates of the Gay Games while Figure 6.7 shows the number of countries participating as well as the number of sports offered. Together, these graphs show that the Gay Games has established itself as a solid international sporting event, which promotes inclusivity along with athletic excellence.

In North America, sports continue to be a focus in colleges and universities. The National Collegiate Athletic Association (NCAA) governs the largest number of collegiate athletics programs in the United States. There are three divisions or categories of athletic programs. Division I is the largest division with the greatest number of athletic teams and scholarships. Division I programs must offer at least 14 sports, 7 for women and 7 for men or 6 for men and 8 for women. There are a total of 335 member

FIGURE 6.6
Gay Games Athlete Participation

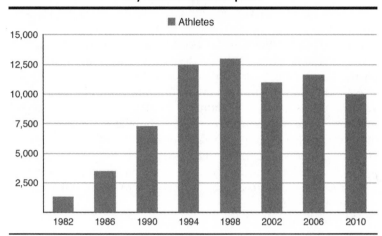

FIGURE 6.7
Gay Games: Country Participation and Sports

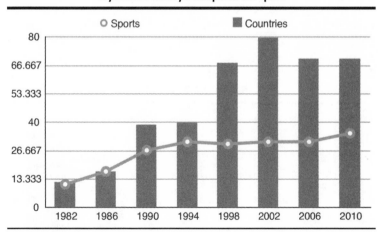

institutions within Division I. Division I schools that are part of the Football Bowl Subdivision (FBS) are the only exception, required to offer 16 teams. There are 120 schools that belong to this category. The 118 schools that make up the Football Championship Subdivision (FCS) of Division I still host football programs but offer the normal 14 teams. The remaining 97 members of Division I do not host football programs. Division I programs are the most competitive level of collegiate athletics. Division II schools are generally smaller and are required to offer 10 sports. Each male and female sport counts as a sport. There are approximately 100,000 athletes in Division II schools with very few of them receiving full-tuition scholarships, but most athletes are on partial scholarship. Currently, there are 281 institutions fully active as Division II. Division III is the least competitive, but the schools in this division contain the most number of schools and athletes. There are 436 active institutions whose student-athletes make up approximately 40 percent of the total number of NCAA student-athletes. NCAA student-athletes have grown steadily over the years, making sports a major component of North American education. Figure 6.8 shows the growth of NCAA student-athletes since 2006.

Another trend in North America is participation in outdoor sports. Millions of people engage in outdoor sport activities each year. Such sports as adventure racing, BMX bicycling, cross-country skiing, surfing, and trail running are popular choices among many North Americans. Figure 6.9 shows the participation rates of these representative outdoor sports from 2006 to 2010. BMX bicycling has experienced 30 percent growth going

FIGURE 6.8
NCAA Athlete Participation

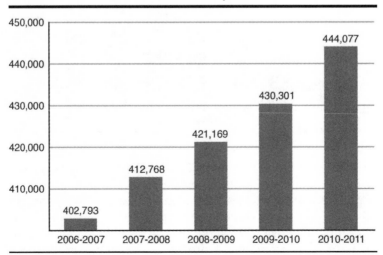

FIGURE 6.9
Outdoor Sports Participation

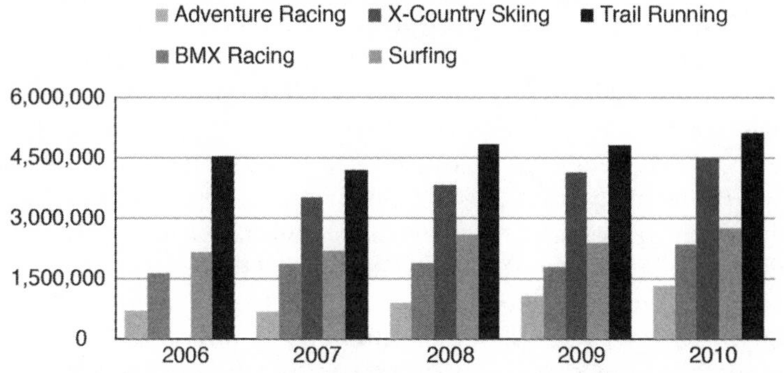

from 1.7 million participants to 2.4 million while surfing has maintained its appeal as a lifestyle sport with 2–3 million participants per year since 2006. Endurance sports have become extremely popular in North America. Adventure racing has experienced significant growth from about 725,000 participants in 2006 to almost 1.4 million in 2010. Cross-country skiing and trail running are some of the most popular outdoor sports with participation rates of 4.5 and 5.1 million in 2010.

The Business of Sport

Growth in sport business is indeed a global reality. Worldwide, people engage in sport as elite athletes, spectators, industry professionals, recreational athletes, or some combination of these. More competitions allow many opportunities for elite athletes to compare themselves to the best in the world, allowing some to earn considerable sums of money doing so. Sports are also entertainment for millions of fans around the world. Staging sporting events, preparing teams and athletes to compete, and providing the means for people to participate require a plethora of industry-related professionals and such entities as coaches, athletic trainers, team owners, referees, officials, media representatives, governing body administrators, facilities, sporting goods manufacturers, retail shops, fitness centers, and sport-specific apparel. As sport has become embedded in global cultures, sport business has experienced significant growth. Using England as an example, Figure 6.10 shows the growth of consumer spending on sport from 1985 to 2008 in U.S. dollars and adjusted for inflation.

The data from Figure 6.10 reveal the steady growth of consumer spending on sport-related goods and services. According to the same report, total consumer spending on sport as a percentage of total consumption rose from 2 percent in 1985 to 2.3 percent in 2008, representing overall growth despite the economic conditions of the mid-2000s. Concurrently, sport industry employment in England also increased. As noted in Figure 6.11, more people have sport-related jobs in 2008 than in 1985, with an increase from 304,000 employees in 1985 to just over 440,000 in 2008. The study notes that these numbers also represent a higher percentage of jobs in England that can be attributed to the sport industry, rising from 1.3 percent in 1985 to 1.8 percent in 2008 (see Figure 6.11).

Sporting-related consumer spending results from a variety of sporting-related activities and sales. For instance, sporting goods wholesale revenue and retail sales revenue comprise a significant portion of sporting-related revenues in the United States.

FIGURE 6.10
Sport-Related Consumer Expenditures In England (in U.S. Dollars)

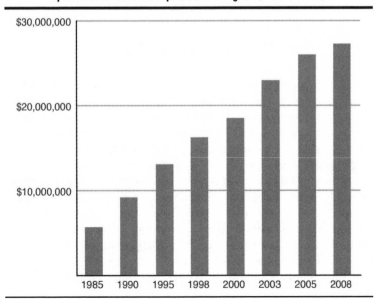

FIGURE 6.11
Sport-Related Employment in England

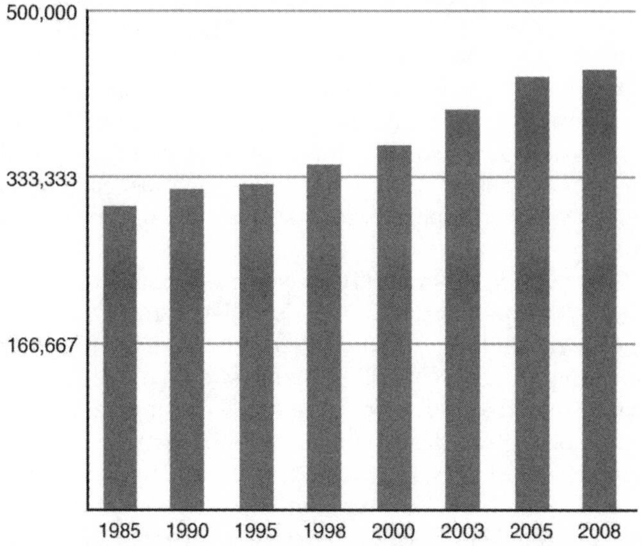

As Table 6.2 shows, despite the high profile of spectator sports, selling sporting goods is perhaps one of the most lucrative areas of the sports industry. In the United States, over $74 billion in revenue results from manufacturers selling sporting goods, and retail sales are similarly strong at $40 billion while spectator sports bring in approximately $30 billion. The sporting goods industry employs people in product design, marketing, sales, and manufacturing. This side of the sports industry is one of the most globalized components of sport with companies often headquartered in the United States or Europe while manufacturing is frequently based in Asia. Also, one of the fastest growing segments in the sport industry is health clubs and fitness centers. In Europe, the estimated number of health club members is approximately 44 million, which generates more than $31 billion in club fees annually. In the United States, approximately 50 million health club members generate just over $20 billion in club fees. As these clubs continue to be popular, such industry professionals as athletic trainers are more in demand. Finally, another important segment of the sport industry is the multiple governing bodies for sport. In Table 6.2, examples of the NCAA and NASCAR show that governing bodies also bring in substantial sums for establishing the rules, organizing events, and overseeing their respective sports.

Not only is consumption and employment in sport increasing, but corporations are aligning themselves with sports and sport events at increasingly higher levels of commitment. Corporations' desires to be involved with high-profile sports and sporting events is reflected in the number of large, global corporations signing on as sponsors. Table 6.3 shows the most current list of sponsors for major sport organizations and high-profile sport events.

The Olympic Program (TOP) is one of the most prestigious levels of sport sponsorship at the global level. To be a TOP sponsor means committing millions of euros to the Olympic program by donating to the IOC. TOP companies receive exclusive rights to use the Olympic rings and name in advertising. In total, sponsorship money provides over 40 percent of the revenues for the IOC, which goes to support programs worldwide. NASCAR, FIFA, and the NCAA also have ongoing sponsors to support their efforts. The number of races sanctioned by NASCAR and the frequency of events results in over 40 regular sponsors. FIFA secures sponsorship money to support oversight of international events and global development of soccer. The NCAA is a North American entity governing intercollegiate athletic programs in hundreds of colleges and universities. While sport sponsorship supports specific sport organizations, it also is crucial to such specific events as the FIFA World Cup and the NFL Super Bowl.

TABLE 6.2
Sports Equipment Sales and Industry Revenue

Sports industry revenue	
Wholesale revenues, U.S. sporting goods manufacturers	$74.2 Billion in 2010
Retail sporting equipment sales	$40 Billion in 2011
Spectator sports	$31.4 Billion in 2011
European health club revenue	$31 Billion in 2010
U.S. health club revenue	$20.3 Billion in 2010
NCAA sports revenue	$757 Million in 2011/2012
NASCAR revenue	$645.4 Million in 2010

Source: Table compiled by author from data available at http://www.plunkettresearch.com/sports-recreation-leisure-market-research/industry-statistics.

TABLE 6.3

Sponsors for International and North American Sport Events and Organizations

2010 and 2012 Olympic Games Top partners	National Football League Super Bowl 2012	FIFA partners	2014 FIFA World Cup sponsors	2011 NASCAR official sponsors	NCAA
Coca-Cola	2nd Story Software	Adidas	Budweiser	3M	AT&T
Acer	American Honda Motor	Coca-Cola	Castrol	Bank of America	Capital One
Atos Origin	Anheuser-Busch InBev	Hyundai-Kia Motors	Continental	Camping World	Coca-Cola
Dow	Audi of America	Emirates	Johnson & Johnson	Canadian Tire	Buick
GE	Best Buy	Sony	McDonald's	Chevrolet	Enterprise
McDonald's	Bridgestone Americas	Visa	oi	Cintas	The Hartford
Omega	Careerbuilder		Seara	Coca-Cola	Infiniti
Panasonic	Cars.com		Yiingu Solar	Coors Light	LG
Procter & Gamble	Century 21			Craftsman Tools	Lowe's
Samsung	Chrysler			Diageo	Planters
Visa	Coca-Cola			DIRECTV	Reese's
	Dannon Yogurt			Diageo	Unilever
	General Motors			Dodge	UPS
	GoDaddy.com			DRIVE4COPD	
	H & M			DuPont	
	Hyundai			Exide	
	Kia Motor			Featherlite Coach	
	Mars Inc's M&M's			Featherlite Trailers	
	Paramount Pictures			Ford Trucks	
	PepsiCo's Doritos			Freescale	
	PepsiCo Beverages			Freightliner Trucks	
	Relativity Media			Growth Energy	
	Skechers			Gillette	
	Teleflora			Goodyear	
	Toyota			Head & Shoulders	
	Toyota's Lexus			Mars Inc.	
	Universal Pictures			Mobil 1	
	Volkswagon			McLaren	

(Continued)

TABLE 6.3 (*Continued*)

2010 and 2012 Olympic Games Top partners	National Football League Super Bowl 2012	FIFA partners	2014 FIFA World Cup sponsors	2011 NASCAR official sponsors	NCAA
	Walt Disney Pictures			Nabisco (Kraft)	
				Nationwide	
				Office Depot	
				Old Spice	
				O'Reilly's	
				Safety-Kleen	
				SIRIUS XM Radio	
				Sprint	
				Sunoco	
				Toyota	
				Unilever	
				UPS	
				Visa	
				K & N	
				Whelen Engineering Inc.	

Source: Table compiled by author from data obtained from the following Web sites: http://www.olympic.org/Documents/IOC_Marketing/OLYMPIC_MARKETING_FACT_FILE_2011.pdf; http://adage.com/article/mediaworks/super-bowl-buying-super-bowl-2011/146802/; http://www.fifa.com/worldcup/organisation/partners/index.html; http://www.ncaa.org/wps/portal/ncaahome?WCM_GLOBAL_CONTEXT=/corp_relations/corprel/corporate+relationships/corporate+alliances/partners.html; http://www.nascar.com/guides/sponsors/.

Sponsors of sport events hope to reach a wide audience in order to maximize their return on investment. One way in which sport events look to provide fans with the best sport experience possible is to build state-of-the-art stadiums to host large numbers of people in comfortable ways. While the building of stadiums remains controversial, new stadiums continue to be built at exorbitant costs. Figure 6.12 illustrates the fact that most stadiums are multimillion dollar projects with the most recent North American stadiums costing over $1 billion.

The National Stadium in Beijing, known locally as the Bird's Nest, cost $423 million and was the symbol of the Beijing 2008 Olympics. It seats approximately 80,000 people. Its design includes several features meant for sustainability. There is a rainwater catching system after which the rainwater is purified and

FIGURE 6.12
Stadium Costs in U.S. Dollars

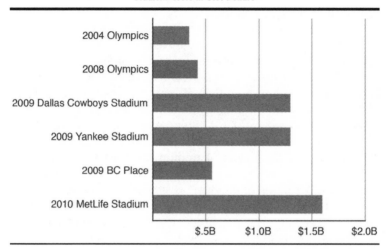

used for all facilities in the stadium. To control the stadium's temperature, pipes under the playing field gather heat in the winter and remain cool throughout the summer. While some stadiums are built from the ground up, many stadiums simply undergo major renovations. These renovations can easily cost several million dollars. The Athens Olympic Stadium was a re-model project, completed just in time for the 2004 Olympics. Canada's BC Place was an older stadium that underwent sub-stantial renovation for the 2010 Winter Olympics. Renovations begun in 2007 and completed in 2010 are estimated at $563 mil-lion. Renovations included the world's largest retractable roof, refurbished locker rooms, a new turf field rated as the world's best, 1,140 HDTV screens throughout the stadium so spectators can watch the action while at the concessions stands, wider seats, more concessions, and North America's second largest HD center-hung scoreboard. BC Place hosts more than 200 events each year. The Dallas Cowboys Stadium and the New York Yankees stadium are other examples of expensive renovations. The Cow-boys Stadium is the world's largest domed stadium and features an HD center-hung display that goes from one 20-yard line to the other. The New York Yankees renovation featured many ele-ments that were made to look like the original 1923 stadium but with new technology and improved comfort for fans. Finally, the most expensive NFL stadium to date is the new MetLife Stadium. At a cost of $1.6 billion, this stadium has unique attributes. Special louvers and lighting systems allow colors and banners to change to match the colors of the two teams who share this space: the New York Giants and the New York Jets.

Certainly, professional sports hold a prominent place in the world, but the popularity of the "Big 4" professional leagues in North America allow players in all four leagues to earn millions of dollars annually. The average player salaries for the four major leagues as reported in 2011 by Steve Aschburner, feature writer for NBA.com, are as follows: (1) the NBA at $5.15 million for 2010–11, (2) the MLB at $3.34 million for 2010, (3) the NHL at $2.4 million for 2010–11, and (4) the NFL at $1.9 million for 2010. As Aschburner notes, figures can be difficult to assess. First, average salaries get skewed upward due to the few extremely high salaries that most teams pay in order to acquire or keep top players. Figure 6.13 illustrates the average annual salary of the highest paid player in each of the major leagues.

An average must be reported in order to compare the figures since players have contracts for different numbers of years. For Figure 6.13, the average was calculated by dividing the total contract value of the highest paid player by the number of years in the contract. The notable aspect of these salaries compared to league averages is the extent to which teams are willing to sign

FIGURE 6.13
Average Annual Salary of Highest Paid Player in North American Major Leagues

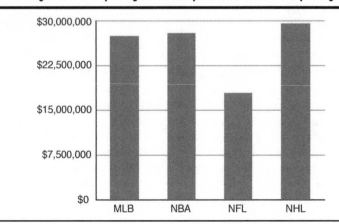

star players at salaries that dwarf average salaries in each of the leagues. The NHL pays its highest-paid player approximately 12 times what the average hockey player makes. These discrepancies become even more pronounced if one considers the median salary of each league. The median salary might be a better indicator of what professional athletes really make since it is the number that half the salaries are above and half are below, meaning that extremely high salaries do not affect the results. In every league, the highest-paid players are paid so much more than the average player that the median is always below the average salary. Yet, players and owners have agreed to use averages in collective bargaining agreements. No matter which method is used, the average professional athlete makes about 40 times the average salary of an American. Second, it could be argued that the NBA and the NFL are not really dealing with similar team profiles based on numbers, making comparisons irrelevant. NBA teams have 15 players while NFL teams have 53 players among whom to divide total amounts dedicated to player salaries. MLB and the NHL have rosters of 25 and 23 respectively. One argument in favor of the discrepancies is that since there are fewer NBA players, it makes them more valuable overall.

When league revenues are considered relative to players' salaries, the business of professional sports leagues becomes more apparent. Figure 6.14 shows the 2010/2011 major league revenues for MLB, NBA, NFL and the NHL.

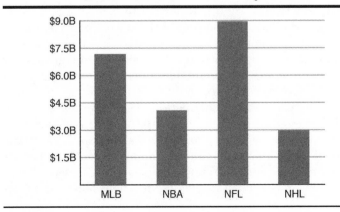

FIGURE 6.14
2010/2011 North American Professional League Revenues

These revenues are in the billions of U.S. dollars; therefore, comparing the average salaries to these revenue figures is nearly impossible because of the difference between millions and billions of dollars. In these instances, calculations can be made, which reveal that approximately 59 percent of total league revenue goes players' salaries whereas 2.4 percent of NHL total revenue is devoted to players' salaries. MLB and the NFL spend 35 percent and 36 percent of total league revenue respectively. What happens to the balance of the revenue? League owners receive a share, and the teams themselves benefit through revenue-sharing contracts. Given these revenue figures and relative salaries, even considering the highest paid athletes, leagues are bringing in billions of revenue each year. With these numbers in mind, the efforts of mayors to pass along stadium costs to taxpayers seem misdirected. Although the simplistic accounting presented here does not take into account the complexity of funding North American professional sport teams, there is no doubt that professional sports not only constitute an important part of American culture, but also economic activity.

Politics, Performance, and Ethics in Sport

While sport is clearly a personal pursuit as well as a business, it is also like any other sphere of social life in that political and ethical elements weave intricately throughout its history and current practice. Throughout the history of the Olympics, boycotts have occurred because of ideological stances on issues of human rights. Although more rare, athletes have used their status to make political statements or refuse to participate in regular sport practices for religious reasons. Athletes have always been pushing the limits of performance, and today is no exception. In this pursuit of excellence and better performances, athletes often face ethical choices about how they will improve their performances. Some scholars argue that performance-focused sport has made the use of PEDs almost an imperative in some sports. Pushing to the limits also results in serious injury, and concerned athletes and medical professionals are asking questions about the ethics of submitting athletes to unnecessary risk, especially in the case of concussion. In order to support human rights and counter practices of cheating or unsportsmanlike conduct, many sport organizations work hard to support ethical decision making, positive relationships, or sportsmanship through sport.

Politics

Governments have consistently tied sport to politics, often making important decisions for athletes based on their desire to make a political statement. The Olympic Games have long been a stage upon which countries have made political statements. Yet, not all political statements arise out of similar concerns. In order to understand the intersection between sport, specifically the Olympics, and politics, it is important to look at the types of boycotts that have occurred. There is much variety in the reasons why countries boycott such sporting events as the Olympics. Some concerns stem from ideological disagreements about the best types of government—for example, democratic governments or communist regimes. Other concerns arise out of human rights, such as the exclusion of South Africa from the Olympic Games for 32 years because of apartheid. Other instances involve one country boycotting an Olympics because of a national disagreement with another country.

Olympic Boycotts and Politics

Document 6.1 lists some of the most important Olympic boycotts and political issues. The descriptions provide insights into the types of politics and issues that precipitate such actions. Very often the athletes feel that the boycott is unfair while the boycott itself is meant to point out an issue of unfair or harmful practices.

1956 Melbourne

Lichtenstein, the Netherlands, Spain, and Sweden boycotted the games in protest of the Soviet invasion of Hungary. Egypt, Lebanon, and Iraq also boycotted as a result of the Suez crisis. The People's Republic of China refused to participate due to the inclusion of the Republic of China (Taiwan).

1964 Tokyo

South Africa was banned by the IOC from taking part due to its oppressive apartheid regime. This ban lasted until 1992.

1968 Mexico City

In Mexico City, 10 days before the Olympics began, students protesting against the government were surrounded by the army who opened fire, killing 267 and injuring more than 1,000. During the Games, American athletes Tommie Smith and John Carlos were expelled for raising their fists in a "black power" salute on the winners' podium.

1972 Munich

11 Israeli athletes were taken hostage by Palestinian terrorists 'Black September', to protest against the holding of 234 Palestinian prisoners in Israel. The terrorists murdered two of their captives, then, as the result of a bungled rescue attempt by the authorities, the remaining nine captives were killed alongside three of their captors.

1976 Montreal

26 African countries boycotted the Games in response to New Zealand's inclusion. Earlier that year a New Zealand team had undertaken a three-month rugby tour of segregated South Africa, but the IOC refused to ban them. The Republic of China (Taiwan) team was also barred from entering the country, then allowed to enter if they agreed not to compete as "the Republic of China"; the Taiwanese considered this unacceptable and withdrew.

1980 Moscow

Due to the Soviet invasion of Afghanistan, President Carter called upon the U.S. Olympic Committee to boycott the Games. The Olympic Charter requires such committees to "resist all pressures of any kind whatsoever, whether of a political, religious or economic nature," but theory and practice diverge. The Americans stayed home, and in total 62 countries including West Germany and Japan refused to attend. In all, 80 nations participated in the Games, down from 122 nations in Munich. The USSR won 195 medals, but allegations of cheating tainted this astonishing result.

1984 Los Angeles

14 countries, including the USSR, boycotted the Games in what was widely seen as revenge for the Moscow Games four years earlier, though the official line was that they had security concerns. Ironically, China chose this year to return to the Games after a 32-year absence.

1988 Seoul

After failing to be recognized as cohost of the Games, North Korea (which was still technically at war with the South) boycotted the Games, with Cuba and Ethiopia joining them in solidarity. However, there were no widespread boycotts for the first time since 1972.

1992 Barcelona

It was a rare Olympic games with no boycotts. The Soviet Union had broken up, and the new Russian republics competed under one banner. The Berlin Wall had been torn down— so East and West Germany competed together as a united country. South Africa returned to the Games after the end of apartheid and 32 years of sporting isolation.

2008 Beijing

There was talk of a boycott to the Beijing Olympic Games due to China's treatment of the Tibetan people and other human rights abuses, though no major protest eventuated.

Source: Top End Sports. Available at http://www.topendsports.com/events/summer/boycotts.htm. Used with permission from the author.

On occasion, athletes make political or religious statements, sometimes to the detriment of their athletic careers. Understanding the history of athlete protests and the types of protests bring to light the interconnection between sports, politics, and religion. Some athletes refuse to participate in an athletic event or part of a ceremony because of religious reasons. When supported in these beliefs and actions, athletes can often continue to have productive athletic careers. Table 6.4 highlights 10 notable protests by athletes. This list makes clear the types of protests athletes have engaged in the 20th and 21st centuries. The descriptions provide insights into how these protests are received. Some displays of protest are accepted, but many displays of protest result in athletes being ostracized in some manner despite the fact that often their protests mobilize discussions around social justice issues and serve a larger cause.

Eric Liddell and Shawn Green are excellent examples of athletes refusing to participate in an event for religious reasons. Although extremely unhappy with Liddell's decision not to run the 100 meters because one of the heats fell on Sunday, Great Britain's Olympic Committee was able to make accommodations and allow Liddell the opportunity to race in the 400 meters. Shawn Green's insistence to respect Yom Kippur was accepted, allowing Green to have a successful career. Other athletes do not always receive the same respect. In the case of Mahmoud Abdul-Rauf (formerly Chris Wayne Johnson), his Islamic beliefs were less tolerated. Abdul-Rauf's refusal to acknowledge the Star Spangled Banner positioned him as controversial. Politics and anti-Islamic sentiment as the result of 9/11 seem evident in the discrepancy in the treatment of these athletes.

Other athletes protest in the name of a much larger cause. Muhammad Ali, Tommie Smith, and John Carlos are three of the most notable athletes willing to take a political stance even if it threatened their athletic careers. Ali's protest was against the Vietnam War in 1967. His refusal to be drafted into the Army resulted in many antiwar supporters feeling validated. Ali's refusal to participate in the war stemmed from his refusal to kill others so that white people could dominate people of color. After a long struggle, the Supreme Court overturned Ali's draft conviction in 1971. Ali remained controversial for many years, but was honored as a courageous athlete who was willing to speak out in support of human rights and asked to light the Olympic flame during the 1996 Olympic Games in Atlanta. Tommie Smith and John Carlos also used their athletic success during the 1968 Olympic Games in Mexico City as an opportunity to raise global awareness about the oppression of blacks in the United States.

Whether religious, political, or human rights oriented, both countries and individual athletes have used sporting events or their athletic reputations to speak out for a cause in which they believe. Some scholars make the point that with the current

TABLE 6.4
Political Protests and Religious Affirmations by Athletes

1924	Eric Liddell	Eric Liddell refuses to run the 100 meters because one of the heats falls on Sunday, a day of rest for this devoted Christian. Although the 100 meters is Liddell's best event in which he is expected to win the gold medal, Liddell races the 400 meters instead. Liddell runs the race the only way he knows how—a full-out sprint—winning the gold medal. Liddell's story is captured in the Hollywood movie *Chariots of Fire*.
1960	Taiwanese Olympic Athletes	The People's Republic of China stands beside its decision to not attend the Rome Olympics because the IOC was not banning The Republic of China (Taiwan), which was ruled by an entirely different government and was an antagonist of Mao's, from the Olympics. Because Western countries do not approve of the People's China, the IOC asks that the Republic of China (Taiwan) march under the name Taiwan or Formosa, making sure that in no way is this nation connected to the People's China. Despite being overtly anti-politics when it came to the Olympics, Brundage finds himself accused of being a communist sympathizer by the United States, who wants nothing to do with China in any form. Politically, the situation escalates when the Taiwanese athletes do not appreciate having to change their name and march into the stadium during the opening ceremonies with a sign that reads "Under Protest." Avery Brundage has to be convinced not to ban them from participating.
1967	Muhammad Ali	Muhammad Ali is the heavyweight champion of the world in 1967. In that same year, Ali is drafted into the Army to join the Vietnam War. In one of the most famous political acts by an athlete, Ali refuses to enlist because of his religious beliefs. He argues that he does not believe in the war and will not fight. Ali is stripped of his championship title and suspended for three years from competition. Ali's actions spur political discussions around the country.
1968	Tommie Smith and John Carlos	At the 1968 Mexico City Olympics, American sprinters Tommie Smith and John Carlos win the gold and bronze medals respectively. When the athletes receive their medals, they both raise their right hands covered in black socks, an act that symbolizes black power, solidarity, and brings attention to the oppression of blacks in America. Smith and Carlos are booed when leaving the podium and expelled from the Olympic Games the next day. While their actions are controversial, it raises awareness about the treatment of black Americans and other minorities in the United States. Today, a statue of Smith and Carlos lies on the campus of San Jose State University in honor of their courage to stand up for human rights.
1993–2007	Shawn Green	Throughout his baseball career, Shawn Green never competes on Yom Kippur, the holiest day of the Jewish calendar. Instead, he reserves that day for fasting and prayer as is the custom for this day. Green demonstrates that his religious beliefs are more important than any game even though Yom Kippur often occurs during pennant races.

(Continued)

TABLE 6.4 (*Continued*)

1996	Chris Wayne Johnson later known as Mahmoud Abdul-Rauf	Starting in 1996, Mahmoud Abdul-Rauf (formerly Chris Wayne Johnson) refuses to stand for "The Star-Spangled Banner" before NBA games. Abdul-Rauf states that the U.S. flag is a symbol of tyranny and oppression, which come in conflict with his Islamic beliefs. Abdul-Rauf is suspended for one game in March 1996, but the NBA works out a compromise with Abdul-Rauf. They allow him to close his eyes and pray while standing. In this instance, unlike Shawn Green, Abdul-Rauf's actions are ultimately seen as too controversial, and he only plays three more seasons with 62 starts.
2002	Pat Tillman	Pat Tillman refuses a $3.6 million contract with the Cardinals and enlists in the U.S. Army. Tillman feels that joining the Army is the right choice following the 9/11 attacks. Tillman stands up for his religious and political beliefs at the time to forego an athletic career. After Tillman is killed in friendly fire, many of his closest army friends report that Tillman had shifted his views and was adamantly against the war at the time of his death.
2004	Carlos Delgado	Carlos Delgado, Toronto's first baseman, refuses to stand for "God Bless America" during the 7th inning stretch of Major League Baseball games. Delgado is protesting the United States' involvement in Iraq and Afghanistan. His protest is based on the belief that lives were lost for no good reasons. Delgado is booed when he plays in New York. Delgado's convictions appeared to be less important when he was traded to the New York Mets in 2006. He started standing for the anthem again.
2010	Albert Pujols and Tony LaRussa	Albert Pujols and his manager, Tony LaRussa, attend the "Restoring Honor" rally held by Glenn Beck, a conservative and religious proponent. Beck's message is to restore America through a rebirth of faith and trust in God. Beck is a vehement critic of Obama and the American progressive movement. Pujols's and LaRussa's support of Beck results in criticism from fans.
May 5, 2010	Phoenix Suns	Arizona passes a new immigration law to stop rampant illegal immigration across their state. The owner of the Phoenix Suns, Robert Sarver, feels that the law is racially thoughtless. Sarver uses his team to make a political statement. On Cinco de Mayo, Sarver intentionally had his team wear jerseys that read "Los Suns." Reportedly the team unanimously supported this decision.

Source: Table compiled by author from data available at http://bleacherreport.com/articles/446420-ten-athletes-who-made-major-political-and-social-statements.

commercialization of sport, nations and athletes are less willing to make political statements for fear of losing their sponsorship contracts. Despite the fact that there is a history of the mixing of sport and politics, it remains to be seen whether or not commercialization is a constraining factor keeping sport and politics more separate for athletes than it has historically been.

Performance

With the commercialization of sport, there is increasingly more pressure for athletes to perform at higher levels. Athletic performances are improving, and the progression of world records illustrates this steady progress. There are various reasons for continually better performances, but improved understandings of training methods and technological advances are two key factors. In order to put the performance progression into perspective, Table 6.5 is a selective list of some of the current world records as compared to historical data.

Not only is it important to understand the progression but also some of the possible contributors to those progressions. The progressions for ultrarunning and marathon show that over time, long distance runners are still making improvements. In 2011, there were four instances in which male marathoners ran a sub 2:04. One possible contributing factor is the large number of runners in the world. Currently, there are over 600 officially sanctioned marathons in the United States and approximately 500 in the rest of the world hosting thousands of runners in each event. The larger the pool of marathoners, the greater the competition, thus driving better and better performances.

Swimming and speed skating have also benefited from improvements in training methods. Yet, for these two sports, technological advances in gear have also made a significant difference. During the 2008 Olympics in Beijing, 23 out of the 25 world records were achieved with swimmers wearing Speedo's LZR Racer. Evident in Table 6.5 is the number of world records during the 2008 Olympic Games. Swimmers wearing the Speedo LZR claimed a total of 38 out of 42 world swimming records in 2008. Due to these statistics, the Federation Internationale de Natation (FINA) banned the swimsuit in 2009. In November 2011, Speedo introduced a new swimsuit, the Fastskin3 swimwear system. The system consists of goggles, cap, and swimsuit. The cap and goggles are designed to reduce drag while the swimsuit is made of material that reduces drag. Many swimmers expected to be in the London 2012 Olympics will be wearing this new system. For speed skaters, the revolutionary clap skate was invented in the mid1980s but took off in 1996/1997. The clap skate consists of a hinged blade as opposed to the traditional fixed blade. The idea is that the blade stays in contact with the ice for a longer time, allowing the skater to maintain speed. By 1997/1998, most skaters

TABLE 6.5
Progressions in Athletic Performances

Historical data	Current records
Ultrarunning In 1996, Eric Clifton ran the Rocky Raccoon 100-mile race and set a course record with 13 hours 16 minutes and 2 seconds. Clifton averaged just under an 8-minute per mile pace for 100 miles.	In 2011, Ian Sharman ran the same Rocky Raccoon 100-mile race, establishing a new course record of 12 hours 44 minutes and 33 seconds. He averaged 7:38 pace for 100 miles. This is the fastest 100-mile time in the world.
Men's marathon 2:05:42—Khalid Khannouchi (MOR)—Chicago 1999 2:05:38—Khalid Khannouchi (USA)—London 2002 2:04:55—Paul Tergat (KEN)—Berlin 2003 2:04:26—Haile Gebrselassie (ETH)—Berlin 2007 2:03:59—Haile Gebrselassie (ETH)—Berlin 2008 * Geoffrey Mutai (KEN) ran a 2:03:02 in the 2011 Boston Marathon, but since it is a net downhill course, it does not qualify for a world record.	2:03:38—Patrick Makau (KEN)—Berlin 2011
Women's marathon 2:20:43—Tegla Loroupe (KEN)—Berlin 1999 2:19:46—Naoko Takahashi (JPN)—Berlin 2001 2:18:47—Catherine Ndereba (KEN)—Chicago 2001 2:17:18—Paula Radcliffe (GBR)—Chicago 2002	2:15:25—Paula Radcliffe (GBR)—London 2003
Swimming—men's 100 meters freestyle 47.84 Pieter van den Hoogenband (NED) 2000 Olympic Games 47.50 Alain Bernard (FRA) 2008 European Championships 47.24 Eamon Sullivan (AUS) 2008 Olympic Games 47.20 Alain Bernard (FRA) 2008 Olympic Games 47.05 Eamon Sullivan (AUS) 2008 Olympic Games	46.91 César Cielo (BRA) 2009 World Championships
Swimming—women's 100 meters freestyle 53.52 Jodie Henry (AUS) 2004 Olympic Games 53.42 Lisbeth Lenton (AUS) 2006 Australian Championships & Commonwealth Games Trials 53.30 Britta Steffen (GER) 2006 European Championships 52.88 Lisbeth Trickett (AUS) 2008 Australian Championships & Olympic Trials 52.85 Britta Steffen (GER) 2009 German Championships 52.56 Britta Steffen (GER) 2009 German Championships	52.07 Britta Steffen (GER) 2009 World Championships
Speed Skating—men's 5000 meters 6:34.96 Johann Olav Koss (NOR) 1994	6:03.32 Sven Kramer (NED) 2007

(Continued)

TABLE 6.5 (Continued)

Historical data	Current records
6:30.63 Gianni Romme (NED) 1997	
6:22.20 Gianni Romme (NED) 1998	
6:21.49 Gianni Romme (NED) 1998	
6:18.72 Gianni Romme (NED) 2000	
6:14.66 Jochem Uytdehaage (NED) 2002	
6:09:68 Chad Hedrick (USA) 2005	
6:08.78 Sven Kramer (NED) 2005	
6:07.48 Sven Kramer (NED) 2007	
6:07.40 Enrico Fabris (ITA) 2007	
Speed Skating—women's 5000 meters	
7:03.26 Gunda Niemann (GER) 1994	6:42.66 Martina Sáblíková (CZE) 2011
6:59.61 Claudia Pechstein (GER) 1998	
6:58.63 Gunda Niemann-Stirnemann (GER) 1998	
6:57.24 Gunda Niemann-Stirnemann (GER) 1999	
6:56.84 Gunda Niemann-Stirnemann (GER) 2000	
6:55.34 Gunda Niemann-Stirnemann (GER) 2000	
6:52.44 Gunda Niemann-Stirnemann (GER) 2001	
6:46.91 Claudia Pechstein (GER) 2002	
6:45.61 Martina Sáblíková (CZE) 2007	

Source: Information compiled by author from data available at the following Web sites: http://fun2run-penang. blogspot.com/2011/09/mens-marathon-world-record-progression.html; http://www.scmsom.se/results/statistics/ Development%20OG%20and%20WC%20Men.htm; http://www.scmsom.se/results/statistics/Development%20OG% 20and%20WC%20Women.htm; http://en.wikipedia.org/wiki/World_record_progression_100_metres_freestyle; http://en.wikipedia.org/wiki/World_record_progression_5,000_m_speed_skating_men; http://en.wikipedia. org/wiki/World_record_progression_5,000_m_speed_skating_women.

were wearing the clap skate. The drop in times in the 5,000 meter distance is shown in Table 6.5. Johann Olav Koss claimed the previous five world records in this distance. Yet, once Gianni Romme adopted the clap skate, there is a drop of four seconds from 1994 to 1998. Similarly for the women, the world record in 1998 is almost four seconds faster than the 1994 world record. After 1998, world records were consistently broken, but by smaller amounts, because all the skaters had adapted to clap skates and training methods were responsible for the increases.

Ethics

With increased pressures to win, potential sponsorships, and prize money, there is a growing concern that athletes will do anything to raise their performance, including the use of performance enhancing drugs (PEDs). Currently, professional baseball and cycling receive the most media attention when it comes to PEDs even though they each have a long history of drug use. Tables 6.6 and 6.7 list the athletes associated with PEDs from both baseball and cycling. Table 6.6 is a summary of MLB players during the period known as "The Steroid Era" of baseball from 1990 to 2010. It features players who were either mentioned as PED users in the Mitchell Report, who admitted to PED use, who have been implicated by others, or those who were officially suspended.

TABLE 6.6
MLB Players Associated with Performance Enhancing Drug Use from 1990–2010

Mitchell Report	Admitted	Implicated by others	MLB suspensions
47 Players	16 players	34 players	27 players
Ricky Bones—Steroids	Ken Caminiti—Steroids	Mark McGwire—Steroids	Alex Sanchez—Unknown
Alex Cabrera—Steroids	Bobby Estalella—Steroids & HGH	Manny Alexander—Steroids	Jorge Piedra—Unknown
Larry Bigbie—Steroids & HGH	Jason Giambi—Steroids & HGH	Chuck Finley—Steroids	Agustin Montero—Unknown
Jack Cust—Steroids	Jeremy Giambi—Steroids	Barry Bonds—Steroids	Jamal Strong—Unknown
Tim Laker—Steroids	Armando Rios—Steroids & HGH	Marvin Bernard—Steroids & HGH	Juan Rincon—Unknown
Josias Manzanillo—Steroids	Benito Santiago—Steroids & HGH	Randy Velarde—Steroids	Rafael Betancourt—Unknown
Todd Hundley—Steroids	Gary Sheffield—Steroids	Wilson Alvarez—Steroids & HGH	Rafael Palmeiro—Stanozolol (Steroid)
Mark Carreon—Steroids	Jose Canseco—Steroids & HGH	Bret Boone—Steroids	Ryan Franklin—Unknown
Hal Morris—Steroids	Tom House—Steroids	Ozzie Canseco—Steroids	Mike Morse—Unknown
Matt Franco—Steroids	Wally Joyner—Steroids	Juan Gonzalez—Steroids & HGH	Carlos Almanzar—Unknown
Rondell White—Steroids & HGH	Paxton Crawford—Steroids & HGH	Dave Martinez—Steroids	Felix Heredia—Unknown
Chuck Knobloch—HGH	Jim Leyritz—HGH	Ivan Rodriguez—Steroids & HGH	Matt Lawton—Boldenone (Steroid)
Gregg Zaun—Steroids	David Segui—HGH	Tony Saunders—Steroids & HGH	Yusaku Iriki—Unknown
David Justice—HGH	John Rocker—HGH	Miguel Tejada—Steroids	Jason Grimsley—Steroids & HGH
F. P. Santangelo—Steroids & HGH	Paul Byrd—HGH	Lenny Dykstra—Steroids & HGH	
Glenallen Hill—HGH	Shane Monahan—Steroids		
Mo Vaughn—HGH			
Denny Neagle—Steroids & HGH			
Ron Villone—HGH			
Chris Donnels—Steroids & HGH			
Todd Williams—Steroids			
Phil Hiatt—Steroids & HGH			
Todd Pratt—Steroids			
Kevin Young—HGH			

(Continued)

TABLE 6.6 (Continued)

Mitchell Report	Admitted	Implicated by others	MLB suspensions
47 Players	16 players	34 players	27 players
Mike Lansing—Steroids & HGH	Ken Caminiti—Steroids	Dave Hollins—Steroids	Guillermo Mota—Unknown
Cody McKay—Steroids	Bobby Estalella—Steroids & HGH	Roger Clemens—Steroids & HGH	Juan Salas—Unknown
Kent Mercker—HGH	Jason Giambi—Steroids & HGH	Andy Pettitte—HGH	Ryan Jorgensen†—Unknown
Adam Piatt—Steroids & HGH	Jeremy Giambi—Steroids	Brian Roberts—Steroids	Dan Serafini—Unknown
Jason Christiansen—HGH	Armando Rios—Steroids & HGH	Jay Gibbons—Steroids	Eliezer Alfonzo—Unknown
Mike Stanton—HGH	Benito Santiago—Steroids & HGH	Gary Matthews Jr.—HGH	Humberto Cota—Unknown
Stephen Randolph—HGH	Gary Sheffield—Steroids	Jerry Hairston Jr.—HGH	Henry Owens—Unknown
Paul Lo Duca—HGH	Jose Canseco—Steroids & HGH	Darren Holmes—Steroids & HGH	JC Romero—Androstenedione
Adam Riggs—Steroids an HGH	Tom House—Steroids	Rick Ankiel—HGH	Sergio Mitre—Androstenedione
Bart Miadich—Steroids	Wally Joyner—Steroids	Troy Glaus—Steroids	Kelvin Pichardo—Unknown
Fernando Vina—Steroids & HGH	Paxton Crawford—Steroids & HGH	Scott Schoeneweis—Steroids	Manny Ramirez†—HCG
Kevin Brown—Steroids & HGH	Jim Leyritz—HGH	Matt Williams—Steroids & HGH	Edinson Volquez—Clomiphene
Eric Gagne—HGH	David Segui—HGH	Jose Guillen—Steroids & HGH	Ronny Paulino—Unknown
Mike Bell—HGH	John Rocker—HGH	Ismael Valdez—Steroids	
Matt Herges—HGH	Paul Byrd—HGH	Magglio Ordonez—Steroids & HGH	
Gary Bennett, Jr.—HGH	Shane Monahan—Steroids	Alex Rodriguez—Steroids	
Jim Parque—Steroids		Mike Piazza—Steroids	
Brendan Donnely—Steroids		Todd Greene—Steroids	
Chad Allen- Steroids		Sammy Sosa—Unknown	
Jeff Williams- Steroids		David Ortiz—Unknown	
Howie Clark- HGH			
Nook Logan—HGH			
Dan Naulty—Steroids & HGH			

Source: Table compiled by the author from information available at http://www.baseballssteroidera.com/.

The 2007 Mitchell Report stirred controversy and was responsible for the pervasive sense that baseball was riddled with illegal drug use. While these lists cover a 20-year period, 124 players represent 17 percent of the total number of MLB players in any given year. This percentage is far below what the general public perceives is the reality in baseball; however, it has only been since 2006 that a new program, the Joint Drug Prevention and Treatment Program aimed at improving drug testing protocols, has been adopted by MLB. Professional cycling has also experienced much media attention with regard to PEDs. This relatively recent change in attitude toward drug use in cycling has proven difficult for the sport. For a sport that once openly accepted drug use as part of the endeavor, the transition to a "drug free" sport has caused cycling to have a roller coaster relationship with sponsors and fans. The types of transgressions in cycling are numerous, ranging from the illegal practice of blood doping, to stimulants, steroids, and blood expanders. Detection of banned substances is difficult given the range of substances and the rate at which new drugs appear. Furthermore, it can take over a year for a decision to be made about suspensions. It took the Court of Arbitration for Sport (CAS) over a year and a half to officially declare Alberto Contador guilty of substance abuse. Such issues related to PEDs raise legitimate concerns about winners at any given time, causing cycling to lose credibility with fans and making sponsors less willing to align themselves with athletes and teams. Table 6.7 lists those athletes from 2008 to 2011 who were either suspended from their teams at the time or suspended for life following a decision by the CAS.

Similar to baseball, the actual number of athletes officially banned compared to the number of athletes involved in these sports appears to be relatively small. Historically, detecting banned substances has proved extremely problematic, and these small numbers of officially banned athletes does not likely reflect actual numbers of athletes using PEDs. At the very least, media attention has caused both fans and sponsors to question the integrity of these sports. It remains to be seen whether or not fans and sponsors will demand "clean" athletes or accept "modified" athletes in the pursuit of better performances.

Another growing concern in sport participation is the willingness of athletes to sustain injury while playing sport. A look into youth sport from 2001 to 2009 reveals that visits to the emergency department increased by 62 percent from 2001 to 2009. Table 6.8 shows the total number of reported concussions determined by emergency room visits from 2001 to 2009 as well as the percentages of concussions associated with specific sports and organized by gender.

TABLE 6.7
Professional Cyclists Suspended from Competition or Teams for a Period of Time

2008	2009	2010	2011
25 Cyclists	16 Cyclists	27 Cyclists	9 Cyclists
Alessandro Petacchi	Alejandro Valverde	Alberto Contador	Alexandr Kolobnev
Camilo Gomez	Antonio Colom	Alessandro Colo	David Clinger
Carlos Ospina	Christian Pfannberger	Dan Staite	Lisban Quintero
Hernandez	Clément Lhotellerie	David García Dapena	Lorenzo Bernucci
Danilo Di Luca*	Danilo Di Luca*	Ezequiel Mosquera	Marco Arriagada
Dmitry Fofonov	Davide Rebellin	Francesco De Bonis	Oscar Sevilla
Eddy Mazzoleni	Gabriele Bosisio*	Gabriele Bosisio*	Pasquale Muto
Emanuele Sella	Hector Guerra	Huesolessandro Ballan	Patrik Sinkewitz
Floyd Landis	Isidro Nozal	Jair Fernando dos Santos	Riccardo Riccò*
Giovanni Barriga	Mikel Astarloza	Jao Paulo de Oliveira	
Giovanni Carini	Nuno Ribeiro	Joao Benta	In 2012 Alberto Contador
Hernán Buenahora	Olaf Pollack	Kacper Szczepaniak	was officially stripped of his
Igor Astarloa	Stefan Schumacher	Li Fuyu	winning titles in the 2010
Jimmy Casper	Thomas Dekker	Lucas Onesco	Tour de France and 2011
Juan Guillermo Castro	Tom Boonen*	Manuel Vazquez	Giro D'Italia.
Leonardo Piepoli	Tyler Hamilton	Mario Costa	
Manuel Beltrán		Mauro Santambrogio	
Maria Moreno		Mickaël Larpe	
Maximiliano Richeze		Niklas Axelsson	
Michael Rasmussen		Óscar Sevilla	
Moisés Dueñas		Pawel Szczepaniak	
Ondrej Sosenka		Pietro Caucchioli	
Paolo Bosson		Ricardo Serrano	
Rafael Montiel		Roy Sentjens	
Riccardo Riccò*		Rui Costa	
Tom Boonen *		Thomas Frei	
		Vania Rossi	

* Cyclists with multiple suspensions from 2008 to 2011
Source: Table compiled by the author from information available at http://en.wikipedia.org/wiki/List_of_dop
ing_cases_in_cycling#2011.

Findings show that young males are over two times more likely than young females to experience a traumatic brain injury (TBI) while playing sport. Males between the ages of 10 and 18 are much more likely to be concussed than when they are younger. For girls, the largest jump in TBIs is when they are between the ages of 5 and 9 years. By the time girls and boys reach the ages between 10 and 14, the sports resulting in the most number of

TABLE 6.8
Reported Youth Sport–Related Concussions by Age, Gender, and Sport 2001–2009

≤ 4 years		5–9 years		10–14 years		15–19 years		≤ 19 years total number of concussions	
Male	Female	Male	Female	Male	Female	Male	Female	Male	Female
Playground 35.3%	Playground 47.8%	Bicycling 23.6%	Playground 30.3%	Football 20.7%	Bicycling 12.2%	Football 30.3%	Soccer 16%	Football 24,431	Playground 7,136
Bicycling 17.8%	Bicycling 14.4%	Playground 18.9%	Bicycling 20.7%	Bicycling 19.1%	Basketball 11.1%	Bicycling 9.7%	Basketball 14.6%	Bicycling 20,285	Bicycling 5,928
Baseball 7.3%	Baseball 6%	Baseball 8.8%	Baseball 4.7%	Basketball 9.2%	Soccer 11%	Basketball 9%	Gymnastics 9.1%	Playground 9,568	Soccer 4,767
Scooter 5.1%	Trampoline 4.8%	Football 6.5%	Scooter 4.6%	Baseball 7%	Horseback 7.7%	Soccer 6.7%	Softball 7%	Basketball 9,372	Basketball 4,615
Swimming 4.8%	Swimming 4.9%	Basketball 4.5%	Swimming 4.4%	Skateboard 6%	Playground 6.2%	ATV 5.6%	Horseback 6.2%	Baseball 8,030	Horseback 2,853
Other 29.7%	Other 23.7%	Other 37.9%	Other 35.2%	Other 37.9%	Other 51.9%	Other 38.7%	Other 47.1%	Other 51,284	Other 25,011
Total # 9,020	Total # 5,386	Total # 25,362	Total # 11,391	Total # 43,449	Total # 16,824	Total # 45,140	Total # 16,709	Total # 122,970	Total # 50,310

Source: Table compiled by author from data from the report "Nonfatal Traumatic Brain Injuries Related to Sports and Recreation Activities Among Persons Aged ≤ 19 Years—United States, 2001–2009" found at the Center for Disease Control and Prevention available at http://www.cdc.gov/mmwr/preview/mmwrhtml/mm6039a1.htm?s_cid=mm6039a1_w#tab3.

concussions are very different, reflecting the opportunities in organized sport for each gender. Boys aged 10 to 14 are much more likely to experience TBI in football, a trend that continues into the next age range of 15–19 years. What is important to note is that as children get older, many more sporting opportunities arise. The possibility of concussions from a wide variety of sports tends to increase as indicated by the large percentages of TBIs reported in the "other" categories. Still, reports such as this by the Center for Disease Control and Prevention (CDC) raise ethical questions about children's sport participation. The question is not whether or not children should play sport, but under what circumstances and with what attitude. Many head injuries are preventable. The report points to a few important steps that can be taken. Since bicycling is responsible for a large number of these concussions, helmet protection when riding bicycles is highly recommended. Continued emphasis on skills, safety, and sportsmanship can also reduce concussion rates. Perhaps one of the more controversial steps is simply to be overly cautious, take kids out of the play if concussion is suspected, and become more aware of the symptoms and signs of concussion despite the difficulty in assessing concussion.

Teaching sportsmanship in aggressive sports can be problematic. For football, an adversarial attitude is often promoted in order to increase athletes' aggression toward opponents. Still, there are many involved in sport who believe that promoting sportsmanship is desperately needed in today's sport culture. Some organizations work at the grassroots level to promote sportsmanship throughout all levels of athletic competition. These organizations are crucial to creating sport as a positive experience. Athletes for a Better World (ABW) is one such organization, which works diligently at providing overt connections between sport and life.

The Code for Living

Athletes for a Better World publishes "The Code for Living" on their Web site. This code is a good example of how specific behaviors and attitudes can be outlined for young athletes. Document 6.2 is the Code for Living, which outlines the principles of sport that can apply to life.

Because I am a role model and have the opportunity and responsibility to make a difference in the lives of others, I commit to this

Code. I will take responsibility and appropriate actions when I fail to live up to it.

Members of Athletes of a Better World are those individuals who affirm and seek to live by the following:

As an **INDIVIDUAL:**

I will respect the dignity of every human being, and will not be abusive or dehumanizing of anyone either as an athlete or as a fan.

I will develop my skills to the best of my ability and give my best effort in practices and competitions.

I will compete within the spirit and letter of the rules of my sport.

As a member of a **TEAM:**

I will place team goals ahead of personal goals.

I will follow the team rules established by the coach.

I will be a positive influence on the relationships on the team.

As a member of **SOCIETY:**

I will display caring and honorable behavior off the field and be a positive influence in my community and world.

I will give of my time, skills, and money as I am able for the betterment of my community and world.

Source: http://www.abw.org/the-code-for-living/. Used by permission of Athletes for a Better World.

Gender, Race, and Ethnicity in Sport

Two of the prominent discussions in this book revolve around who is playing sport and who is leading it. Categories examined include gender, race, and ethnicity. In order to gain a deeper understanding of the major trends in sport participation and sport leadership, it is helpful to examine the numbers. In this section, the following trends are examined: (1) participation by gender in the Olympics and in North American collegiate sports; (2) participation by race and ethnicity in North American collegiate, professional sports, and outdoor sports; (3) leadership in North American collegiate sport by gender and race and ethnicity; and (4) media coverage of sport by gender. These selected data provide valuable insights into the demographic profile of sport, demonstrating that sport remains largely white and male despite increased participation by women and people of color in recent history.

The Olympic Games remains the world's largest multisport event. The Summer and Winter Games occur every four years in alternating even years. Two notable trends have emerged in Olympic participation in the past two decades as shown in Figure 6.15.

First, winter Olympic participation has grown for both men and women, but women have experienced the greatest gains. The Winter Olympics has always been a much smaller event compared to the Summer Olympics. Women in the 2010 Olympic Games in Vancouver totaled about 1,000 participants, comprising almost 40 percent of the total number of the 2,500 athletes. Men's participation numbers have remained steady since the 2002 Winter Olympics, but women's participation has slowly increased, which has resulted in a gradual percentage increase. Second, women's participation in the Summer Olympics has also grown in the past two decades, almost doubling from 1992 to 2008. The percentage of women participating in Beijing 2008 was about 42 percent or 4,746 female athletes compared to 6,450 male

FIGURE 6.15
Olympic Games Participation by Gender

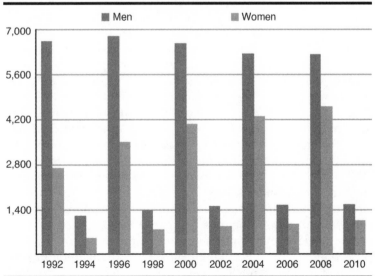

athletes. As noted in Figure 6.15, the decrease in men's participation in Summer Olympic sports since 1996 creates a seemingly larger increase in percentage of women's participation despite modest gains in actual numbers. Still, mandates from the IOC that require all new sports inducted into the Olympic Games to offer sports for both men and women have helped increase opportunities for women to compete in the Olympics. The 2012 Olympic Games in London will be the first time that the number of sports offered for men and women are equal. Discrepancies remain with respect to the number of events offered within the sport categories. In 2008, there were 137 events offered for women compared to 175 events offered to men with 10 mixed events offered. Figure 6.15 confirms the increase in opportunities for women to compete in the Olympic Games, but many scholars believe that significant discrepancies remain and efforts to promote women's inclusion in international sporting events need to continue.

Another area of significant gains for sport participation among women is in intercollegiate athletics. While NCAA institutions do not represent 100 percent of collegiate sport colleges and universities, the trends in NCAA schools are promising. Out of 444,077 students participating on NCAA championship sports teams, women now make up about 43 percent of the total. Figure 6.16 shows that the average number of women and men per NCAA institution participating in championship sports during the school year 2010–2011 was at an all-time high.

Despite the recent increase in men's participation, women's participation has grown 13 percent over the past two decades. In 2010–2011, the average NCAA member institution had approximately 414 student-athletes: 236 males and 178 females. Compared to the early 1980s, the growth since the 1990s has resulted in an average of 79 more female athletes and 10 more male athletes per NCAA institution. While indoor track and field had more female athletes than any other collegiate sport, soccer became the sport with the most number of female athletes beginning in 1999. One of the primary reasons for the growth in women's sport participation has been the addition of women's teams. Since the 1990s, 4,641 women's teams have been added to NCAA collegiate athletics programs compared to 3,272 men's teams. Women's soccer makes up the majority of new programs added since the 1990s with 635 new teams. Such trends reinforce the idea that if opportunities are created for women in sport, they will participate.

FIGURE 6.16
Average Number of Student-Athletes by Gender Per NCAA Institution

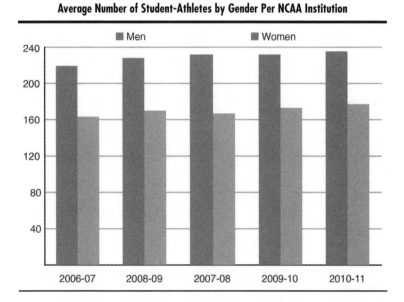

When analyzing the data regarding race and ethnicity in intercollegiate sports, it is clear that more white athletes are participating than any other group. Whether male or female, over 60 percent of the total number of NCAA Division I athletes have been white for the past four years. It appears that opportunities for going to college and playing intercollegiate athletics remain limited for persons of color. Table 6.9 shows the breakdown of NCAA Division I participation by gender and race/ethnicity.

African America men are the second largest group to participate in intercollegiate athletics, making up approximately 25 percent of total male participants. The combined remaining ethnicities represented in intercollegiate athletics have been consistently less than 10 percent for both male and female athletes.

When athletes move on to the professional leagues, the trends change. It is important to remember that professional athletes are comprised of less than 1 percent of the total number of intercollegiate athletes. Making it to the professional leagues is incredibly difficult. Those that do make it include a far greater percentage of athletes of color than is the case with intercollegiate athletics. Figure 6.17 shows the relative numbers of professional athletes broken down by race, ethnicity, or nationality.

TABLE 6.9
NCAA Division I Student-Athletes by Gender and Race/Ethnicity

	2006–2007		2007–2008		2008–2009		2009–2010	
	Men	Women	Men	Women	Men	Women	Men	Women
White	64.2%	72.1%	64.3%	71.9%	63.8%	71.3%	62.5%	70.6%
African American	24.7%	15.7%	25%	15.9%	24.8%	16.0%	24.9%	16.0%
Latino	3.8%	3.7%	3.9%	3.7%	4.0%	3.9%	4.2%	4.2%
American Indian/Alaska Native	0.4%	0.4%	0.4%	0.4%	0.4%	0.4%	0.4%	0.4%
Asian/Pacific Islander	1.6%	2.3%	1.5%	2.5%	1.9%	2.4%	2.0%	2.4%
Two or More races			0.2%	0.3%	0.5%	0.7%	1.0%	1.1%
Other		5.8%	4.3%	5.2%	4.7%	5.3%	5.0%	5.2%

Source: Table compiled by author from data available at http://tidesport.org/RGRC/2010/2010_College_RGRC_FINAL.pdf.

FIGURE 6.17
Racial Breakdown of Professional Athletes (Combined MLB, MLS, NBA, NFL, WNBA)

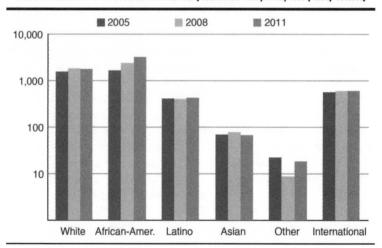

Since 2008, the number of white, Latino, Asian, and international athletes involved in North American professional sports has remained fairly consistent. African American athletes involved in professional leagues have increased. A closer look at the North American professional leagues gives an idea about the disproportionate numbers of African American athletes participating in football and men's and women's basketball. While the majority of the MLB and MLS players are white, the majority of the NFL, NBA, and WNBA players are African American. Table 6.10 illustrates this distribution.

The concentration of athletes of color in football and basketball give the appearance that sports provides ample opportunities for people of color to participate. Media coverage of these sports lends support to the idea that racial equity has been achieved in sports. Yet, given the data from intercollegiate and professional sports regarding race and ethnicity, it is clear to see that white athletes dominate organized sports in North America.

A similar trend is noted in such nonorganized sports as outdoor sports. Looking at the data for people aged 6 years to older than 45, Table 6.11 shows that there is consistently a greater percentage of Caucasians participating in outdoor activities.

Out of the total number of Caucasians surveyed in 2008, 2009, and 2010, over 55 percent of Caucasian respondents indicate that they participate in outdoor activities from ages 6 to 44 years. Pacific Islander and Hispanic participant rates are just slightly less than those of Caucasians. African American participation rates drop significantly after 17 years of age to rates between 30 and 36 percent. For African Americans aged 13–17 years, there has been a steady increase in outdoor participation. Running, jogging, and trail running are the preferred outdoor activities of African Americans, Hispanics, and Pacific Islanders while fly fishing and salt water fishing is preferred by Caucasians. While the survey does not explain these preferences, it could be argued that fishing

TABLE 6.10
2011 Racial Breakdown Professional Leagues

	MLB	MLS	NBA	NFL	WNBA
White	61.5%	52%	17%	31%	21%
African American	8.5%	26%	78%	67%	69%
Latino	27.0%	20%	4%	1%	3%
Asian	2.1%	1%	1%	2%	0%
Other	0.7%	1%	< 1%	< 1%	> 1%
International	27.7%	038%	17%	2%	6%

Source: Data compiled by author from information available at the following Web sites: http://tidesport.org/RGRC/2011/MLS_RGRC_FINAL.pdf; http://tidesport.org/RGRC/2011/RGRC_NFL_2011_FINAL.pdf; http://tidesport.org/RGRC/2011/WNBA_RGRC_FINAL.pdf; http://tidesport.org/RGRC/2011/2011_NBA_RGRC_FINAL%20FINAL.pdf.

TABLE 6.11
Participation in Outdoor Recreation in North America by Ethnicity

	Age 6–12	Age 13–17	Age 18–24	Age 25–44	Age 45+
2010					
African American	48%	52%	35%	34%	26%
Asian/Pacific Islander	59%	55%	53%	53%	32%
Caucasian	67%	65%	60%	59%	40%
Hispanic	54%	53%	49%	51%	35%
2009					
African American	39%	44%	35%	34%	24%
Asian/Pacific Islander	62%	53%	50%	51%	34%
Caucasian	67%	65%	60%	58%	42%
Hispanic	50%	52%	45%	49%	30%
2008					
African American	54%	38%	29%	36%	25%
Asian/Pacific Islander	60%	60%	51%	48%	32%
Caucasian	67%	65%	59%	57%	41%
Hispanic	50%	53%	48%	45%	29%

Source: Data compiled by author from information available from the following Web sites: http://www.outdoorfoun dation.org/pdf/ResearchParticipation2011.pdf; http://www.outdoorfoundation.org/pdf/ResearchParticipation 2010.pdf; http://www.outdoorfoundation.org/pdf/ResearchParticipation2009.pdf.

is a more expensive sport, and that these preferences could be due partially to differences in socioeconomic status, which tends to follow racial and ethnic demographics. These participation rates for outdoor activities are important for understanding the trends in leisure activities versus organized sport activities. Leisure activities follow trends similar to organized sports in that while youth participation rates for people of color are either improving or remaining fairly steady, Caucasians still participate at higher rates.

The dominant presence of white males is even more pronounced when analyzing the trends in leadership positions in sport. Data from the NCAA illustrates the overwhelming prevalence of white males in sport leadership in North America. Figure 6.18 shows that the percentage of female head coaches declines from 1992 to 2010.

In 2010, just over 40 percent of head coaches of female teams were women. Compared to 1972 when 90 percent of all female teams were coached by women, the 2010 data represents a sig-

FIGURE 6.18
NCAA Coaches by Gender

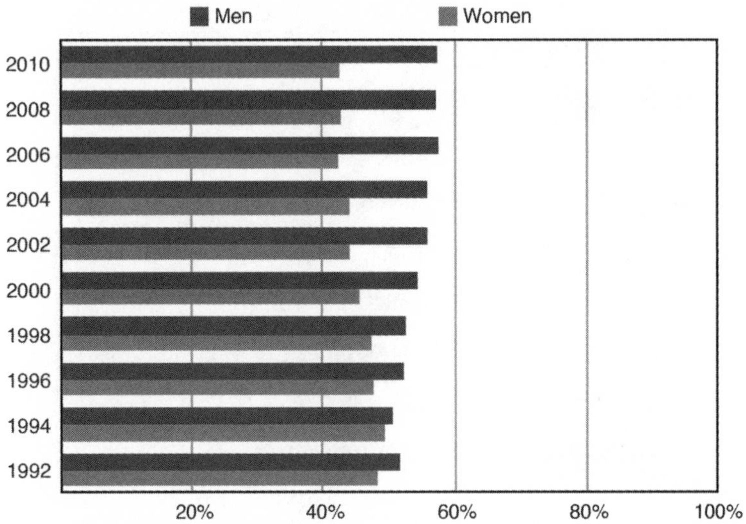

nificant decline in female leadership in intercollegiate athletics. What the data does not show is that the actual number of female head coaches has increased to an all-time high of 3,874 female head coaches of female teams in 2010. While the addition of female teams over the past two decades has provided more opportunities for women to be head coaches, men continue to get a larger proportion of those jobs compared to women. The Acosta and Carpenter study from which Figure 6.18 was compiled note that the gender of the athletics director makes a difference with respect to gender of head coaches hired. Athletic departments with a female athletic director are more likely to have more female head coaches while the number of female head coaches will be lower in athletics departments in which the athletic director is male. Figure 6.19 illustrates how overwhelmingly male-dominated collegiate athletic administration continues to be.

Except for the years 2004 and 2008, over 60 percent of all NCAA athletic directors were male. According to the Acosta and Carpenter study, Division I has the fewest female athletic directors at 36 while Division III has 133 female athletic directors. With more sports being added to NCAA institutions, there have

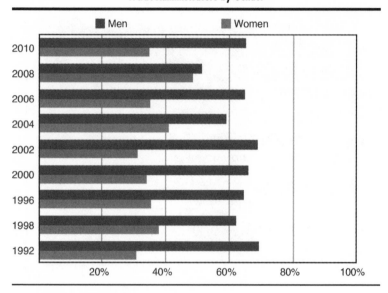

FIGURE 6.19
NCAA Administrators by Gender

been increasing numbers of sport administrative positions available and more opportunities for women to be involved in sport administration, but men are still being hired at higher rates than women. Women cite that the top reason they are interested in sport administration is the perceived support for women's athletic programs from university administration. The top three reasons for women not moving into athletic administration are cited as time requirements, amount of travel, and job availability. There is an average of 3.94 athletic administrators per campus with women comprising an average of 1.41 athletic administrators per school. While 98.1 percent of schools have at least one female administrator, women in athletic administration are often isolated and serve as the solitary female voice in an entire athletic department. Figures 6.18 and 6.19 present concrete data that primarily men make decisions, influence values, and set goals for intercollegiate sports programs.

Further data support the assertion that sport leaders are also predominately white. Table 6.12 clearly shows that although women make up a very small number of head coaches in NCAA athletics, people of color make up even smaller percentages.

Some progress has been made since 2006 in terms of the total percentage of African American male head coaches of women's sports, moving from 3.6 percent to 3.9 percent. But the percentage of African American male head coaches for men's teams is declining. Latino and Asian male or female head coaches for either men's or women's teams have never exceeded 1.8 percent. There has been a slight increase in percentage points for male Latino head coaches of men's teams. This trend is predominantly due to the hiring of more Latino head coaches for baseball, where 2.6 percent of the head coaches are Latino.

Breaking the percentages down by division, whites comprised 87.7 percent, 89.5 percent, and 91.9 percent of all head coaching positions in Divisions I, II, and III, respectively. Taking a look at specific sports, there were seven African American head coaches in Football Bowl Series schools as of 2008. African American head basketball coaches made up the greatest percentage

TABLE 6.12
NCAA Division I Head Coaches by Race

	Men's sports		Women's sports	
	Men	Women	Men	Women
2008–2009				
White	87.1%	2.1%	52.8%	34.9%
African American	6.3%	0.6%	3.9%	3.3%
Latino	1.8%	0%	1.2%	0.5%
Asian	0.7%	0%	0.7%	0.4%
Other	1.2%	0%	1.4%	0.9%
2007–2008				
White	87.1%	2.1%	54.3%	35.3%
African American	6.5%	0.7%	3.7%	3.3%
Latino	1.6%	0%	1.3%	0.8%
Asian	0.9%	0%	0.9%	0.5%
Other	1%	0%	1.2%	0.4%
2005–2006				
White	87.8%	2.8%	54.3%	35.3%
African American	6.7%	0.6%	3.6%	3.0%
Latino	1.1%	0%	1.2%	0.4%
Asian	0.4%	0%	0.8%	0.3%
Other	0.6%	0.2%	0.5%	0.6%

Source: Table compiled by author from information available from http://tidesport.org/RGRC/2010/2010_College_RGRC_FINAL.pdf. Information from 2006–2007 not recorded.

at 21 percent in 2008, which was down 4.2 percent from the 2005–2006 season. Although female head coaches of women's teams are rare, of the female head coaches, 87.7 percent, 89.5 percent, and 91.9 percent in Divisions I, II, and III, respectively, were white. When looking at specific sports, African American women comprised 11.4 percent of head coaching positions for women's basketball in Division I schools, which represents the largest percentage of any sport as well as all other sports combined for female head coaches. These percentages stand in contrast to the over 50 percent of African American female students making up collegiate basketball teams.

The percentages of people of color in NCAA administrative positions are less than those of coaching positions. Table 6.13 shows that NCAA athletic directors are overwhelmingly white.

In the three academic years shown, the total percentages of African American, Latino, Asian, and other race/ethnicity Division I athletic directors went from 6.9 percent to 11.2 percent. This represents some progress with respect to sport administration diversity. It is notable, however, that there are no Asian athletic directors in the entire NCAA Division I. According to the 2010 Racial and Gender report Card for college sport from the Institute for Diversity and Ethics in Sport, the percentages of white athletic directors increase in Division II and III schools. In 2008–2009, whites held 88.8 percent of Division I schools, 92.7 percent of Division II, and 96.2 percent of Division III schools. In Division I schools, athletic director positions were 7.4 percent African American, 2.2 percent Latino, 0 percent Asian, and .9 percent

TABLE 6.13
NCAA Division I Athletic Directors by Gender and Race/Ethnicity

	2008–2009		2007–2008		2006–2007	
	Men	Women	Men	Women	Men	Women
White	81.8%	7.0%	83.8%	6.2%	85.8%	7.3%
African American	6.7%	0.7%	6.2%	1.0%	5.0%	0.5%
Latino	1.9%	0.3%	1.6%	0.3%	0.9%	0%
Asian	0.0%	0%	0%	0%	0%	0%
Other	1.3%	0.3%	0.6%	0.3%	0.5%	0%

Source: Table compiled by author from information available from http://tidesport.org/RGRC/2010/2010_College_RGRC_FINAL.pdf.

Native American. Division II school athletic directors consisted of 3.1 percent African Americans, 3.1 percent Latinos, .8 percent Asians, and no Native Americans. For Division III schools, African American athletic directors accounted for 2.2 percent of the total, Latinos were .4 percent, Asians were .6 percent, and Native Americans were .2 percent. According to the Institute for Diversity and Ethics in Sport, racial diversity has improved in NCAA athletic programs due to improved hiring practices. The evidence is clear that when hiring practices allow for greater inclusivity with respect to applicants that a more diverse athletic staff is likely to result.

On a final note, while sport participation is increasing for women and increasing albeit slightly for people of color in North America, North American media remains focused on the "Big 3" sports of football, basketball, and baseball. Table 6.14 highlights findings from Messner and Cooky's 20-year longitudinal study of sports media coverage. Their study was conducted in the Los Angeles area by following local programming, adding ESPN's *SportsCenter* in 1999. Findings show that women's sport has declined significantly in the past two decades to 1.6 percent of the media coverage from network news and highlights. This is a significant decline from 1999, the year the USA Women's Soccer team won the FIFA World Cup, when women's sports coverage was at 8.7 percent.

In 2009, 100 percent of lead stories were stories about men's sports. Network news covered a higher percentage of women's sports than ESPN's *SportsCenter*, a program dedicated entirely to sports. While 96.2 percent of airtime was devoted to men's sports in 2009, a total of 72 percent of all airtime, main and ticker, were focused on football, men's basketball, and baseball. Messner

TABLE 6.14
Airtime Devoted to Sports by Gender

	1989	1993	1999	2004	2009
Neutral/Both	3.0%	1.1%	3.1%	2.4%	2.1%
Men	92.0%	93.8%	88.2%	91.4%	96.3%
Women	5.0%	5.1%	8.7%	6.3%	1.6%

Source: Table compiled by author from information available in the following study: Messner, Michael and Cheryl Cooky. 2010. *Gender in televised sports: News and highlights shows, 1989–2009.* Center for Feminist Research, University of Southern California.

and Cooky assert that this high percentage of total airtime is facilitated by the media running stories about men's football, basketball, and baseball, either professional or college, when not in season. Local networks covered no stories of the WNBA when out of season compared to 60 stories covering the NBA when they were out of season. When in season, networks covered 3 WNBA stories and 51 NBA stories, which amounted to more airtime despite fewer stories. Not only is media coverage of women's sports declining, but the "Big 3" male sports dominate airtime.

Messner and Cooky note that in 1971, only 294,000 U.S. high school girls played interscholastic sports, compared with 3.7 million boys. In 2009, 3.1 million girls played high school sports compared to 4.4 million boys. The researchers acknowledge that the Internet and other sports programming have opened up more opportunities for people to see women's sports as well as other nonmainstream sports. Still, they assert that networks news and highlights are important avenues through which people receive sports information and shape how we value sport. Arguments that networks are "giving viewers what they desire" seems misdirected in the case of network news according to Messner and Cooky since network news is watched by a much broader audience than a sports-specific television channel. On a more promising note, trivializing or sexualized coverage of women' sports during network news has mostly disappeared. Messner and Cooky conclude that change will only come about if approached from a variety of angles. Sports organizations can provide media with more news of women's sports, and fans can demand more coverage of women' sports. Clearly, the issue of media coverage is driven by gender ideology, which remains a complex issue in which social expectations and economics are intertwined.

7

Directory of Organizations

This chapter describes 95 sport organizations—both international and from the United States—that are integral to youth sport development, athlete participation, athlete performance and safety, and sport business. For easy reference, the chapter is divided into seven sections according to major themes previously addressed. The first section is comprised of professional sport organizations whose main purpose is to serve both the athletes and spectators by providing league play and organizing championship events. The second section spotlights sport organizations that serve amateur athletes in the Olympic and niche sports. These organizations also establish rules of play and determine by what standards athletes are eligible for competition. The third section focuses on youth sport organizations in the United States whose purpose is to promote good character and improved safety for physically active youth. The fourth grouping describes organizations established around the business of sport. These organizations are dedicated to supporting professionals in a wide array of such sport business components as media, information, sports agency, entertainment, luxury suites, ticketing, marketing, sports equipment, and law. The fifth section consists of organizations dedicated to the performance of athletes through such means as sport science, sport psychology, and sports medicine. It includes organizations committed to helping athletes recover from injury or learning to enter an ideal competitive mental state. The sixth section includes associations concerned with sport for development, antidoping, sportsmanship, ethical sport leadership development,

211

and athletes' rights. The final grouping consists of organizations specifically directed toward helping marginalized groups participate fairly in sport.

Professional Sport Organizations

Fédération Internationale de Football Association (FIFA)
http://www.fifa.com/
E-mail: http://www.fifa.com/contact/index.html

FIFA exists to develop football (soccer) around the world, promote goodwill among diverse people, and organize such high-profile events as the World Cup and the Women's World Cup. Given that football (soccer) is played by millions of people around the world, FIFA embraces the view that football can serve as a unifying force in the world by functioning as a tool for social and human development.

Major League Baseball (MLB)
http://mlb.mlb.com/index.jsp
E-mail: http://mlb.mlb.com/mlb/help/contact_us.jsp

Professional baseball is one of the oldest professional sports leagues in the United States. From 1871 to 1875, the National Association organized professional games, but it was not until 1876 and 1901 that the National League and the American League, respectively, were founded. In 2000, the two leagues merged into MLB, which consists of 30 teams: 29 from the United States and 1 from Canada. The MLB also organizes minor and development leagues, partnering with many youth organizations as well as running international development camps. The World Series is the name of the MLB playoffs that crown a World Champion at the end of each season.

National Association of Stock Car Racing (NASCAR)
http://www.nascar.com/
E-mail: http://support.nascar.com/ics/support/default.asp?dept
    ID=5483

Bill France Sr. established NASCAR on February 15, 1948. NASCAR exists to hold many different levels of racing series on raceways across the United States. NASCAR hosts the Sprint Cup Series, the most important and prestigious motorsports series in the United States. The Sprint Cup series consists of the world's top drivers in 36 races each season. NASCAR's desire to reach out to a more global audience has resulted in two international series, the Canadian Tire Series and the Mexico Series.

National Basketball Association (NBA)
http://www.nba.com/home/index.html
E-mail: http://www.nba.com/email_us/contact_us.html

The National Basketball Association oversees professional basketball events, schedule, rules, and policies in the United States. Formed in 1949 through the merging of the Basketball Association of America and the National Basketball League, the NBA has evolved into a league of 30 teams, including both American and international players. With their recent year-long community and fan engagement program, the NBA hopes to reach more than 15 million fans through 2012.

National Football League (NFL)
http://www.nfl.com/
E-mail: http://www.nfl.com/contact-us

The National Football League had its beginnings as the American Professional Football Association in 1920 and consisted of 11 teams. In 1922, the named changed to the National Football League. The NFL organizes games among 32 teams divided evenly into two conferences, the American Football Conference (AFC) and the National Football Conference (NFC). During the 2010–2011 season, the NFL was the most attended sports league in the United States, averaging 66,960 fans per game. The NFL playoffs culminate in the most watched sport event in the United States, the Super Bowl.

National Hockey League (NHL)
http://www.nhl.com/
E-mail: http://www.nhl.com/ice/feedback.htm

The National Hockey League was founded on November 26, 1917, and consisted of only five teams, all of which were from Canada. Today, the NHL consists of 30 teams, divided evenly into six divisions with three divisions in one of two conferences, the Western and the Eastern. NHL players are recruited internationally although the NHL is fully situated in North America. The NHL playoffs end with the Stanley Cup Finals and a league champion who wins the Stanley Cup.

Women's National Basketball Association (WNBA)
http://www.wnba.com/
E-mail: http://www.wnba.com/contact_us/contact_wnba.html

The WNBA, a U.S. professional league for female basketball players, was established on April 24, 1996, and commenced their first league games in June 1997. The season extends into early October, ending in playoffs and a season champion. Given the short season compared to men's professional sports, many of the WNBA players from the 12 WNBA league teams compete on international teams in the off-season. These teams are located across the globe, including teams in Europe, Asia, Australia, and Israel.

Women's Professional Soccer (WPS)
http://www.womensprosoccer.com/
E-mail: http://www.womensprosoccer.com/about/contact-us

The Women's Professional Soccer Association was founded in 2007, but began play on March 29, 2009. WPS is the women's soccer league in the United States, comprised of six teams, all of which are located in the eastern United States. While teams have emerged and shut down since its inception, the WPS's mission is to become the premiere women's soccer league in the world.

Women's Tennis Association (WTA)
http://www.wtatennis.com/page/Home
E-mail: http://www.wtatennis.com/page/Contact

The Women's Tennis Association was established in 1970 when nine female tennis players signed $1 contracts to play in inaugural Virginia Slims of Houston tournament on September 23, 1970. Today, the WTA leads the world in terms of professional sport for women. Over 2,400 players from 99 nations compete at 53 events and 4 Grand Slams in 32 countries each year. In 2010, 5 million people attended women's tennis events while others viewed women's tennis on international sports networks. The $87 million in prize money per year remains a fraction of many high-profile male professional athletes.

Amateur Athletic Organizations

American Ultrarunning Association (AUA)
http://www.americanultra.org/
E-mail: aua@americanultra.org

The American Ultrarunning Association is a nonprofit organization that is committed to the promotion of ultrarunning in the United States. It hosts the U.S. National Championships as well as fields teams to international competitions. AUA is also a member of the International Association of Ultrarunners (IAU) and USA Track & Field (USATF). It is committed to serving athletes as efficiently as possible, employing fewer than 10 staff and board members.

Boston Athletic Association (BAA)
http://www.baa.org/
E-mail: info@baa.org

Established in 1887, the Boston Athletic Association organizes, promotes, sets qualifying times and courses, and hosts the Boston Marathon. In 1985, John Hancock Financial Services became a primary sponsor, providing substantial prize money to attract the world's best marathoners. This strategy has worked, and the Boston Marathon is a cultural and financial success, growing from just over 4,000 participants in 1986 to almost 39,000 runners in 2010.

International Association of Athletics Federation (IAAF)
http://www.iaaf.org/
E-mail: http://www.iaaf.org/aboutiaaf/contacts/feedback.html

Near the end of the 19th century, sport was burgeoning, and athletics was becoming more popular with athletes around the world. In response to the demand for more organized worldwide athletic events to showcase the world's top athletes, the International Amateur Athletic Federation was founded in 1912 by 17 national athletic federations. An important task of this organization was to codify the rules, standards of measurement, and program of events.

International Association of Ultrarunners (IAU)
http://www.iau-ultramarathon.org/
E-mail: nadeem.khan@iau-ultramarathon.org

The International Association of Ultrarunners was founded in 1984. Committed to developing the sport of ultrarunning (ultramarathon), the IAU hosts four major events each year. The IAAF recognizes the 100k World Championships as an official event. Today, more than a thousand ultramarathon races occur over the globe. Due to phenomenal growth, there are more than 50 federations worldwide and more than 100,000 athletes compete in official ultra races internationally each year.

International Olympic Committee (IOC)
http://www.olympic.org/
E-mail: pressoffice@olympic.org

Pierre de Coubertin created the International Olympic Committee on June 23, 1894, consisting of 13 member countries. Its headquarters are located in Lausanne, Switzerland. The IOC organizes the Olympic and Paralympic Games. While the Summer and Winter Olympics each occur four years apart, they are alternated so that an Olympics occurs every two years. Other purposes of the IOC are to support Olympic national governing bodies, promote the Olympic movement, support sport worldwide, and advance the Olympic values of excellence, friendship, and respect.

International Skateboarding Federation
http://www.internationalskateboardingfederation.org/
E-mail: president@internationalskateboardingfederation.org

The International Skateboarding Federation was founded in 2004 in order to promote such lifestyles as self-expression, passion, and freedom. Its practical purpose is two-fold. It functions as the primary organization negotiating the possible inclusion of skateboarding into the Olympics. It also garners sponsorship for

es
me top

several major events worldwide including the ISF World Championships each year.

International Triathlon Union (ITU)
http://www.triathlon.org/
E-mail: http://www.triathlon.org/about/contact_us/

Due to significant growth, there was interest in adding triathlon to the Olympic program in 1988. In order to organize for possible inclusion in the Olympics and to set standard distances, the International Triathlon Union was founded 1989. After many years of successful international events, triathlon debuted at the 2000 Summer Olympic Games in Sydney, Australia. The Olympic distance is 1.5 km swim, 40 km bike, and 10 km run. The ITU is headquartered in Vancouver, Canada.

London 2012
http://www.london2012.com/
E-mail: http://www.london2012.com/contact-us.php

London 2012 was established as the local organization hosting the 2012 Summer Olympic Games. London 2012 desires to create the most accessible Games in which everyone is encouraged to participate and enjoy the Olympic Games. The legacy London 2012 wants to leave is the inspiration for people to take on new activities, achieving more than they ever thought possible. The Games was inspiration for the United Kingdom to develop many local programs that promote sport and fitness.

National Association of Intercollegiate Athletics (NAIA)
http://naia.cstv.com/
E-mail: http://naia.cstv.com/member-services/about/staff.htm

The National Association for Intercollegiate Athletics not only organizes collegiate events in North America but is also committed to the idea that sports can be an important educational component of a total college education. With over 650,000 student-athletes at nearly 300 member colleges and universities throughout the United States and Canada, the NAIA is divided in 25 conferences and offers 23 championships in 13 sports. The NAIA was the first organization to include black colleges and students in championships, include women in national championships, and develop an initiative focused on character development.

National Collegiate Athletic Association (NCAA)
http://www.ncaa.org/
E-mail: http://www.ncaa.org/wps/wcm/connect/public/ncaa/
    home/contact+the+ncaa

The National Collegiate Athletic Association (NCAA) was established in 1906 in the United States as a response to the increasing injuries and deaths incurred in football. Its original purpose was to provide guidelines for play that would ensure the safety of student-athletes. Today, the NCAA directs 89 championships in 23 sports. Over 400,000 student-athletes compete in three divisions (I, II, III), representing more than 1,000 colleges and universities. The NCAA sets general collegiate rules, determines conference regulations, including gender equity requirements, governs recruiting rules, seeks sponsorship and negotiates media rights for its popular events such as March Madness, an event consisting of playoffs in men's Division I Basketball.

National Skateboard Association (NSA)
http://skatensa.com/
E-mail: http://skatensa.com/contact

National High School Skateboard Association (NHSSA), founded in California in 2006 by Jeff Stern, became the National Skateboard Association. Stern's initial idea of an organization grew out of a desire to provide more ways for skateboarders to showcase their skills in California. The NHSSA/NSA helped mobilize the development of high school teams and events where these teams could come together and compete. Stern is committed to staying true to skateboarding culture by soliciting input from the skaters and valuing independence and freedom of expression.

Sochi 2014
http://sochi2014.com/en/
E-mail: http://sochi2014.com/en/team/committee/contacts/

Sochi 2014 is the local organizing committee for the 2014 Winter Olympic Games. Their vision includes embracing change and passion, embarking on new opportunities, and promoting growth, transformation, and personal fulfillment. Innovation is the key word for Sochi 2014, looking to technology and creativity to bring in the new future, especially for Russia. The legacy they hope to leave for Russia is a raised awareness of Olympic history and ideals. They have implemented this educational effort at the public, academic, and professional levels.

United States Olympic Committee (USOC)
http://www.teamusa.org/
E-mail: http://www.teamusa.org/usoc-contacts

The passage of the Amateur Sports Act in 1978 officially gave responsibility to the U.S. Olympic Committee for organizing all sports related to the Olympic movement. The mission of the USOC is to help all Olympic and Paralympic athletes achieve their dreams of competing at the highest level. They support the national governing bodies for each sport and oversee the bidding process to host the Olympic and Paralympic Games by U.S. cities. The USOC serves as a support in all such areas for athletes as training, physiological testing, grants for attending college, transition out of sport, and fundraising. The USOC is the only Olympic National governing body in the world that is privately funded.

Youth Sport Organizations

Boys and Girls Clubs of America
http://www.bgca.org/Pages/index.aspx
E-mail: http://www.bgca.org/Pages/Contact.aspx

The Boys and Girls Clubs of America had its beginnings as a boys club first established in 1860. The organization grew throughout the 19th and early 20th century, helping boys develop character and providing educational support. In 1990, recognizing that girls also needed similar support, the current name was adopted. Today, the Boys and Girls Clubs of America provide after-school activities and support directed at helping underprivileged children and young adults get the adult support they need to help them enter college. Sports activities are a focus for encouraging physical activity, healthy lifestyles, and character development.

National Association for Girls and Women in Sport (NAGWS)
http://www.aahperd.org/nagws/
E-mail: NAGWS@aahperd.org

The National Association for Girls and Women in Sport operates under the umbrella of the American Alliance for Health, Physical Education, Recreation and Dance (AAHPERD), which emerged from an organization directed at the betterment of physical activity for physical education in 1899. Since then, the NAGWS has focused more deliberately on sport for girls and women. Their efforts consist of advocacy, research, leadership development, and educational outreach. Specific activities include raising awareness regarding legal, political, and social justice issues affecting girls and women in sport as well as efforts directed at improving more opportunities for girls and women in sport.

National Federation of State High School Associations (NFHS)
http://www.nfhs.org/
E-mail: http://www.nfhs.org/ContactUs.aspx

The National Federation of State High School Associations oversees establishment of rules and policies for state high school in the United States. Their purpose extends beyond codification of guidelines. NFHS offers extensive resources for coaches including coaching education and accreditation. NFHS provides coaches with access up-to-date training and such sports medicine information as special concussion training. Another important element of their services is a program directed toward character development among high school athletes and teaching coaches how they can best support athletes as students.

National Program for Playground Safety (NPPS)
http://www.uni.edu/playground/
E-mail: playground-safety@uni.edu

Established in 1995, the National Program for Playground safety is the only organization that oversees issues around playground safety. According to NPPS, over 200,000 children are injured on playgrounds annually. NPPS focuses on educating about S.A.F.E. playgrounds. S.A.F.E. stands for supervision, age-appropriate, fall surfacing, and equipment maintenance. NPPS conducts playground safety inspections and educates playground supervisors and adults about the important of having S.A.F.E. playgrounds.

National Youth Sports Safety Foundation (NYSSF)
http://www.health.gov/nhic/nhicscripts/Entry.cfm?HRCode=
   HR2693
E-mail: NYSSF@aol.com

Located in Boston, Massachusetts, and established in 1989, the National Youth Sports Safety Foundation is the only organization in the United States solely dedicated to reducing the number of injuries youth incur due to sports and physical activities each year. NYSSF educates a wide array of such professionals as health professionals, program administrators, coaches, and parents who work with young athletes. The organization also directs efforts toward educating youth about how to stay healthy and avoid injury while playing.

President's Council on Fitness, Sports, and Nutrition
http://www.fitness.gov/
E-mail: http://www.fitness.gov/contact-us.html

A United States government-funded organization committed to health and fitness was established in 1959. This early organization changed its name to President's Council on Physical Fitness and Sports in 1968 in order to emphasize the importance of not only physical activity but also of sports to healthy living. In response to growing concerns about nutrition, the name was changed to the President's Council on Fitness, Sports, and Nutrition in 2010 to include this aspect of health. The goals of the organization are to educate, empower, and encourage healthy living through physical activity and nutrition knowledge throughout the United States so that the next generation of children is healthier than the current. Programs are administered through public school systems.

Sports Business and Media

American Bar Association Forum on the Entertainment and Sports Industries
http://www.americanbar.org/groups/entertainment_sports.
   html
E-mail: Teresa.Ucok@americanbar.org

American Bar Association Forum on the Entertainment and
Sports Industries has the specific purpose of educating lawyers
in the legal principles and aspects of entertainment and sports
law. The organization exists as a forum for the discussion of
current legal issues in sport law as well as issues related to entertainment and sports law. Sports law is one aspect of a larger
entertainment focus. The organization has seven governing
members, all of whom are dedicated to encouraging excellence
in the practice of law within these specific fields.

Associated Press Sports Editors (APSE)
http://apsportseditors.org/
E-mail: http://apsportseditors.org/contact-us/

On June 4, 1974, in New York City, the Associated Press Sports
Editors was founded as a result of discontent with the regular
Associated Press's (AP) untimely sports news releases. Since
then, APSE has grown and become a leader in setting the industry standards of journalism in sport. A conference is held
each year in different locations in the United States in order to
give sports journalists from smaller cities a chance to make it
to a conference. In 1982, workshops on sports journalism were
added to the conference program and have been well received.
The APSE has set standards and been a negotiator regarding
ethics, locker room access, and credentialing with the U.S. Olympic Committee. More important, in 1993, the APSE instituted the
Sports Journalism Institute, directed toward providing female
and minority college journalism students for a week of instruction and practical experience.

Association of Luxury Suite Directors (ALSD)
http://alsd.com/
E-mail: http://alsd.com/content/contact-us

The Association of Luxury Suite Directors was established in
1990 to provide a central organization that could connect sellers
and buyers of luxury suites in sports stadiums in North America with plans to reach out globally. Included in this network
of luxury suite partners are suppliers and food and beverage
concessions. ALSD organizes and supports suite directors and
team/facility executives in the work they do in order to maximize profits. More significantly, ALSD is committed to ensuring

that patrons receive outstanding service and have an exceptional experience.

Association of Professional Sales Agents (Sport and Leisure Industries) (APSA)
http://www.apsa.org.uk/
Email: http://www.apsa.org.uk/contactus

Association of Professional Sales Agents (Sport and Leisure Industries) represents sales agents in the United Kingdom who trade in sports equipment and peripheral materials. APSA agents do not represent athletes but rather sell sports products from such various sport industries as outdoor, leisure, and golf. Members of APSA are experienced in the sports industry and know the details about the trends in each particular industry. APSA functions within the Federation of Sports and Play Association.

Federation of Sports and Play Association (FSPA)
http://www.sportsandplay.com/
Email: info@sportsandplay.com

The Federation of Sports and Play Associations is an organization in the United Kingdom that represents over 400 member companies in the sports and play industries among 17 associations. Their purpose is to act as a liaison between sports and play companies and such governmental agencies as government partners, governing bodies, and national associations. FSPA serves as the collective voice of a variety of industry companies, providing expertise about the industry, counseling about legal issues within the industry, and actively lobbying on behalf of sports and play companies.

Information Display and Entertainment Association (IDEA)
http://www.ideaontheweb.org/
E-mail: info@ideaontheweb.org

The Information Display and Entertainment Association was founded in 1982. Its purpose is to be the primary association for professionals in the big screen/event industry. Members of IDEA represent a wide range of stakeholders from sports teams to public facilities to international manufacturers involved in the sports and entertainment industries. Members include baseball, basketball, football, hockey, soccer, arenas, stadiums, and universities. IDEA offers resources to all people involved in such game-day operations as Web site, newsletters, awards programs, and an annual conference.

IMG Worldwide
http://www.imgworld.com/home.aspx
E-mail: http://www.imgworld.com/contact-us.aspx

IMG Worldwide began as International Management Group in 1960 when Mark McCormack became the sports agent for Arnold Palmer. Today, IMG is the world's leading representing agency in global sports, fashion, and media. IMG has almost 3,000 employees in over 30 countries internationally. They offer a wide array of such services as negotiating collegiate marketing, media, and licensing rights, international sports media rights, and branding. Also, IMG represents elite athletes, coaches, and industry experts. MG Academies also offers multisport training and education to more than 12,000 young athletes from 80 countries annually.

International Association for Sport Information (IASI)
http://sportinfo.ning.com/
E-mail: http://sportinfo.ning.com/main/authorization/signUp?

The International Association for Sport Information organization was founded in 1960 in Rome. Its purpose is to support those who keep international documentation about sports as well as promote the sharing of this information to physical educators, sport scientists, people who make documentaries, and sport researchers. In addition, IASI gives advice about how to plan, operate, and develop new sport information centers around the globe. One program, Share the Knowledge Project, is a direct effort on the part of IASI to globally spread information about sport. It is a joint venture with the Human Kinetics publisher in which books on sport science, physical education and other sport books are distributed to institutions around the world that do not otherwise have the resources to buy these books.

International Association of Skateboard Companies (IASC)
http://skateboardiasc.org/
E-mail: http://skateboardiasc.org/contact/

The International Association of Skateboard Companies was created in 1995 and is made of skateboard manufacturers, distributors, contest organizers, private skateparks, and individuals. IASC is a nonprofit trade organization that is committed to keeping the needs of skateboarders and the skateboard industry in mind when acting on behalf of these entities. Their goal is to promote skateboarding worldwide while maintaining the culture and integrity of skateboarding.

International Association of Venue Managers (IAVM)
http://www.iavm.org/
E-mail: http://www.iavm.org/cvms/contact.asp

In 1924, the Auditorium Managers Association was established in order to deal with the emerging stadiums and arenas around the United States. This organization later grew into the International Association of Venue Managers (IAVM), seeing the need to incorporate and disseminate knowledge more globally. As a result of so many public stadiums, venues, sport arenas, and other public gathering places, IAVM fills the gap with respect to educating and promoting individuals to work in the management of these public but often both publically and privately funded spaces. IAVM is committed to being the premiere source for all public assembly related research, information, services, and life-safety issues worldwide.

International Ticketing Association (INTIX)
http://www.intix.org/
E-mail: info@intix.org

The International Ticketing Association has its beginnings in the Box Office Management International (BOMI) organization, which was established in 1980. Serving the needs of the United States and Canadian ticketing professionals, BOMI changed its name to the International Ticketing Association (INTIX) in 1997 when technology revolutionized ticketing. Today, INTIX is a nonprofit membership organization committed to leading the forum for the entertainment ticketing industry. INTIX represents over 1,100 ticketing, sales, technology, finance, and marketing professionals who work in arts, sports, and entertainment. INTIX's mission is to education for members about the latest trends in ticketing, supply access to the latest technology, provide a code of ethics, present networking opportunities, and make available a friendly forum for those professionals new to ticketing.

National Sporting Goods Association (NSGA)
http://www.nsga.org/i4a/pages/index.cfm?pageid=1
E-mail:http://www.nsga.org/i4a/pages/index.cfm?pageid=3285

The National Sporting Goods Association (NSGA) is a member organization that serves as a resource to sporting goods industry professionals in a wide variety of ways. They provide a searchable job list, a learning center for educating professionals about the industry, conferences for networking and sharing information, such sporting goods directories as buyers' guides and wholesalers, research reports on topics such as branding, sport and leisure activities participation rates, and cost of doing business survey results, media contacts, and publications.

Outdoor Industry Association (OIA)
http://www.outdoorindustry.org/
E-mail: http://www.outdoorindustry.org/about.contact.html

Established in 1989, the Outdoor Industry Association provides trade services for over 4,000 manufacturers, distributors, suppliers, sales representatives and retailers in the outdoor industry. OIA is the premier trade association for outdoor companies, hosting biannual trade shows in the United States. OIA operates under the values of quality, service, and innovation, working diligently to ensure the business health of specialty retailers and supply chain. OIA endeavors to raise the standards of the industry, increase outdoor participation, strengthen business markets, and improve profitability of its members. To this end, OIA creates many annual reports about who is participating in what outdoor sports and for what reasons in order to keep the industry as a whole better informed about trends.

Sports Lawyers Association (SLA)
http://www.sportslaw.org/
E-mail: http://www.sportslaw.org/contact.cfm

The Sports Lawyers Association was founded in 1975 by a group of five lawyers. The impetus was the escalating animosity between sports agents and teams. Lloyd E. Shefsky had the foresight to suggest a third party organization to which the fighting parties could turn in order to resolve disputes, primarily over salary. An SLA lawyer mitigated the *Curt Flood* case, which opened the door to the idea of a free agent, at which point player salaries went from minimum wage to whatever they could negotiate. Today, SLA is an international organization that provides education about sports law, serves as a forum for discussion on current sports law issues, and promotes ethical conduct with regard to practicing sports law.

Organizations Dedicated to Sports Medicine, Injury, Rehabilitation, and Psychology

American Alliance for Health, Education, Recreation, and Dance (AAHPERD)
http://www.aahperd.org/
E-mail: http://www.aahperd.org/about/contactus.cfm

AAHPERD promotes and supports a wide range of physical activity. Their mission is to be a leader in research, education, and best practices with respect to creating healthy, safe, and active lifestyles. To this end, AAHPERD specifically creates and shares professional guidelines, practices, and ethics with professionals, offer opportunities for professional growth through conferences and workshops, advance knowledge through funding research and disseminating research, and promote public understanding by serving as a liaison among government agencies associated with promoting physical activity.

American College of Sports Medicine (ACSM)
http://www.acsm.org/
Email: http://www.acsm.org/about-acsm/contact-us

The American College of Sports Medicine (ACSM) has more than 45,000 members and certified professionals worldwide, making it the largest organization dedicated to sports medicine and exercise science. Its purpose is to advance scientific research in sports medicine so that educators and practitioners can help athletes and physically active people maintain performance, fitness, and healthy lives.

American Orthopedic Society for Sports Medicine (AOSSM)
http://www.sportsmed.org/
E-mail: http://www.sportsmed.org/Contact_Us/

Founded in 1972, AOSSM was initially an organization of 75 members devoted to the sharing of knowledge about sports-related injuries, clinical problems, and working solutions. AOSSM purchased the *American Journal of Sports Medicine* in 1975, turning it into one of the most respected sports medicine journals in the world. AOSSM holds conferences for physicians to meet, exchange ideas, and collaborate annually as well as provides online resources for physicians.

Association for Applied Sport Psychology (AASP)
http://www.appliedsportpsych.org/
E-mail: http://www.appliedsportpsych.org/About/Contact-AASP.html

The Association for Applied Sport Psychology was founded in 1986 with an initial membership of about 1,200. AASP is currently the world's largest professional organization dedicated to the development of research, theory, and applied practice of sport psychology. AASP is a resource for athletes, coaches, teams, parents, and others who are physically active, involved in sport, or rehabilitating from injury. ASSP maintains ethical guidelines of practice for all members. It is the only North American professional organization that offers certification to those desiring to become a practitioner in applied sport and exercise psychology.

Exercise and Sport Science Australia (ESSA)
http://www.essa.org.au/
E-mail: info@essa.org.au

Exercise and Sport Science Australia is the premier professional organization that supports people working in the field of exercise and sport science. It is dedicated to the overall health of Australians as well as high performance of Australia's elite athletes. As a unified organization, ESSA provides leadership and advocacy on important issues in sport and exercise science. It also fosters a collaborative community through annual conferences, promotion of excellence in practice, education, training, and research.

Human Kinetics (HK)
http://www.humankinetics.com/Home
E-mail: http://www.humankinetics.com/contactus

In 1974, Rainer Martens created Human Kinetics, a publishing company, in order to publish the proceedings from the North American Society for the Psychology of Sport and Physical Activity Conference. Today, Human Kinetics remains committed to publishing journals, textbooks, books for the general public, videos, and course materials dedicated to supporting physical activity and sport management programs. Human Kinetics is the largest publisher in the world serving this audience with over 320 employees and revenues of $37 million annually.

International Federation of Sports Medicine (FIMS)
http://www.fims.org/
E-mail: http://www.fims.org/en/general/contact/

In 1920, at the St. Moritz Winter Olympics, the Association International Medico-Sportive (AIMS) was founded as a response to the growing demand for sports medicine physicians in support of high-performance athletes. Its primary function in these early years was to work with international sports federations and the International Olympic Committee to provide exceptional medical care for Summer and Winter Olympic athletes. Today, FIMS consists of national sports medicine associations across all five continents. FIMS remains committed to helping athletes achieve optimal performance through education and support in health, nutrition, high-quality medical care, and training.

International Sports Sciences Association (ISSA)
http://www.issaonline.com/
E-mail: http://www.issaonline.com/contact-issa/

The International Sports Sciences Association was created in 1988 as a distance education institution and certifying agency for personal trainers. Today it offers nine certification courses and has over 180,000 students and alumni in 85 countries around the globe. Their vision is to provide the highest quality personal trainer education so that globally people may lead healthier lives.

National Academy of Kinesiology (NAK)
http://www.nationalacademyofkinesiology.org/
E-mail: http://www.nationalacademyofkinesiology.org/contact-us

The National Academy of Kinesiology has its roots in the American Academy of Kinesiology and Physical Education, which was founded in 1926. After several name changes and evolution in purposes, today the NAK's dual purpose is to support scholarly research in human movement and physical activity and encourage practical applications of these findings. NAK encourages professional and scholarly productivity, synthesis of information through conferences and publications, and philosophical discussions regarding values and issues of human movement and physical activity.

National Athletic Trainers Association (NATA)
http://www.nata.org/
E-mail: http://www.nata.org/contact

The National Athletic Trainers' Association, founded in 1950 in the United States, is a worldwide professional membership association for certified athletic trainers and supporters of the profession. NATA's mission is to enhance the quality of care provided by trainers and move the profession forward. NATA links this community by providing career resources, certification programs, and professional resources and connections.

National Center for Catastrophic Sport Injury Research
http://www.unc.edu/depts/nccsi/
E-mail: mueller@email.unc.edu

Located at the University of North Carolina in Chapel Hill since 1965, the National Center for Catastrophic Sport Injury Research has been the premier center for collecting and reporting sports injury data for high school and college sports in the United States. The research and data collection tracks death and permanent disability injury involving brain and/or spinal cord injuries. Grants from the National Collegiate Athletic Association, the American Football Coaches Association, and the National Federation of State High School Associations fund the research.

National Strength and Conditioning Association (NSCA)
http://www.nsca-lift.org/
E-mail: nsca@nsca-lift.org

Established in 1978 in the United States, the National Strength and Conditioning Association is now an international nonprofit educational association with almost 30,000 members in 52 countries worldwide. NSCA offices are located around the globe as well in Japan, Korea, Italy, Shanghai, and Spain. They provide education for the major strength and conditioning certification exams. Their educational formats are technologically advanced so that they may reach a broad audience. The NSCA provides access to training videos, conference Web sites, conference proceedings and videos, podcasts, webinars, and journals. The NSCA serves professionals in sport science, athletic, health, and fitness industries, who utilize strength and conditioning programs to improve the health and athletic performances of the general public as well as elite athletes.

North American Society for the Psychology of Sport and Physical Activity (NASPSPA)
http://www.naspspa.org/
E-mail: http://www.naspspa.org/contact-us

NASPSPA is a professional organization specifically dedicated to the research and dissemination of information regarding the development, learning, and control of motor behavior as well as sport and exercise psychology. Sport psychology focuses on high performance, whereas exercise psychology is directed at helping people continue daily exercise. NASPSPA hosts an annual conference and produces an online newsletter, both of which are aimed at information sharing and the advancement of the motor behavior and psychological aspects of sport and physical activity.

Sport for Development, Character, Ethical Behavior, and Athletes' Rights

American Sport Education Program (ASEP)
http://www.asep.com/
E-mail: info@hkusa.com

As one of seven distinct divisions within Human Kinetics, which was founded in 1974, the American Sport Education Program was an expansion of the American Coaching Effectiveness Program (ACEP), which was created in 1976. ASEP remains focused on educating coaches so that coaches learn to value the athlete over winning. Today, education programs committed to this ideal are available for officials, sport administrators, parents, and athletes. ASEP offers curricula for each high school sport, consisting of Coaching Principles, Sport First Aid, and Coaching Technical and Tactical Skills. Online courses are offered as well, enabling ASEP to realize their dream of reaching as many coaches, parents, and athletes as possible.

Athletes for a Better World (ABW)
http://www.abw.org/
E-mail: http://www.abw.org/contact-us/

Founded by Fred Northup in June of 1998, Athletes for a Better World was a response to a growing concern that sports was creating "characters," not developing "character." Northrup felt as though young athletes needed specific guidance in order for them to develop in positive ways, especially given the pressures to win even at the earliest stages in sport. ABW's sole purpose is to promote sport as a positive experience through which character, teamwork, and citizenship can be developed through explicit commitment to a "Code for Living" that ABW created.

Canadian International Development Agency (CIDA)
http://www.acdi-cida.gc.ca/home
E-mail: info@acdi-cida.gc.ca

The Canadian International Development Agency is an effort on the part of the Canadian government to help eliminate poverty.

As part of their commitment to this goal, CIDA has established several programs aimed at helping youth living in poverty find ways to better their lives. For instance, CIDA has sponsors sport programs directed toward learning about healthy living, helping children whose parents have died of HIV/AIDS learn to live more healthy lives through sport involvement and use sport programs to empower girls and women.

Citizenship through Sports Alliance
http://www.stlsports.org/sportsmanship/
E-mail: salexander@stlsports.org

Citizenship Through Sports Alliance is a good example of a grassroots effort aimed at promoting sportsmanship at the youth levels. The organization functions as the home of the Sportsmanship Initiative, a division of the St. Louis Sports Commission. The alliance grew out of a concern that over 70 percent of youth drop out of sport before age 13 because of an overemphasis on winning, exceedingly high performance expectations of parents, early specialization, and a lack of fun sport experiences. Utilizing a sportsmanship pledge, the Citizenship through Sports Alliance reaches out to coaches, parents, officials, athletes and fans asks them to sign the pledge, an act reinforcing their commitment to respect, civility, integrity, and fair play in sport.

Court of Arbitration for Sport (CAS)
http://www.tas-cas.org/news
E-mail: http://www.tas-cas.org/address

The Court of Arbitration for Sport began as an idea in 1981 under the direction of the newly elected IOC President, Juan Antonio Samaranch. Realizing that there was a clear need for arbitration of disputes among international organizations and athletes, the IOC officially ratified the statutes of the CAS in 1983, allowing it to become an official court on June 30, 1984. CAS operates within the budget of the IOC. While no persons are obligated to use the services of this court, it is open to all international athletes and governing organizations. There are two types of cases submitted to the CAS: commercial and disciplinary. Commercial disputes consist of those relating to sponsorship, television rights, staging of sports events, and employment and agency contracts. The majority of disciplinary cases involves doping but also includes issues around athlete violence and abuse toward referees.

Institute for International Sport (IIS)
http://www.internationalsport.org/
E-mail: http://www.internationalsport.org/contact.cfm

The Institute for International Sport was created in 1986 by Daniel E. Doyle Jr., who had played basketball in Europe as a basketball player during the 1960s and 1970s. Doyle realized the potential for sport to instill goodwill and promote friendship among international competitors. IIS has established various programs including the development of the annual National Sportsmanship Day, the Scholar-Athlete Games, and the World Youth Peace Summit.

International Olympic Academy (IOA)
http://ioa.org.gr/
E-mail: http://ioa.org.gr/

As early as 1927, Pierre de Coubertin thought that an academic center for the study of the Olympic movement should be established to maintain the efforts and legacy of the Olympic Games. On June 14, 1961, the International Olympic Academy was officially created and later built in ancient Olympia. The IOA takes an interdisciplinary approach to studying Olympism, the ideals associated with the ancient Olympics revived through the modern Olympics.

International Olympic Truce Center
http://www.olympictruce.org/Default.aspx
E-mail: about@olympictruce.org

The International Olympic Committee established the International Olympic Truce Center in 2001 as part of the larger Olympic legacy efforts. The Olympic Truce has been around since 776 BC when the first Olympic Games occurred. Today the International Olympic Truce Center's aims are to uphold the ancient Olympic Truce, which is the idea of imagining peace as was evident during the ancient Olympics when rival regions would put aside their differences. The organization supports both global and local initiatives through online activities, publications, and field trips.

International Platform on Sport and Development
http://www.sportanddev.org/
E-mail: info@sportanddev.org

International Platform on Sport and Development is a site where people can learn about sport and development. The Platform facilitates information sharing about sport for development movements to all stakeholders. It also promotes good practices in sport for development movements (S&D) and fosters relationships among all people interested in this movement.

National Association of Collegiate Directors of Athletics (NACDA)
http://www.nacda.com/
E-mail: http://www.nacda.com/nacda/nacda-staff.html

The National Association of Collegiate Directors of Athletics is the professional organization serving collegiate administrators. The NACDA hosts an annual conference, produces publications, advocates for the profession, and enhances opportunities for gender and ethnic minorities in collegiate athletic administration. Also, the NACDA develops networking opportunities and educational initiatives for present and future collegiate administrators.

National Consortium for Academics and Sports (NCAS)
http://ncasports.org/
E-mail: http://ncasports.org/about/contact-us/

The mission of the National Consortium for Academics and Sports is to pursue social justice through sport participation. Focused on values-based thinking, NCAS provides workshops to sport administrators and collegiate athletes on such various topics as how to engage with diversity, think differently about violence in sport, and consider how personal actions reflect more broadly on the athletic department as a whole. In addition, NCAS also promotes National Student-Athlete day on April 6, a day honoring all student-athletes' achievements and the positive values associated with sport participation.

People to People Sport Ambassadors
http://www.peopletopeople.com/OurPrograms/Sport/Pages/
    default2.aspx
E-mail: http://www.peopletopeople.com/AboutUs/Pages/Contact
    Us.aspx

The People to People Sport Ambassadors program is part of a
larger organization, People to People, which organizes international exchanges and gatherings in order to promote global understanding. The programs for sport ambassadors are based on
the training camp idea. Young soccer athletes, aged 12–17, can
participate in training camps offered worldwide. The People to
People Sport Ambassadors soccer program allows these athletes
to work with outstanding coaches, play with international teammates, play in Olympic-style tournaments, and use professional
facilities. The organization also coordinates with the Washington School of World Studies so that sport ambassadors can earn
academic credit while participating in intensive sport programs
around the world.

Sport Management Resources (SMR)
http://www.sportsmanagementresources.com/
E-mail: http://www.sportsmanagementresources.com/contact

Sport Management Resources is a consulting organization that
helps athletic directors identify issues within their organization
through comprehensive data collection. SMR works with scholastic and collegiate programs within the United States. They
specialize in taking a holistic perspective by integrating financial
goals, social issues, and athletic and academic goals when working with organizations.

Sports Legacy Institute
http://www.sportslegacy.org/
E-mail: http://www.sportslegacy.org/index.php/contact-sli

The Sports Legacy Institute was founded on June 14, 2007, in
Boston, Massachusetts, by Christopher Nowinski and Dr. Robert
Cantu. Its mission is to improve the study, treatment, and preven-
tion of traumatic brain injury in athletes and other at-risk groups.
SLI works in conjunction with Boston University School of Medi-
cine, together forming the Center for the Study of Traumatic

Encephalopathy. SLI offers educational programs about brain trauma and provides online information about concussion as well as host events for raising awareness and funds to support the ongoing research.

United Nations Office on Sport for Development and Peace
http://www.un.org/wcm/content/site/sport/
Email: http://www.un.org/wcm/content/site/sport/home/
    unplayers/unoffice/contact

Since 2003, the United Nations (UN) General Assembly has supported a vision and specific programs built around sport as a means to help developing countries. The UN recognizes the potential of sport to mobilize people in ways that other activities do not. The UN's sport for development programs are directed at fostering social ties and economic development in poor areas of the world. Their efforts are focused on participation, not elite sport, and include the overarching goals of eradicating poverty through transfer of sport skills to life, empowering girls and women, encouraging youth to attend school because of sport, and reducing child mortality and the spread of HIV/AIDS due to increased health awareness through sport.

United States Anti-Doping Association (USADA)
http://www.usada.org/
E-mail: http://www.usada.org/contact

The United States Anti-Doping Agency was founded in 2000 to function as the primary anti-doping agency serving Olympic and Paralympic athletes in the United States. The USADA educates athletes about the harmful effects of and compromised integrity associated with doping as well as supports detection research. Through resources and education, the USADA's efforts are focused on deterrence by protecting those athletes not involved in doping.

World Anti-Doping Association (WADA)
http://www.wada-ama.org/en/
E-mail: http://www.wada-ama.org/en/Footer-Links/Contact/

The World Anti-Doping Association was established in 1999 to be the international anti-doping agency. Its mission is to create a drug-free sport world. Supported by a combination of international governments and sport-organizing bodies, WADA has developed an anti-doping code, which is aimed at preventing athletes from engaging in doping practices in sport. WADA has also developed international standards and best practices for sport organizations so that they may better monitor athletes and enforce violations of the doping code. WADA also updates and provides a list of banned substances.

Organizations Representing Marginalized Groups in Sport

Australian Women's Sport and Recreation Association
http://www.australianwomensport.com.au/
E-mail: http://www.australianwomensport.com.au/default.asp?
    PageID=25&n=Contact+Us

Australian Women's Sport and Recreation Association is a nongovernmental nonprofit organization established in 2005 serving girls and women in Australia. It aims are to promote physical activity and sport participation for all girls and women throughout Australia. Its purpose is to advocate for girls and women and educate the general public in order to influence policy development, participation rates, and professional opportunities for girls and women in sport.

Black Coaches and Administrators (BCA)
http://www.bcasports.org/
E-mail: http://www.bcasports.org/index.php?option=com_rsfo
    rm&view=rsform&formId=5&Itemid=191

The Black Coaches and Administrators organization was created in 1988 in order to provide support to ethnic minorities wanting to move into leadership positions in either professional, collegiate, or high school sports. The BCA offers a positive vision aimed at unifying efforts to raise awareness of the high-quality sport leaders within ethnic groups. Specifically, the BCS addresses issues particular to ethnic minorities gaining employment, offer scholarships for professional development and education, and create alliances with youth groups.

Black Entertainment and Sport Lawyers Association (BESLA)
http://www.besla.org/
E-mail: info@BESLA.org

Starting out as the Black Entertainment Lawyers Association (BELA) in 1980, the name changed to the Black Entertainment and Sports Lawyers Association (BESLA) in 1986 due to an increased demand for negotiations within the sport industry. Today, BESLA is an international organization consisting of a highly diverse group of lawyers and industry executives that offer an expert group of sports industry professionals. BESLA is committed to creating more opportunities both economically and socially for ethnic minorities and providing a solid network of professionals dedicated to assisting in the legal and business affairs for sports industry employment for people of color.

Black Sports Agents Association (BSAA)
http://www.blacksportsagents.com/
E-mail: http://www.blacksportsagents.com/contactus.php

The Black Sports Agents Association, established in 1996 by the Rev. Jesse Jackson and other influential sports industry professionals, grew out of the recognition that black athletes were wanted as star athletes but had very little bargaining power in contract negotiations. BSAA is an international organization dedicated to advancing the credibility of African American player representatives and promoting the economic and social status of black players. BSAA also functions as a resource for African American player representatives in terms of ethical guidelines and best practices while being a unified voice for player representatives around the globe.

Today, the association welcomes the participation of all members of sports-related communities whose common goal is the understanding, advancement, and ethical practice of sports management and representation

Black Women in Sport Foundation (BWSF)
http://www.blackwomeninsport.org/
E-mail: http://www.blackwomeninsport.org/ContactUs.htm

The Black Women in Sport Foundation was established in 1992 to promote character building, self-discipline, and teamwork by reaching out on a grassroots level to women of color. Facing a disproportionate number of economic barriers, the organization is committed to working in local urban areas by providing life skills development through sport, hosting workshops, and offering mentors to women of color.

Canadian Association for the Advancement of Women and Sport (CAAWS)
http://www.caaws.ca/
E-mail: http://www.caaws.ca/e/about/contact_us.cfm

The Canadian Association for the Advancement of Women and Sport (CAASWS) takes a comprehensive approach to advancing physical activity, health, and sport in the daily lives of girls and women in Canada. They offer 10 programs aimed at increasing participation. These programs vary according to the specific issue or group being addressed. Examples include programs aimed at helping indigenous people see the benefits of physical activity, encouraging older women to participate, and promoting inclusivity by educating about the harmful effects of homophobia in sport.

Center for the Study of Sports in Society
http://www.northeastern.edu/sportinsociety/
Email: sportinsociety@neu.edu

The Center for the Study of Sports in Society was founded in 1984 by Richard Lapchick. Residing at Northeastern University, the center is dedicated to creating safe, healthy, inclusive environments for all people involved in sport. Their work is predicated on the belief that raising awareness of issues in sport as well as providing resources to people will allow sport organizations to use more effectively leverage sport as a means for improving conditions for more people. The center has initiated multiple programs aimed at these goals, most recently establishing the Athletes for Human Rights initiative (AHR) in 2005.

Challenged Athletes Foundation
http://www.challengedathletes.org/site/c.4nJHJQPqEiKUE/
    b.6449023/k.BD6D/home.htm
E-mail: caf@challengedathletes.org

The Challenged Athletes Foundation was established in San Diego in 1997 after an athlete was paralyzed during a triathlon. Since then, the foundation has worked to help disabled athletes enjoy sport to the fullest of their ability. Their vision includes helping disabled athletes receive the same respect as able-bodied athletes, to serve disabled athletes with integrity, and to raise awareness in the community. The foundation offers several programs as well as grants to achieve their mission.

Disabled Sports USA (DS/USA)
http://www.dsusa.org/
E-mail: http://www.dsusa.org/contactus.html

Disabled Sports USA was created in 1967 by Vietnam veterans to help those disabled by war. Today, Disabled USA functions as a nationwide network of locally based centers, which are open to anyone who is permanently disabled. As a part of the U.S. Olympic Committee, DS/USA supports rehabilitative programs for a wide variety of sports as well as organizes competitions for Paralympic hopefuls. Their goal is to provide opportunities for disabled persons to become more independent, confident, and physically fit.

Federation of Gay Games
http://www.gaygames.com/
E-mail: http://www.gaygames.com/index.php?id=contact

Dr. Tom Waddell conceived of the Gay Games in 1980 as a way to counter the image that being gay and being an athlete were contradictory. Since the first Gay Games in San Francisco in 1982, the Gay Games have been dedicated to bringing together the LGBT community and friends in order to empower, raise awareness, and advocate for improved social, economic, and political inclusion of LGBT people globally. The Gay Games are held every four years in cities across the world. The 2010 Gay Games in Cologne had almost 10,000 athletes from 60 countries participating in 41 sports. The next Gay Games will be held in Cleveland and Akron, Ohio, in 2014.

Institute for Diversity and Ethics in Sport
http://tidesport.org/
E-mail: rlapchick@bus.ucf.edu

The Institute for Diversity and Ethics in Sport was established in 2002 as part of the De Vos Sport Business Management Graduate Program at the University of Central Florida. The institute is a resource regarding racial and gender issues in sport for collegiate and professional sports. Annually, the institute produces racial and gender reports of hiring practices of coaches and sport management positions at the collegiate and professional levels, tracks graduation rates of student-athletes at NCAA schools, conducts diversity training for sport administrators in conjunction with National Consortium for Academics and Sports, and examines other social issues such as exploitation of student-athletes, gambling, performance-enhancing drugs, and violence in sports.

International Association for Physical Education for Girls and Women (IAPESGW)
http://www.iapesgw.org/
E-mail: klofstrom@caaws.ca

Founded in 1949, IAPESGW has members from 45 countries across all continents. The main goals of the organization are to be a resource for its members who work in physical education, provide opportunities for professional development, and facilitate international cooperation among practitioners across the globe. IAPESGW also works at the international level to influence policy making as more national governing bodies become committed to supporting women in sport.

International Paralympic Committee (IPC)
http://www.paralympic.org/index.html
E-mail: http://www.paralympic.org/IPC/Contacts/

Established on September 22, 1989, the International Paralympic Committee is the global governing body overseeing development of and competitions for people with physical disabilities. The IPC organizes the Winter and Summer Paralympic Games, which occur approximately 2–3 weeks after the Olympic Games in the same location.

National Association of Collegiate Women Athletic Administrators (NACWAA)
http://www.nacwaa.org/
E-mail: http://www.nacwaa.org/contact

NACWAA had its beginnings in 1979 with the formation of the Council of Collegiate Women Athletic Administrators (CCWAA). The name changed to NACWAA in 1992 to reflect more accurately the nationwide advocacy work in which it was involved. Today, with membership of more than 1,700, NACWAA remains committed to increasing athletic and administrative opportunities for women and promoting progressive and positive attitudes toward women in sports. NACWAA also provides such services for their members as mentorship and networking opportunities, scholarships for professional development, leadership training, and career path guidance.

North American Gay Amateur Athletic Alliance (NAGAAA)
http://www.nagaaasoftball.org/
E-mail: commissioner@nagaaasoftball.org

The North American Gay Amateur Athletic Alliance was established in 1977 to promote more inclusive sports competition with a focus on participation of the gay, lesbian, bisexual, and transgender (GLBT) community. In particular, the NAGAAA hosts 37 softball leagues, comprised of over 10,000 members, throughout the United States and Canada. NAGAAA offers such national and international sports competitions as the NAGAAA Gay Softball World Series (GSWS).

Special Olympics
http://www.specialolympics.org/
E-mail: http://www.specialolympics.org/contact.aspx

On July 19–20, 1968, the first International Special Olympics Summer Games took place in Chicago, Illinois. By 1971, the International Olympic Committee approved their use of the word "Olympics," only one of two organizations approved to do so. Today, Special Olympics is a worldwide organization, which operates in Africa, Asia Pacific, East Asia, Europe/ Eurasia, Latin America, the Middle East/North Africa, and North America. It is dedicated to helping athletes with intellectual disabilities compete with dignity, a feeling of acceptance, and hope that they can reach their potential. They help local Special Olympics organizations carry out their work and host Winter and Summer Special Olympic Games, which take place every four years.

The Women's Sports Foundation (WSF)
http://www.womenssportsfoundation.org/
E-mail: http://www.womenssportsfoundation.org/home/
contact-us

The Women's Sports Foundation was founded in 1974 by Billie Jean King, the famous women's tennis player. The purpose of WSF is to advocate for women in sport and physical activity. WSF takes a variety of approaches to carry out their mission. They support such programs as GoGirlGo!, which is a specific curriculum designed to be carried out at local levels to help sedentary young girls become more physically active. WSF supports female athletes through achievement awards and travel grants to aspiring female athletes who cannot afford the travel expenses to important competitions. Finally, WSF complies and disseminates important research and political stances on gender equity, Title IX, GLBT equity, and health and fitness for women.

United States Association of Blind Athletes (USABA)
http://www.usaba.org/
E-mail: http://usaba.org/index.php/about-us/staff/

In 1976, Dr. Charles Buell founded the United States Association of Blind Athletes (USABA). The purpose of USABA is to support visually impaired athletes in their pursuit of physical activity and athletic competition. USABA is part of the United States Olympic Committee. USABA offers programs at the national and local levels specifically aimed at providing sporting opportunities for the visually impaired in such sports such as track and field, nordic and alpine skiing, biathlon, judo, wrestling, swimming, tandem cycling, powerlifting, and goalball (a team sport for the blind and visually impaired).

United States Paralympic Team
http://usparalympics.org/
E-mail: http://usparalympics.org/contact_us

The United States Paralympic Team is the governing body for all competitive athletes who are physically or visually impaired. As part of the USOC, the U.S. Paralympic Team partners with local Paralympic sports clubs, local community sport organizations, medical facilities, and government agencies to open up more opportunities for the physically impaired to pursue physical activity and competitive sport. Given that more than 21 million Americans have a physical or visual disability, the goal of the U.S. Paralympic Team is to increase the 130 clubs across the United States dedicated to serving these athletes to 250 clubs by the end of 2012.

USA Deaf Sports Federation
http://www.usdeafsports.org/
E-mail: HomeOffice@usdeafsports.org

The USA Deaf Sports Federation had its beginnings in 1945 but officially was established in its current form in 1997. USADSF is the official governing body in the United States dedicated to serving deaf athletes. As part of the USOC, they organize multiple competitions and support deaf athletes competing worldwide in 22 sports. World competitions area offered in many sports as well as the Summer Deaflympic Games.

Wheelchair and Ambulatory Sports USA (WASUSA)
http://www.wsusa.org/
E-mail: http://www.wsusa.org/index.php?option=com_contact&
    task=view&contact_id=16&Itemid=637

Wheelchair and Ambulatory Sports USA was originally created in 1956 as a response to helping disabled war veterans become physically active again. After a few name changes, the current WASUSA became official in 2009. In support of athletes with physical disabilities, WASUSA provides access to international competitions, conducts regional and national competitions, makes available resources, provides education about being physically active, and facilitates community-based outreach programs.

Women's Basketball Coaches Association (WBCA)
http://www.wbca.org/
E-mail: http://www.wbca.org/contact-us/

The Women's Basketball Coaches Association (WBCA) was established in 1981. The WBCA is a professional organization bringing together collegiate, high school, junior high school, club, youth, national, international and Olympic coaches as well as former players, members of the media, sports information directors, officials and fans of women's basketball in order to raise the level of respect for women's basketball in the United States. Their services include offering conferences, producing publications, distributing important information about Title IX and NCAA rules changes, and assisting in career development.

Women in Sports and Events (WISE)
http://www.womeninsportsandevents.com/handler.cfm?CFID=
    5035585&CFTOKEN=70241177
E-mail: http://www.womeninsportsandevents.com/handler.
    cfm?cat_id=21030

Women in Sports and Events is the premier professional organization in the United States serving as a resource and voice for all businesswomen in sports and events. WISE serves it members by offering events, ongoing meetings in local chapters, and mentoring programs. WISE's goal is to assist women in learning about the issues and challenges of pursuing a career in sports and events so that they may recognize opportunities and move forward more easily in their careers.

8

Print and Nonprint Resources

This chapter includes selected and annotated bibliographies of print and nonprint resources. Reference works, books, and journal and magazine articles comprise the print resources while the nonprint resources consist of databases, DVDs/videotapes, and Internet sites. In order to more easily locate information, the print resources are organized by four categories: an overview of sport; sport business; sport professionals, technology, and health; and social and political aspects and issues in sport. The nonprint resources are organized by three categories: general sport; sport business and sport professionals; and social, political, and ethical issues in sport.

Print Resources

Overview of Sport
Reference Works
Applegate, L. 2002. *Encyclopedia of Sports and Fitness Nutrition*. New York: Three Rivers Press, 432 pp.

This encyclopedia provides a comprehensive guide to sport nutrition and performance. Highlighting key concepts of creating personalized nutrition plans and integrating them with fitness programs, the author covers important information in nontechnical language.

Bartlett, R., C. Gratton, and C. Rolf, eds. 2006. *Encyclopedia of International Sport Studies*. London: Routledge, 3 vols. 1520 pp.

This reference work includes a wide variety of entries as a general guide to the developments in sport. Entries include key aspects of sports medicine, sport science, and technology in sport. Entries also include discussions in sport sociology and sport psychology.

Berkshire Encyclopedia of World Sport. 2005. (vols. 1–4). Great Barrington, MA: Berkshire Publishing Group, 4 vols. 1816 pp.

This reference book covers sport from prehistoric times through the 21st century, discussing youth sports, community-based sports, and professional sports. Topics include the business of sports, social issues in sport, and sports psychology.

Booth, Douglas, and Holly Thorpe. 2007. *Berkshire Encyclopedia of Extreme Sports.* Great Barrington, MA: Berkshire Publishing Group, 450 pp.

This encyclopedia offers an in-depth reference to the characteristics, philosophy, functions, and history of extreme sports. It covers such extreme sports as bungee jumping, snowboarding, skateboarding, dirt biking, skysurfing, and street luge. It considers the future growth of these sports as individualistic sports representing an ideology in contrast to those of the big-time team sports such as basketball, baseball, and football.

Cashmore, E. 2000. *Sports Culture: An A–Z Guide.* New York: Routledge, 482 pp.

These encyclopedic entries cover the growth of sport with respect to broadcasting, merchandising, iconography, and commercialization. Focusing on individual issues, key events, and organizations, this reference book has over 170 entries that put progress in sport into historical and cultural perspectives.

Christensen, K.A., A. Guttmann, and G. Pfister, eds. 2001. *International Encyclopedia of Women and Sports.* New York: Macmillan, 3 vols. 1350 pp.

This three-volume reference is the largest and most comprehensive work about women's sports ever published. Articles on individual sports, sports medicine and women's health, societal and cultural issues, biographies, and historical country profiles offer unique understanding. Such health issues such as eating disorders, nutrition, and bone density, and such social issues as body image, gender equity, and Title IX legislation are among the issues covered in 430 articles.

Edgington, K., T. Erskine, and J. M. Welsh. 2011. *Encyclopedia of Sports Films.* **Lanham, MD: Scarecrow Press, Inc., 564 pp.**

The authors provide a listing of sport films from 1925 to 2010. Each entry includes production crew, cast members, running time, and such available format as videotape or DVD. Over 200 entries include more lengthy summaries and themes. Primarily, the films are fictional although some are based in historical events, but a few documentaries are included.

Frank, A. M. 2003. *Sports and Education: A Reference Handbook.* **Santa Barbara, CA: ABC-CLIO, 226 pp.**

The author critically examines the role of sports in academic institutions within the United States. The book is a balanced, serious consideration of whether or not the United States should remove sports from the academic agenda, similar to other countries. Both positives and negatives of sports within educational settings are well thought out.

Gaschnitz, Michael K. 2007. *Statistical Encyclopedia of North American Professional Sports: All Major League Teams and Major Non-Team Events Year by Year, 1876 through 2006,* **2nd ed. Jefferson, NC: McFarland, 1820 pp.**

This reference work is a four volume, comprehensive statistical accounting of football, baseball, basketball, hockey, and soccer leagues in North America Entries include leaders in common statistics, championship results, significant rule changes, recipients of major awards, and athletes inducted into the halls of fame.

Levinson, D., and K. Christensen. 1998. *Encyclopedia of World Sport: From Ancient Times to the Present.* **New York: Oxford University Press, 488 pp.**

More than 200 sports are featured in this extensive reference work. Besides the major sports, there are the arcane ones like korfball and boomerang throwing. Importantly, a larger picture of games and competition emerges that includes discussions about ethics, drug use, media, and commercialization.

Nelson, M. R. 2008. *Encyclopedia of Sports in America: A History from Foot Races to Extreme Sports.* **Westport, CT: Greenwood Press, 2 vols. 608 pp.**

The editor looks at the development and influence of sports in American culture, noting changes over the decades. Such topics as race, gender, ethnicity, and social class provide social context for the events, sport icons, commercial developments, and fan culture noted in this reference work.

Swayne, L. E., and M. Dodd. 2011. *Encyclopedia of Sports Management and Marketing.* **Los Angeles: Sage Publications, 4 vols. 1960 pp.**

This four-volume reference work focuses on sport economics, budgeting, leadership, law, human resources, and marketing. Celebrity endorsements, sport event sponsorship, and using sport as a branding strategy comprise the entries dealing with the promotion of nonrelated sport products.

Wiggins, D. K., ed. 2004. *African Americans in Sports.* **Armonk, NY: Sharpe Reference, 2 vols. 440 pp.**

This set features alphabetically arranged articles on the history, influence, and accomplishments of African American players and institutions.

Sport Business
Books
Barney, R. K., S. R. Wenn, and S. G. Martyn. 2002. *Selling the Five Rings: The International Olympic Committee and the Rise of Olympic Commercialism.* **Salt Lake City: University of Utah Press, 384 pp.**

Thorough research yields a wealth of information about the inside history of how the International Olympic Committee has evolved into one huge, commercialized enterprise. The people, the process, the politics, and the ethics of this corporate entity are examined.

Carter, D. 2010. *Money Games: Profiting from the Convergence of Sports and Entertainment.* **Stanford, CA: Stanford University Press, 304 pp.**

The author explores the blurring of the sports industry and the entertainment industry, commenting on the future direction of sports. He highlights how this mergence has played a crucial role in the continued growth of the sport industry, discussing such recent trends as fantasy leagues, video sport games, technological interactions with mobile devices that track workouts, and the growing number of commercials capitalizing on sport to convey desired messages.

Clotfelter, C. T. 2011. *Big-Time Sports in American Universities.* **New York: Cambridge University Press, 342 pp.**

The author incorporates recent research on intercollegiate sports to make sense of the positives and negatives associated with having sports play such a large and integral part of many higher educational institutions in the United States.

Davis, J. A. 2012. *The Olympic Games Effect: The Value of Sports Marketing in Creating Successful Brands.* **Hoboken, NJ: Wiley, 256 pp.**

This book details the various ways in which the Olympics offer a unique branding and marketing opportunity to corporations. Going back to the ancient Olympics, the author engages the reader in a historical context that identifies the legacy of the Olympics, a key component in branding.

Delaney, K. J., and Rick Eckstein. 2003. *Public Dollars, Private Stadiums: The Battle over Building Sports Stadiums.* **New Jersey: Rutgers University Press, 248 pp.**

The authors chronicle recent debates over the funding of sport stadiums. The book includes interviews with sports professionals, looks at recent research that shows sport stadiums are not necessarily financially sound, and reveals the new arguments for sports stadiums around social and community values.

Gold, J. R., and M. M. Gold. 2011. *Olympic Cities: City Agendas, Planning, and the World's Games, 1896–2016,* **2nd ed. New York: Routledge, 464 pp.**

The author assesses the developments and legacies that the Olympic Games have left for host cities on a business and cultural level, noting their interdependence. Three major sections are covered: the Olympic festivals, planning and management, and impact on select host cities from Berlin in 1936 to speculation on the 2016 Olympic Games in Rio de Janeiro.

Hagstrom, Robert G. 2001. *The NASCAR Way: The Business That Drives the Sport.* **New York: Wiley, 230 pp.**

This book is an in-depth look at NASCAR, the second most watched sport in the United States. It details the business acumen behind NASCAR, highlighting the creation of demand for the sport by deliberately limiting the number of races. It underscores the reasons why corporations seek out sponsorship deals with NASCAR.

Horrow, R., and K. Swatek. *Beyond the Box Score: An Insider's Guide to the $750 Billion Business of Sports.* **New York: Morgan James Publishing, 224 pp.**

The authors have extensive experience in the sports business, offering insights from their over three decades of direct dealings with athletes, owners, commissioners, and the media.

Lee, J. W. 2010. *Branded: Branding in Sport Business.* **Durham, NC: Carolina Academic Press, 370 pp.**

This book profiles key brands and their relationships with sport. It highlights the successes as well as the failures, providing insights into the sport branding business with real-world examples.

Rosner, S., and K. L. Shropshire. 2011. *The Business of Sport,* **2nd ed. Sudbury, MA: Jones and Bartlett Learning, 770 pp.**

This comprehensive book covers business related topics for professional, Olympic, and intercollegiate sports. It focuses on the multibillion dollar entities that control or govern sport, bringing forth economic, political, and social issues in the process.

Sheard, R., R. Powell, P. Cook, and P. Bingham-Hall. 2005. *The Stadium: Architecture for the New Global Culture.* **Berkeley, CA: Periplus Editions, 208 pp.**

This book discusses 18 of the world's famous sport stadiums. The authors discuss the increased cultural and iconic significance of the stadium throughout the 21st century. Through in-depth discussions of the stadia, they show how stadia have been financially, geographically, culturally and spiritually central to modern society.

Zimbalist, A. S. 2006. *The Bottom Line: Observations and Arguments on the Sports Business*. Philadelphia, PA: Temple University Press, 312 pp.

This book is a collection of journal articles and essays written by the author between 1998 and 2006 focused on the economics of sport. It covers such topics as the financing of new stadiums, the economic value of professional teams, revenue sharing in professional leagues, the cost of college sports programs, and governmental involvement in policing steroid use by professional athletes.

Journal and Magazine Articles

"50 Most Influential People In Sports Business." 2010. *Street & Smith's Sportsbusiness Journal* 13, no. 33, 8 pp.

The 50 most influential people in sports business include National Football League Commissioner Roger Goodell, ESPN/ABC Sports President George Bodenheimer, National Basketball Commissioner David Stern, Major League Baseball Commissioner Bud Selig, NFL Players Association Executive Director Demaurice Smith, and NBC Universal Sports & Olympics Chairman Dick Ebersol.

"Degrees in Sports Business." 2011. *Street & Smith's Sportsbusiness Journal* 14, no. 9, 9 pp.

This article provides an overview of all the degrees offered in the United States in the field of sports.

Eisenberg, Christiane. 2006. "FIFA 1975–2000: The Business of a Football Development Organisation." *Historical Social Research* 31, no. 1, 14 pp.

This article examines FIFA's rise from an organizing body to a very lucrative business through television deals and the globalization of soccer. It also comments on the internal politics that arose as FIFA moved through these changes.

Hui, Wang. 2011. "Analysis of Modern Sports Marketing of Post-Olympic Era." *Journal of Human Sport & Exercise* 6, no. 2, 6 pp.

Chinese sport businesses are busy building and broadening brand loyalty after the splashy introduction of so many products and services at the Olympic games in Beijing. Demand grows; profitability rises.

Humphreys, Brad R., and Jane E. Ruseski. 2009. "Estimates of the Dimensions of the Sports Market in the US." *International Journal of Sport Finance* 4, no. 2, 19 pp.

Having investigated the participation, viewing, and the supply and demand sides of sport business in the United States, the authors project that the value of sport business in 2005 ranged from $44 to $60 billion. Over 1 million employees worked at about 50,000 sport business firms.

Inoue, Yuhei, Aubrey Kent, and Seoki Lee. 2011. "CSR and the Bottom Line: Analyzing the Link Between CSR and Financial Performance for Professional Teams." *Journal of Sport Management* 25, no. 6, 44 pp.

In a rare assessment of any link between corporate social responsibility (CSR) and corporate financial performance in sport business, these authors studied four major U.S. leagues. No positive correlation was found; a negative link existed. The authors posit that the stakeholders simply were not aware enough of the benefits of corporate social responsibility.

Layden, T. 2002. "What Is This 34-Year-Old Man Doing On A Skateboard? Making Millions." *Sports Illustrated* 96, no. 24, 9 pp.

The author profiles Tony Hawk, the most famous skateboarder in the world, and his path to creating one of the most successful sports marketing businesses based in extreme sports.

Lee, Sanghak, and Paul M. Pedersen. 2009. "Commercialization and Automobile Racing in the United States: A Case Study of the Rise of the National Association for Stock Car Auto Racing (NASCAR)." *International Journal of Applied Sports Sciences* 21, no. 2, 6 pp.

This study analyzed the history of NASCAR and the success story that made stock car auto racing the second most popular and commercially successful sport business in the United States. The major factors behind NASCAR's popularity were the sport's fundamental friendliness and fairness. The evolved factors behind its sport business financial success were the speedways, sponsorships, television, geographic and ethnic expansion, globalization, and cultivation of young fans.

Mitra, Shakya. 2010. "The IPL: India's Foray Into World Sports Business." *Sport in Society* **13, no. 9, 19 pp.**

How a sport business has revenues of $4.13 billion in 2010 along with being almost the highest paying league in the world within three short years of inception is a stunning story. This article attempts to identify what ingredients have led to this solid enterprise, currently based on a league composed of 20 cricket teams.

Trotter, Jim. 2011. "The Fighter." *Sports Illustrated* **114, no. 8, 5 pp.**

This article discusses the abilities of DeMaurice Smith, executive director of the labor union of the National Football League (NFL) Players Association (NFLPA), to be an effective negotiator in the 2011 collective bargaining talks.

Other Types of Print Works
Fédération Internationale de Futbol Association. 2010. *FIFA Financial Report.* **Available at http://www.fifa.com/aboutfifa/officialdocuments/index.html, 116 pp.**

This report summarizes the three-year period leading up to the 2010 World Cup. It highlights the facts and figures for the fiscal year 2010.

International Olympic Committee. 2010. *Olympic Marketing Fact File.* **Available at http://www.olympic.org/ioc-financing-revenue-sources-distribution, 51 pp.**

This report outlines the overall marketing objectives of the International Olympic Committee as decided in 2009. It also provides an overview of Olympic partnership revenues and such distributions as those from the TOP program, broadcasting rights, ticketing, and licensing.

International Olympic Committee. 2011. *The Olympic Charter.* Available at http://www.olympic.org/content/The-IOC/Governance/Introductionold/, 95 pp.

This document is the complete bylaws, rules, regulations for staging, and competing in the Olympic Games. It sets the rules by which the International Olympic Committee manages the Olympics as a business.

National Collegiate Athletic Association. 2010. *Revenue Distribution Chart.* Available at http://www.ncaa.org/wps/wcm/connect/public/ncaa/finances/index.html, 1 p.

This chart shows the revenue distribution of the NCAA. It is an overview of total distributions organized by conference.

Tony Hawk Foundation. 2011. *The Public Skatepark Development Guide.* Available at http://publicskateparkguide.org/, 128 pp.

This detailed guide about how to advocate for a public skatepark, plan and design the skatepark, as well as run the skatepark after opening is written for the general skateboard enthusiast who would like to see a local skatepark emerge in their community. This guide is an example of a grassroots approach to the organization of sport facilities.

Sport Professionals, Technology, and Health
Books
Bouchard, Claude, and Eric P. Hoffman, eds. 2011. *Genetic and Molecular Aspects of Sports Performance.* West Sussex: Wiley-Blackwell, 424 pp.

The editors have compiled the most up-to-date research and discussions of the influence of genetics on human athletic performance. Funded by the International Olympic Committee, this volume adds to the extensive medical literature on high-performance sport.

Cashmere, E. 2002. *Sport and Exercise Psychology: The Key Concepts.* New York: Routledge, 320 pp.

This introductory book introduces the vocabulary of sport psychology, the social-psychological character of fans, and key theories common in sport psychology. It uses both historical and modern examples to educate about applied sport psychology for performance.

Fuss, F., A. Subic, M. Strangwood, and R. Mehta, eds. 2012. *Routledge Handbook of Sports Technology and Engineering.* **New York: Routledge, 624 pp.**

This book is the first of its kind to cover major innovations and impacts of technology in sport. It details research and innovation of sports products, the engineering, design, and materials of sports products, instrumentation and measurement in sport, and sport facilities.

Gucciardi, D., and S. Gordon. 2011. *Mental Toughness in Sport: Developments in Theory and Research.* **New York: Routledge, 272 pp.**

The editors bring together key articles about mental toughness in sport. The book examines what mental toughness is, how it is measured, how to develop it, and how to use it in settings beyond sport.

Martens, Rainer. 2004. *Successful Coaching,* **3rd ed. Champaign, IL: Human Kinetics, 508 pp.**

This book is the best-selling general coaching book ever published. It covers a wide range of topics such as coaching philosophy, motivating athletes, physical training, and managing a team.

Meehan, William P. M. D. 2011. *Kids, Sports, and Concussion: A Guide for Coaches and Parents.* **Santa Barbara, CA: Praeger, 192 pp.**

The author speaks from experience and expertise as a medical doctor on concussion, its symptoms, long-term effects, and preventive options, in accessible language. He discusses what a concussion is, how it manifests in various sports, and recent research on safety and the movement to reduce concussions in sport.

National Association for Sport and Physical Education. 2008. *National Standards for Sport Coaches,* **2nd ed. Reston, VA: National Association for Sport and Physical Education, 42 pp.**

Quality coaching and leadership skills respond to guidance and learning experiences. This book instructs the willing coach in eight basic steps, including philosophy and ethics, to being a professional and competent coach in any sport.

Ruxin, R.H. 2010. *An Athlete's Guide to Agents,* **5th ed. Sudbury, MA: Jones and Bartlett Publishers, 280 pp.**

The author offers parents and high school athletes advice on how to find the right sports agent for negotiating the collegiate recruiting process. While a guide for athletes, the topics such as agent services and fees, insurance, endorsements, and understanding NCAA regulations, make this book a reliable resource about sports agents and their roles.

Shropshire, K.L., and T. Davis. 2008. *The Business of Sports Agents.* **Philadelphia: University of Pennsylvania Press, 224 pp.**

The authors examine the history and development of the sports agent business. They consider the rules and regulations developed to control abuse by professionals and offer advice for how to improve the profession such as reconsidering amateurism and requiring more credentials to become a sports agent.

Thompson, J. 2003. *The Double-Goal Coach—Positive Coaching Tools for Honoring the Game and Developing Winners in Sports and Life.* **New York: HarperCollins, 346 pp.**

Having founded the Positive Coaching Alliance, Thompson here distills those best practices. Coaches can use these lessons and activities immediately to enhance both the functions and the fun of playing sports.

Journal and Magazine Articles

Bamberger, M. 2011. "Best Man." *Sports Illustrated* **114, no. 14, 5 pp.**

This article focuses on International Sports Management's founder, Andrew Chandler. Chandler's personality and personal relationships with his clients are discussed.

Cassidy, Tania. 2010. "Coaching Insights: Holism in Sports Coaching: Beyond Humanistic Psychology." *International Journal of Sports Science & Coaching* **5, no. 4, 5 pp.**

The author aims to provide insights into the term "holistic coaching" by exploring the relationships between coaching behaviors, holism, and humanism. Her aim is to move the discussion of coaching beyond the psychological realm and into one that embraces all aspects of being human.

Conzelmann, A., and S. Nagel. 2003. "Professional Careers of the German Olympic Athletes." *International Review for the Sociology of Sport* **38, no. 3, 21 pp.**

This article examines the correlation between being an Olympic athlete and positions in post athletic career. The authors discuss their findings that the correlation is positive. In this study of 616 former Olympic athletes, the authors show that these athletes secure higher positions in other careers than their nonathletic counterparts.

DeMause, Neil. 2011. "Why Do Mayors Love Sports Stadiums?" *Nation* **293, no. 7/8, 4 pp.**

This article discusses the ways that sport stadiums benefit municipalities, public officials, and city infrastructure. In particular, it focuses on why stadiums tend to be popular projects for city mayors.

Guskiewicz, Kevin M., S. L. Bruce, R. C. Cantu, M. S. Ferrara, J. P. Kelly, M. McCrea, M. Putukian, and T. C. Valovich McLeod. 2004. "National Athletic Trainers' Association Position Statement: Management of Sport-Related Concussion." *Journal of Athletic Training* **39, no. 3, 18 pp.**

This article contains specific guidelines about how to assess a concussion, when to allow a player to return to play, when to see a doctor as a follow-up, and special considerations for young athletes.

Luchs, Josh, George Dohrmann, and David Epstein. 2010. "Confessions of an Agent." *Sports Illustrated* **113, no. 14, 9 pp.**

The author discusses his interview with Josh Luchs, a certified NFL agent for over 20 years. Luchs reveals the idiosyncrasies of being a sports agent, the deals made, and the rules broken just to survive in the business.

Oshust, J. 2002. "Technically Speaking: Technological Advances in NFL Stadia. Ground-Breaking Technology is Undoubtedly

Changing the Way Fans Experience the Game. But Who Stands to Benefit Most From These Advances?" *Stadia* 18, nos. 26–28, 3 pp.

This article discusses the technological advances that NFL stadiums are incorporating as they renovate old or construct new stadiums. The discussion centers around who benefits from these latest advances.

Roper, Emily A., Leslee Fisher, and Craig A. Wrisberg. 2005. "Professional Women's Career Experiences in Sport Psychology: A Feminist Standpoint Approach." *Sport Psychologist* 19, no. 1, 18 pp.

This qualitative study of eight professional women highlighted their career histories and their experiences in sport psychology. Dominant themes were their entrances into sport psychology, their status, their obstacles, the feminist sport psychologist, and their support of women in sport psychology.

Sawicki, Ozzie. 2009. "Sport Performance Technology: An Integral Component of Performance Programming." *Coaches Plan/ Plan Du Coach* 16, no. 4, 45 pp.

This article discusses how Canada could integrate sports technology into their sports system in order to improve athletes' performances. Drawing on comparisons to the United States and Australia, the author suggests that Canada could improve in several areas.

Turocy, Paula Sammarone, Bernard F. DePalma, Craig A. Horswill, Kathleen M. Laquale, Thomas J. Martin, Arlette C. Perry, Marla J. Somova, and Alan C. Utter. 2011. "National Athletic Trainers' Association Position Statement: Safe Weight Loss and Maintenance Practices in Sport and Exercise." *Journal of Athletic Training* 46, no. 3, 15 pp.

This article focuses on the key concepts that athletic trainers should know in order to help manage weight and weight loss with clients. Particular attention is drawn to the fact that athletic trainers often are asked by clients for nutrition advice and should, therefore, be knowledgeable about nutrition, weight management practices, and ways to change body composition.

Wolff, Alexander. 2011. "Sportsman of the Year Mike Krzyzew-ski/Sportswoman of the Year Pat Summitt." *Sports Illustrated* 115, no. 23, 12 pp.

This article focuses on two of the most successful coaches in NCAA history. Drawing on their similarities, the article highlights those aspects that have made these coaches great coaches. Personal relationships with their players and a genuine interest in who they are as people is one aspect discussed.

Other Types of Print Resources

National Association for Sport and Physical Education. 2008a. *Choosing the Right Sport and Physical Activity for Your Child*, 7 pp.

This report details five guidelines that should be used to assess which sport program may be a good fit for your child. While it is produced as a resource for parents, it serves as a solid guide to understanding what makes a strong sport program, one that helps youth develop as athletes and as people.

National Association for Sport and Physical Education. 2008b. *National Coaching Report*, 160 pp.

This report offers a summary of the coaching profession and coaching education, including data on certifying coaches for youth and interscholastic sports. Participation rates and governance guidelines make up a substantial part of the report.

Sport Issues: Character, Youth, High Performance, Politics, and Ethics

Books

Alberts, C. L. 2003. *Coaching Issues and Dilemmas: Character Building Through Sport Participation*. Reston, VA: National Association for Sport and Physical Education, 187 pp.

This book visits the moral and ethical aspects of physical education and training in athletic coaching positions. Character development is valued over less positive values.

Beamish, R. 2011. *Steroids: A New Look at Performance Enhancing Drugs*. Westport, CT: Praeger, 211 pp.

This book places steroid use in a historical context to further understand drug use in modern performance sport. The author advocates for policies that reduce harm rather than proscribe an outright ban on drugs, suggesting that this approach entails more common sense than the current strategies.

Beamish, R., and Ritchie, I. 2006. *Fastest, Highest, Strongest: A Critique of High-Performance Sport.* **New York: Routledge, 194 pp.**

High-performance sports are plagued by doping. The authors discuss this reality and the ethical issues surrounding drug use and drug testing.

Bissinger, H. G. 1990. *Friday Night Lights: A Town, a Team, and a Dream.* **Reading, MA: Addison-Wesley Publishing Company, 357 pp.**

Football shaped the entire culture of a small west-Texas town. Winning was everything. This sport obsession created great and long-lasting social, racial, and gender problems for all involved. This book exposed the harm and saved lives and the community.

Byers, W., with C. Hammer. 1995. *Unsportsmanlike Conduct: Exploiting College Athletes.* **Ann Arbor: University of Michigan Press, 413 pp.**

This expose uncovers the graft and corruption that makes collegiate sports a business that is too lucrative to be criticized. The players are basically unpaid professionals who ought to be operating in an open free market, but are stabled like work horses instead. Byers, having served as NCAA executive director from 1951 to 1987, has personal knowledge from which he speaks.

Coakley, J. 2008. *Sports in Society: Issues and Controversies,* **10th ed. Boston: McGraw-Hill, 704 pp.**

This is the definitive text for the sport sociology course. Fully updated, it includes new photos and fresh references. The connections between sports and health, violence, ethnicity, social class and economics are probed. Athletes, journalists and sociologists provide thoughtful quotations, voicing various viewpoints.

Ehrmann, Joe, Paula Ehrmann, and Gregory Jordan. 2011. *InSideOut Coaching: How Sports Can Transform Lives.* New York: Simon & Schuster, 272 pp.

The author draws on his personal experiences as a collegiate and NFL player to highlight what coaches should do to develop not only athletes' abilities, but also, their sense of self. He makes a strong case for sport being the perfect platform through which life lessons can be learned, as long as people running the sports programs make these aims clear and deliberate.

Engh, F. 2002. *Why Johnny Hates Sports: Why Organized Youth Sports Are Failing Our Children and What We Can Do About It.* Garden City Park, NY: Square One Publishers, 208 pp.

Engh finds that a "Winning is everything" mindset in coaches and parents has often spoiled the sheer fun that play and sport can be and should be. He insists that parents and coaches place much less pressure on children to achieve results and encourages them to help children learn to play fairly, have fun, and be physically active for the enjoyment.

Farrey, T. 2008. *Game On: The All-American Race to Make Champions of Our Children.* New York: ESPN Books, 383 pp.

Making the case that parental obsession with youth sports is harmful to their children, the author suggests that children who are of age 3 through age 14 would be healthier and happier if they were not subjected to the cultural and societal fears and pressures of organized youth sports.

Feezell, R.M. 2004. *Sport, Play and Ethical Reflection.* Urbana: University of Illinois Press. 173 pp.

Sport is play, but rules and traditions expand pure play into character-building experiences. Respect for the total game is the way to eliminate cheating in sports.

Finley, P.S., and L.L. Finley. 2006. *The Sports Industry's War on Athletes.* Westport, CT: Praeger, 198 pp.

From doping to stadium finance, these coauthors find bad forces aligned against athletes. Obsession with profit-driven sport is damaging both individual players and society at large.

Levermore, R., and A. Beacom, eds. 2009. *Sport and International Development*. New York: Palgrave Macmillan, 288 pp.

The articles in this book detail the various ways that sport has been used for development of poorer nations. Using a practical foundation, the articles frame the issues and successes from theoretical lenses, appealing to both practitioners and those interested on an academic level.

Markovits, Andrei S., and Lars Rensmann. 2010. *Gaming the World: How Sports Are Reshaping Global Politics and Culture*. Princeton, NJ: Princeton University Press, 368 pp.

This book focuses on sport as a major global force. It argues that while sport has spawned new identities in terms of a shared global activity, it also has created local identities that often express animosity towards each other. Exploring these tensions, the authors demonstrate the omnipresent influence of sport in today's world.

McCloskey J., and J.E. Bailes. 2005. *When Winning Costs Too Much: Steroids, Supplements and Scandal in Today's Sports*. Lanham, MD: Taylor Trade Publishing, 344 pp.

Sports editor McCloskey and neurosurgeon Bailes look closely at what winning is costing. College recruiting excesses and players' muscle building-even in high schools-are assailed here. The authors also present solutions to the problems with case histories and an appeal for a return to true sportsmanship.

Miah, Andy. 2005. *Genetically Modified Athletes: Biomedical Ethics, Gene Doping and Sport*. New York: Routledge, 232 pp.

The author explores the intersections of human values and ethics in sport. Covering sensitive topics such as genetic modification, the author argues that recent technological advances in sport are part of the continuum that has persisted in sport from the beginning. He asserts that these developments should have no boundaries, which is controversial and much debated.

Selleck, G.A. 2003. *Raising a Good Sport in an In-Your-Face World: Seven Steps to Building Character on the Field—and Off*. Chicago: Contemporary Books, 194 pp.

Turning his back on the violent and win-at-all costs culture that has imbued even little leagues and youth sports, Selleck spells out steps to regain sportsmanship.

Walters, Guy. 2006. *Berlin Games: How the Nazis Stole the Olympic Dream.* **New York: Harper Perennial, 400 pp.**

This book is a detailed account of the two weeks of the 1936 Olympic Games, which are noted as the most political Olympics in its history. The author uncovers the workings of the Nazi agenda to promote Aryan supremacy through these games; and how politicians, diplomats, and Olympic officials manipulated many aspects of these Olympics, which had lasting consequences for future Olympics.

Journal and Magazine Articles

Brand, M. 2006. "The Role and Value of Intercollegiate Athletics in Universities." *Journal of the Philosophy of Sport* **33 (1): 9–20.**

Claiming large, positive benefits from intercollegiate sports, Brand finds that these activities have been undervalued.

Cary, P. 2004. "Fixing Kids' Sports: Rescuing Children's Games From Crazed Coaches and Parents." *U.S. News and World Report,* **5 pp.**

The author summarizes the trends in youth sports and questions the degree to which parents and sport are committing their children to sport. Citing studies that show specialization has increased, fun has decreased, and family dinner time and vacations have decreased, the author captures some of the most pressing concerns around youth sports in the 21st century.

Diacin, M. J., J. B. Parks, and P. C. Allison. 2003. "Voices of Male Athletes on Drug Use, Drug Testing, and the Existing Order in Intercollegiate Athletics." *Journal of Sport Behavior* **26 (1): 1–16.**

Asked about drug use and drug testing, eight male athletes favored drug testing even though there were privacy and fairness issues. Additionally, they perceived many existing difficulties between athletics and academics.

Eitzen, S. 1996. "Ethical Dilemmas in American Sport." *Vital Speeches of the Day* 62 (6): 182–185.

The author loves sport and intends to improve it by a deep focus on its dark side. He would abolish both the Olympics as they exist now and all corporate sponsorship. As a microcosm of society, he argues that sport is currently an opiate rather than an inspiration.

Howe, L.A. 2004. "Gamesmanship" *Journal of the Philosophy of Sport* 31 (2): 212–225.

Bad language and bad behavior are not part of good sportsmanship, excellence or fairness. Howe fits these concepts of gamesmanship into winning and losing in competitive events.

Jones, Martin I., John G.H. Dunn, Nicholas L. Holt, Philip J. Sullivan, and Gordon A. Bloom. 2011. "Exploring the '5Cs' of Positive Youth Development in Sport." *Journal of Sport Behavior* 34, no. 3, 18 pp.

This article summarizes a study conducted on youth sport participants in Canada. Results show that confidence and competence emerge as the most valued prosocial behaviors. Connection, caring, and character are less valued or at least less understood as important values gained from sport.

Myrdahl, Tiffany Muller. 2011. "Politics 'Out of Place'? Making Sense of Conflict in Sport Spaces." *Leisure/Loisir: Journal of the Canadian Association for Leisure Studies* 35, no. 2, 16 pp.

The authors examine sporting spaces as associated with apolitical spaces. They argue that sporting spaces are politicized; however, athletes who make sporting spaces an avenue for politics are often denounced and shunned. The authors follow the case of U.S. college basketball player, Toni Smith, protested against the United States' involvement in Iraq in 2003.

"New Risks In 'Cloaked' Steriods [*sic*]: 'Clean' Athletes Recruited To Discourage Use of Chemical Enhancers." 2004. *Soccer Journal* 49, no. 1, 1 p.

This article is a brief account of the newest designer anabolic steroids and the potential harmful physiological effects. The

American College of Sports Medicine lobbies for 'clean' athletes to be role models and spokespeople for drug free sport.

Nucci, C., and K. Young-Shim. 2005. "Improving Socialization through Sport: An Analytic Review of Literature on Aggression and Sportsmanship." *Physical Educator* **62 (3): 123–129.**

This article reviews previous studies on aggression in sports. The authors make recommendations for how social skills and cooperative behaviors can be built through sports by countering the aggressive behaviors often encouraged through sport.

Parry, J. 2006. "Sport and Olympism: Universals and Multiculturalism." *Journal of the Philosophy of Sport* **33 (2): 188–204.**

The author argues a positive view of sports as a global, universal activity through which universal positive values can be developed. He focuses on how participation in the Olympic Games promotes universal values and makes these values visible and accessible to the global community.

Rogge, J. 2003. "Olympian Efforts." *Harvard International Review* **25 (1Z): 16–20. As a president of the International Olympic Committee, Rogge espouses a utopian view of the benefits of sport in spreading peaceful values.**
Rudd, A. 2005. "Which 'Character' Should Sport Develop?" *Physical Educator* **62 (4): 205–211.**

The author makes a distinction between social character, which is based on values promoted through society, and moral character, which is based on a set of universal principles. He argues that sport develops both types but would be more effective as a way to build character by focusing on moral character.

Other Types of Print Resources

DCMS. 2010. *Plans for the Legacy from the 2012 Olympic and Paralympic Games.* London: DCMS. Available at http://www.sportdevelopment.info/index.php?option=com_content&view=article&id=725:plans-for-the-legacy-from-the-2012-olympic-and-paralympic-games-dec-2010&catid=96:london-2012&Itemid=82.

This report outlines the steps that the United Kingdom will take to ensure that the 2012 Olympic and Paralympic Games will serve as a stepping off point for increased participation in physical activity and sport by youth. Citing that sports participation typically declines significantly between the ages of 16–19 years, plans include targeting this group by incorporating more sport opportunities within educational programs.

Hyman, M. 2010. "A Survey of Youth Sports Finds Winning Isn't the Only Thing." Available at http://www.nytimes.com/ 2010/01/31/sports/31youth.html, 1 p.

This article draws attention to a high school student who polls other youth, asking why they like and play sports. It discusses the overwhelming findings that youth and their parents often have very conflicting reasons for sport participation.

"International Mountaineering and Climbing Federation." 2009. *Mountain Ethics Declaration*. Available at http://www. theuiaa.org/ethics.html, 2 pp.

Growing numbers of nonmainstream sports have ethical concerns and feel compelled to make an overt statement regarding participation. This declaration lists and describes 12 aspects of international climbing that should be considered.

Knight Commission on Intercollegiate Athletics. 2010. *Restoring the Balance: Dollars, Values, and the Future of College Sports*. Available at http://www.knightcommission.org/index. php?option=com_content&view=article&id=503&Itemid=166, 24 pp.

This report discusses ways to make sure that education and development of values remain part of intercollegiate athletics. Revealing that only a handful of collegiate sports programs make money, the report calls for a reconsideration of emphasis in most collegiate programs.

World Anti-Doping Agency. 2011. *World Anti-Doping Code*. Available at http://www.wada-ama.org/en/World-Anti-Dop ing-Program/Sports-and-Anti-Doping-Organizations/The-Code/, 135 pp.

This code guides world efforts to control substance abuse by elite level athletes. It provides policies, rules, regulations, and enforcement protocols for over 1,000 national and regional sport organizations. The International Olympic and Paralympic Committees use this code as their official guidelines for drugs and doping regulations.

Sport Issues: Race, Ethnicity, Gender, Sexuality, and Different Abilities

Books

Adair, D., ed. 2011. *Sport, Race, and Ethnicity: Narratives of Difference and Diversity*. Morgantown: Fitness Info Tech, West Virginia University, 250 pp.

This book is a collection of articles that cover race, ethnicity and aboriginality in comprehensive ways. It discusses a range of topics dealing with the issues in sport bought forth through difference, race, and ethnicity. The range of articles includes multiple perspectives from disciplines such as sociology, political science, history, and cultural theorists.

Aitchison, C., ed. 2007. *Sport and Gender Identities: Masculinities, Femininities and Sexualities*. London: Routledge, 176 pp.

This book is a collection of essays that examine masculinity, femininity, and homophobia in sport. Drawing on studies that explore these topics from a range of disciplines including sociology, social and cultural geography, media studies and management studies, the book offers critical insights into identity formation along these lines as it occurs in sport.

Anderson, E. 2011. *Inclusive Masculinity: The Changing Nature of Masculinities*. New York: Routledge, 208 pp.

The author draws on his own research concerning the different ways that male athletes in today's world conceptualize masculinity in radically different ways than a decade ago. He proposes that more inclusive forms of masculinity are being enacted in certain sporting environments, particularly in college sports in the United Kingdom.

Brittain, Ian. 2010. *The Paralympic Games Explained*. London: Routledge, 192 pp.

This is the first comprehensive book about the development and continuation of the Paralympic Games, the second largest international multisport event in the world. Framing the discussion through medical, social, and bio-social perspectives, the author discusses the history and contemporary impact of the games. Central to the discussion is the concern for changing language regarding disability sport.

Caudwell, J. 2006. *Sport, Sexualities and Queer/Theory.* **New York: Routledge, 192 pp.**

This book is a collection of essays that explore sport experiences of lesbian, gay, transgender, transsexual and intersex people. It considers these experiences within the social and political context of sport.

Hartmann-Tews, Ilse, and Gertrud Pfister. 2003. *Sport and Women: Social Issues in International Perspective.* **London: Routledge/ISCPES.**

This book examines the experiences of women in sport in many different countries around the world. While gains are being made in terms of female sport participation, experiences of women in sport vary tremendously. The authors bring together research data from physically active females in North and South America, Asia, Eastern and Western Europe and Africa.

Kennedy, E., and P. Markula, eds. 2010. *Women and Exercise: The Body, Health and Consumerism.* **New York: Routledge, 317 pp.**

This book is a collection of articles that explore the complex relationship that women have with their bodies, which tends to dissuade them from participating in physical activity. It explores the female perspective on fitness, fat, being a physically active body, and understandings of health.

Long, Jonathan, and Karl Spracklen. 2011. *Sport and Challenges to Racism.* **New York: Palgrave Macmillan, 288 pp.**

This book follows policies, practices in sport, and antiracist movements in sport to offer a broad perspective about how to be change agents in sport. It discusses the challenges to racism in and through sport that have occurred.

O'Reilly, Jean, and Susan K. Cahn. 2007. *Women And Sports In the United States: A Documentary Reader.* **Boston: Northeastern University Press, 406 pp.**

This book is an accounting of the significance of women's participation in sports since Title IX. It weaves together academic studies, magazine articles, political and legal documents, and first-person accounts to explore the experiences, trends, issues, and major successes of women in sports.

Rhoden, W. C. 2006. *$40 Million Slaves: The Rise, Fall, and Redemption of the Black Athlete*. New York: Crown Publishers, 286 pp.

Undeniably, African Americans have been central to the creation and continuation of a global empire of lucrative sport, but black players remain at the edges of power despite multimillion-dollar endorsements and paychecks.

Ruck, Rob. 2011. *Raceball: How the Major Leagues Colonized the Black and Latin Game*. Boston: Beacon Press, 288 pp.

The author discusses the history of baseball's integration of black and Latin ballplayers. Detailing the accounts of how black athletes have declined in baseball while Latin athletes from the Caribbean currently make up approximately 50 percent of the major and minor leagues, the author suggests that participation has done little to change athletes power of their own sporting lives.

Samuels, M. 2011. *Run Like a Girl: How Strong Women Make Happy Lives*. Berkley, CA: Seal Press, 288 pp.

The author tells the true stories of a wide array of women whose lives have been positively changed through sports. The stories relate how these women have used sport as a way to find personal resilience to overcome obstacles in life.

Zeigler, C., and J. Buzinski. 2007. *Outsports Revolution: Truth & Myth in the World of Gay Sports*. Boston: Alyson Books, 286 pp.

The founders of outsports.com tell the story of how the coming out of gay athletes has transformed sport for the LGBT community. Personal stories the myriad of experiences LGBT athletes have had in the history of making sport more open to this community.

Journal and Magazine Articles
Armstrong, Ketra L. 2011. "'Lifting the Veils and Illuminating the Shadows': Furthering the Explorations of Race and

Ethnicity in Sport Management." *Journal of Sport Management* 25, no. 2, 13 pp.

This essay provides an overview of the recent trends of the research and findings concerning racial and ethnic issues in sports.

Brown, Gary. 2011. "Ethnicity Report Reveals Impact of NCAA Diversity Efforts." *NCAA News*, 1 p.

This brief overview of the 2009–2010 NCAA report card on racial and ethnic minorities in leadership positions in collegiate athletics summarizes the recent gains made through the NCAA's efforts to increase diversity.

Caudwell, Jayne. 2011. "'Does Your Boyfriend Know You're Here?' The Spatiality of Homophobia in Men's Football Culture in the UK." *Leisure Studies* 30, no. 2, 16 pp.

Based on interviews with two men involved in an antigay campaign in football in the United Kingdom, this essay raises awareness of the degree to which homophobia in sport can harm. It focuses on the Justin Campaign, which is a grassroots effort to bring forth the real story of the death of a black gay footballer in order to highlight injustice.

Cyphers, L., and K. Fagan. 2011. "Unhealthy Climate." *ESPN Magazine* 14, no. 2, 7 pp.

The authors reveal that the recruiting practices for collegiate women's basketball remains homophobic. Over 50 percent of recruits surveyed said that college representatives asked about their sexuality. NCAA anti-homophobia efforts are discussed within this context.

Davis, Zachary. 2011. "Cream of the Crop." *Sports 'N Spokes Magazine* 37, no. 5, 5 pp.

The author covers the 2011 National Junior Disability Championships (NJDC) held in Michigan. It provides an overview of the sports in which competitions occurred including swimming, archery, and pentathlon. Athletes came from the United States, Bermuda, and Canada.

Hanold, Maylon T. 2010. "Beyond the Marathon: (De)Construction of Female Ultrarunning Bodies." *Sociology of Sport Journal* 27, no. 2, 18 pp.

The author explores the body experiences of high-performance female ultrarunners. Findings show that these women construct various degrees of pain, which helps them sustain training and racing long distances; accept a greater range of body types as legitimate, allowing for a feeling of acceptance and feeling good about their varied bodies; and fell as though they get to experience multiple degrees of femininity and masculinity through their sport, showing the social malleability of the concept of gender.

Lundberg, Neil R., Stacy Taniguchi, Bryan P. McCormick, and Catherine Tibbs. 2011. "Identity Negotiating: Redefining Stigmatized Identities through Adaptive Sports and Recreation Participation among Individuals with a Disability." *Journal of Leisure Research* 43, no. 2, 21 pp.

This study is based on interviews with disabled athletes who participated in adaptive sport programs. They discuss the ways that adaptive programs are structured in such a way as to provide a positive sporting space for these athletes. The athletes affirmed a strong sense of self and competency relative to nondisabled counterparts because of their sport participation.

May, C. 2010. "What's Love Got To Do With It?: (Un)bending Identities and Conventions in Gurinda Chadha's Bend it Like Beckham." *Culture and Religion* 11 (3), 30 pp.

The author explores how post-colonial identities are formed through the tensions among religion, family, race, gender, and sport identities. Using the idea of 'bending' a ball like the soccer player, David Beckham, the author suggests that similar paths, those which curve and turn, represent the real life paths of athletes trying to balance seemingly contradictory identities.

Smith, Earl, and Angela Hattery. 2011. "Race Relations Theories: Implications for Sport Management." *Journal of Sport Management* 25, no. 2, 11 pp.

This essay discusses the reasons why racial minorities are underrepresented in sport administration positions. The authors make suggestions about how to improve racial diversity in sport leadership.

"Something Old, Something New, Something Borrowed, Something Blue." 2011. *Marathon & Beyond* **15, no. 5, 9 pp.**

This article recounts women's participation in running events. Noting the women's only running events that have emerged recently, the article points out the impact that women in running have had over the last two decades.

Taylor, Phil. 2011. "Mixed Messages." *Sports Illustrated* **114, no. 23, 1 p.**

This article makes the case that while many professional players are in support of inclusivity and antigay campaigns, there remain numerous homophobic slurs and comments on a daily basis. He argues that these daily interactions undermine the large scale efforts for inclusivity.

Thomas, Nigel, and Andy Smith. 2009. *Disability, Sport, and Society: An Introduction.* **London: Routledge, 184 pp.**

This book is a critical introduction to the main issues with the development and management of sports for disabled persons. Based on interviews, surveys, and policy documents, this book covers the main areas of concern from adaptive programs to elite level sports for disabled athletes. It frames these concerns within the context of larger society and sport norms.

Other Types of Print Resources

Cooky, C., and M. Messner. 2010. *Women Play Sports But Not on TV.* Available at http://www.womenssportsfoundation.org/en/home/research/articles-and-reports/media-issues/women-play-sports-but-not-on-tv, 35 pp.

This report summarizes the findings of a 20-year study conducted about women's sports coverage on television. Results show that over a 20 year span women's sports coverage has decreased, lowering to less than 2 percent of total sports coverage. When women do appear on television, they are often portrayed in stereotypical ways that reinforce the idea that men are superior to men in sports.

The Institute for Diversity and Ethics in Sport. 2011a. *Racial and Gender Report Card-MLB*. Available at http://tidesport.org/racialgenderreportcard.html, 38 pp.

The report summarizes the hiring practices of Major League Baseball with respect to race, ethnicity, and gender. Many different levels of analysis are detailed.

The Institute for Diversity and Ethics in Sport. 2011b. *Racial and Gender Report Card-MLS*. Available at http://tidesport.org/racialgenderreportcard.html, 29 pp.

The report summarizes the hiring practices of Major League Soccer with respect to race, ethnicity, and gender. Many different levels of analysis are detailed.

The Institute for Diversity and Ethics in Sport. 2011c. *Racial and Gender Report Card-NBA*. Available at http://tidesport.org/racialgenderreportcard.html, 38 pp.

The report summarizes the hiring practices of the National Basketball Association with respect to race, ethnicity, and gender. Many different levels of analysis are detailed.

The Institute for Diversity and Ethics in Sport. 2011d. *Racial and Gender Report Card-NFL*. Available at http://tidesport.org/racialgenderreportcard.html, 49 pp.

The report summarizes the hiring practices of Major League Football with respect to race, ethnicity, and gender. Many different levels of analysis are detailed.

The Institute for Diversity and Ethics in Sport. 2011e. *Racial and Gender Report Card-WNBA*. Available at http://tidesport.org/racialgenderreportcard.html, 30 pp.

The report summarizes the hiring practices of the Women's National Basketball Association with respect to race, ethnicity, and gender. Many different levels of analysis are detailed.

"Problem-Oriented Guides for Police Problem-Specific Guides Series" no. 54. Community Orientated Policing Services: U.S. Department of Justice. Available at http://www.popcenter.org/problems/PDFs/spectator_violence.pdf, 84 pp.

This report serves as a resource and guide for police in dealing with spectator violence at sport events. It was written using input from real situations and research data drawn from international sources.

Tanner, J. 2001. "Women in Sports: Can They Reach Parity with Men?" *Congressional Quarterly Researcher* 11 (18): 401–424. Available at http://library.cqpress.com/cqresearcher/document. php?id=cqresrre2001051100.

From sexist good-ole-boys sport culture to glass-ceilings in media positions, competent female participants in the business, politics, and games of sport find their numbers and revenues growing, but the gains have been painstaking and true sportsmanship has been sparse.

Nonprint Resources

General Sport

Databases

ABI/INFORM is a database focused on trade journals across a wide range of industries. Financial and economic concerns in sport business appear here.

Academic Search Complete has access to over 7,900 periodicals, which includes over 6,800 peer-reviewed journals. Every topic in sport can be found in this database including management, social issues, sport psychology, and special interest articles.

Business Source Complete offers access to both articles in scholarly journals and popular magazines, featuring industry and company reports as well. Articles pertaining to sport management and business can be found here.

Education Research Complete provides a focused database with over 1,500 journals in education. This database is a good source for understanding the educational context with respect to sport such as the tensions between academics and athletics in educational institutions.

Gender Studies Database accesses journals whose primary aim is to publish scholarly work in the area of gender, femininity, masculinity, sexuality, and specific LGBT issues. Insights into sport specific issues around these concepts can be accessed.

JSTOR is a database giving access to over 1,000 academic journals as well as primary sources, images, and letters. It is multidisciplinary covering a wide range of disciplines. Sport topics emerge within each of these disciplines.

Philosopher's Index features articles on philosophy and ethics. Both scholarly articles and books are indexed. Ethical concerns in many areas of sport can be found.

Proquest Research Library has over 4,000 publications including magazine articles, trade publications, and newspapers. Three fourths of the articles are available in full text.

PsychINFO gives access to journal articles, dissertation abstracts, books, and reports pertaining to the field of psychology with overlap into other areas.

SocINDEX is a comprehensive database with access to over 600 journals. Articles pertaining to sport are found within the disciplines covered by this database such as sociology, economic development, ethnic and racial studies, gender studies, social psychology, and substance abuse.

SportDISCUS is a comprehensive database covering sport, physical activity, fitness, exercise, sports medicine, sports science, sports technology, physical education, kinesiology, coaching, training, sport administration, and sport leadership.

Sport Business and Sport Professionals
DVDs/Videotapes
Moneyball. DVD. Culver City, CA: Sony Pictures Home Entertainment, 2012.

This film tells the story of the 2002 Oakland Athletics' manager, who used statistics and mathematical analyses to determine draft picks. Most other managers disapproved of the strategy, but it resulted in the team having an excellent season despite having one of the lowest payrolls.

Sports Agent. DVD. Los Angeles: Tmw Media Group, 2008.

An educational film directed towards high school and college students that highlights the responsibilities and tasks of being a sports agent. It is meant to be a guide to career choices.

Internet Sites

Athletic Insight, http://www.athleticinsight.com/

Athletic Insight is an online journal that offers free access to the abstracts of scholarly articles on sport psychology. It publishes the most up to date information regarding mental training for athletes and coaches.

Sports Business News, http://www.sportsbusinessnews.com/

Sports Business News is a sports news publication that has been in business for over 14 years. It covers all major news in the major leagues in North America, soccer, golf, auto racing, the Olympics, and college sports.

Sport Business Research Network, http://www.sbrnet.com/

Sport Business Research Network provides statistical information on the international level concerning sport participation, fan profiles, sports facilities, sport finance, sporting goods, sponsorship, marketing, media and directories.

Sports Medicine on the Web, http://www.sportsmedicine.com/

Sports Medicine on the Web provides links to peer reviewed, publically accessible articles on al topic in sports medicine. Topics include athletic training, personal training, physical therapy, nutrition and diet, and careers.

The View from Here: The Business of NASCAR, http://blog. vcu.edu/nascar/

Two management professors at Virginia Commonwealth University are NASCAR fans and teach a course on the business of NASCAR. This blog contains scholarly, economic, and management discussions of NASCAR.

Other Types of Nonprint Resources

ATSU Concussion Program. http://www.atsuconcussion.com/ index.html

The Athletic Training Program at Still University provides a comprehensive Web site about concussions. The purpose of the Web site is to provide resources about concussion for parents, coaches, and athletes in order to minimize occurrences and potentially dangerous situations. The Web site offers ideas for prevention and treatment as well as links to other concussion Web sites and concussion studies.

International Olympic Committee. 2010. *Vancouver 2010 Marketing Report.* **Available at http://www.olympic.org/sponsors, 162 pp.**

This electronic magazine describes all the marketing activity for the Vancouver 2010 Winter Olympics. Included are descriptions of the broadcasting entities, ticketing, sponsorship partners, licensing, and the Olympic brand.

Kirschenbaum, D., S. McCann, A. Meyers, and J. Williams. SSE Roundtable #20: The Use of Sport Psychology to Improve Sport Performance. Gatorade Sports Science Institute. Available at http://www.gssiweb.com/Article_Detail.aspx?articleid=59& level=2&topic=12.

This article is in the format of question and answer. Experts answer five basic questions about sports psychology. The topics include how sports psychology has historically been used, its current applications to sports performance today, what are the potential harmful and beneficial effects of sports psychology interventions, and how accessible is sports psychology.

National Collegiate Athletic Association. 2010. *2009–2010 NCAA Membership Report.* **Available at http://www.ncaa.org/ wps/wcm/connect/public/NCAA/Finances/index.html.**

This electronic magazine describes revenues, expenses, programs, distributions, and scholarships of the NCAA. It is a comprehensive financial and descriptive view of the NCAA activities and corporate responsibilities for the academic year 2009–2010.

National Collegiate Athletic Association. 2011. *The Official Licensee List.* **Available at http://www.ncaa.org/wps/wcm/con nect/corp_relations/corprel/corporate+relationships/licensing/ licensees.html.**

This list supplies the names of companies, contacts, specific products and labels for all the companies who have licensing agreements with the NCAA.

Nike. 2011. *Fiscal Year 2015 Revenue Targets.* **Available at http://nikeinc.com/earnings/news/fy15-revenue-target-raised-to-28–30-billion.**

This webpage outlines the strategies Nike hopes to take to increase their revenues for the year 2015. This report lists the brand categories and affiliates with the 2011 fiscal year end projections and percent growth. It describes the brand strategy moving forward to 2015.

Stankovich, Christopher. 2010. *Own the Game: Sport Science Training for Peak Athletic Development!* **[Audible Audio Edition]. Advanced Human Performance Systems, 3hours 9 minutes.**

A guide to high-performance mental skills including getting in the zone, goal setting, motivation, focusing, imagery, overcoming anxiety, and working through performance plateaus and injuries.

Social, Political, and Ethical Issues in Sport
DVDs/Videotapes
The Athlete in Society: What Price Glory? 1993. VHS. Alexandria, VA: PBS Adult Learning Satellite Service.

Former tennis champion Arthur Ashe is among those on a panel discussing ethics and morality in sports.

Chariots of Fire. 1981. DVD. Burbank, CA: Warner Home Video.

This film follows the real life stories of two Olympic athletes competing for Great Britain in the 1924 Olympics. The film juxtaposes the two men as they pursue their Olympic dreams from to very different motivations. Abrahams is a secular Jew more concerned about his difficulty in fitting in with British upper class society. He runs to prove himself worthy. Liddell is a Scottish missionary who believe that God has made him fast and there is an ultimate purpose to his running. In this film based on true stories religion and politics weave throughout these men's Olympic dreams.

Dare to Dream: The Story of the U.S. Women's Soccer Team. 2007. **DVD. New York: HBO Sports.**

This film looks at the successes of the Women's National Soccer Team from 1991 to 2002. It follows players such as Mia Hamm, Julie Foudy, Brandi Chastain, and Michelle Akers, showing how they overcame obstacles to move U.S. Women's soccer into the international light.

How to Teach Character Through Sport. 2007. **DVD. Monterey, CA: Coaches Choice..**

This film is meant to be an educational tool for coaches who wish to incorporate character development into sport participation. It covers development of beliefs about character, how coaches should act, how beliefs become behaviors, and how to teach a value.

Invictus. 2010. **DVD. Burbank, CA: Warner Home Video.**

Racial tension in South Africa is the background to this historically based film. It tells the story of Mandela, who enlisted the captain of the national rugby team to generate support for this sport from blacks as well as whites. Based on the true story, this film shows when sport serves to unite a country strife with racial tension.

It Takes A Team! Making Sports Safe For Lesbian And Gay Athletes. 2004. **VHS. New York: Women's Sports Foundation.**

LGBT activist, Pat Griffin, is director of this 15-minute video produced by the Women's Sport Foundation as part of an educational kit directed at coaches, young athletes, and their parents. It interviews gay and lesbian athletes, providing insights into their struggles and desires for a more inclusive environment in sports.

John Wooden: Values, Victory and Peace of Mind. 2003. **DVD. Santa Fe, NM: Santa Fe Ventures.**

This film highlights John Wooden, who led UCLA to 10 National Championships in basketball. It offers insights into how Wooden developed not only high performing teams, but also confident and capable people beyond basketball.

License to Thrive: Title IX at 35. 2008. DVD. New York: Women Make Movies.

In June of 1972, Congress passed a piece of legislation called Title IX of the Education Amendments, to provide educational access and opportunity for women and young girls throughout the United States. Although most closely associated with sports, no other piece of legislation since the 19th Amendment has been more crucial to opening doors and creating leadership opportunities for women in all arenas, including education, science, math, finance, entertainment, the arts, business, law, and politics.

Media and Sports: Watchdog or Lapdog? 1999. VHS. New York: Insight Media.

Frank Deford, Jennings Bryant, Val Pinchbeck Jr., and Michael Oriard discuss the relationship between sports and media at the First International Conference on Ethics and Sport.

Not Just a Game: Power, Politics & American Sports. 2010. DVD. Northampton, MA: Media Education Foundation.

Dave Zirin, a journalist who has been critical of sports for over a decade, hosts this film about the politics of sport. This documentary points out just how political sports are despite the fact that the average person declares that sports and politics do not mix. The film recounts injustice in and through sport and peoples' efforts in history to change the experiences of marginalized groups for the better in sport.

Playing Hurt: Ethics and Sports Medicine. 2005. DVD. Princeton, NJ: Films for the Humanities and Sciences.

Orthopedic experts discuss athletic injuries from a sports medicine perspective.

Remember the Titans. 2001. DVD. Burbank, CA: Walt Disney Home Video.

This movie recounts the true story of integrating football in Virginia in 1971. A successful white coach is replaced by an African

American coach. Together they model how sport can be integrated by working together and being dedicated to helping their football team overcome racist tensions to become a championship team.

Science and Sports: Performance Enhancing Drugs. **2000. VHS. Dubuque, IA. Kendall-Hunt.**

At the First International Conference on Ethics and Sports, panelists discuss the uses and controversy of performance enhancing drugs in sports.

The Second Step: Warren Macdonald's Epic Journey to Federation Peak. **2008. DVD. Australia: Lysis Films.**

Injured in a hiking accident, Warren Macdonald lost both legs. This film follows Macdonald on his journey to recovery and his eventual 28-day trek to the top of Federation Peak as a double amputee. It is an inspiring story of how one man does not accept the perceived limitations of hiking with different abilities.

The Sociology of Sports in the United States. **2005. DVD. New York: Insight Media.**

The sociology of sports explores the relationship of sport to religion, social roles, citizenship, morality, class, race, gender, and the institutionalization of all sports.

Sports and Justice: Title IX and Gender Equity. **1999. DVD. St. Petersburg, FL: Philosophy Lab.**

Participants in sport discuss the impact of Title IX and perceptions of gender equity in sport.

Tarnished Gold. **2000. VHS. New York: A and E Home Video.**

This documentary delves into the bribery and scandals of the 2002 Winter Olympic Games in Salt Lake City, Utah, revealing the covert interactions that helped bring the Olympics to Salt Lake City.

Training Rules. **2010. DVD. San Francisco, CA: Wolfe Video.**

This documentary follows one woman's journey to understand the reasons for her dismissal from the Penn State women's

basketball team. Intertwined with historical, systematized homophobia, the documentary reveals the harmful consequences of
homophobia for both lesbian and heterosexual athletes.

Internet Sites
Andy Miah. http://www.andymiah.net/

In this Web site Andy Miah brings together all his current research projects about ethics, science, technology, sport, art, and
culture. Miah's cross disciplinary approach places the debates in
sport ethics within a global context.

**Black Athlete Sports Network. http://www.blackathlete.com/
main.shtml**

Black athlete provides news focused on black athletes in professional, college, and Olympic sports. A special features section
highlights black athletes in history and community involvement.
Other features include topics about women and youth in sport.

**Council of Europe. http://www.coe.int/t/dg4/sport/sportin
europe/charter_en.asp**

The Council of Europe has developed a Code of Ethics for sport
participation. This document outlines the policies, rules and
regulations that all European nations will adhere during sport
events and encourage in national sport programs.

Feminist Majority Foundation. http://feminist.org/sports/

This webpage is part of a larger Web site dedicated to gender equity. This webpage contains links to articles about the current impact of Title IX and recent movements and successes for women
in sports. Recent developments in disabled sports with an eye
towards women are also featured on this page.

Institute for Diversity and Ethics in Sport. http://tidesport.org/

The Institute for Diversity and Ethics in Sport is a research center that specializes in compiling and dissemination of trends in
amateur, collegiate, and professional sports. It publishes studies
about graduation rates of student-athletes, racial attitudes, and
the internationally known Racial and Gender Report Cards, a
summary of hiring practices. The Institute also follows ethical

concerns such as gambling and violence in sport. It offers diversity training in conjunction with the National Consortium for Academics and Sports.

Institute for the Study of Youth Sports at Michigan State University. http://www.educ.msu.edu/ysi/

The Institute for the Study of Youth Sports at Michigan State University hosts a Web site that provides unbiased research on youth sports. Specific links to important issues in youth sport are provided for parents and coaches. Other links offer more scholarly material for researchers. The goal of this Web site is to be a resource so that those working with youth in sport learn to maximize the social, psychological, and physical benefits of sport while minimizing adverse effects.

Josephson Institute. http://josephsoninstitute.org/sports/

This Web site provides access to the Josephson Institute: Center for Sports Ethics based in Arizona. The Web site publishes information about how to incorporate sportsmanship into youth sport programs. It hosts documents on how to build athletes' characters and strategies for sportsmanship.

The Next Step. http://www.toolkitsportdevelopment.org/

This Web site has links to reports about the impact of mega sport events on development in poorer countries, summaries of presentations at international sport for development programs conferences, guidelines for how to build sustainable sport organizations committed to the ideals in sport of development programs, and examples of successful sport organizations.

Outsports. http://www.outsports.com/

Outsports is the preeminent Web site dedicated to accomplishments of and newsworthy stories about gays, lesbians, bisexuals, transgender, and transsexual athletes. Topics are organized in a variety of ways: famous gay athletes, sport, feature articles, and other media links.

Sport Journal. http://www.thesportjournal.org/

This online, refereed journal publishes free access articles on a variety of sports topics and issues on physiology, ethics, gender and racial equity, and management. It is produced by the United States Sports Academy, which offers multiple degrees in sport management.

United Nations. http://www.un.org/wcm/content/site/sport/

This site of the United Nations hosts all the news, official documents, and important political actions in the sport for development movement. The Web site provides access to who is involved, the type of programs implemented, and fact sheets.

"Why do You Play Sports?" http://www.sportsreasons.com/

"Why do you play sports?" is a Web site created by a sophomore in high school that reports findings to surveys about why youth play sports. It provides survey results from over 1,000 students in his hometown as well as instructions about how to conduct the survey for others wanting to conduct a similar survey in their own cities.

Women's Sports Foundation. http://www.womenssportsfoundation.org/

The Women's Sports Foundation is the foremost nonprofit organization dedicated to the advancement of women in sport. The foundation serves as a political advocate for women in sports, offers programs that educate about women in sport, sponsors athletes, conducts and disseminates research, and publishes inspirational stories about physically active women.

Women's Sportsnet. http://www.womenssportsnet.com/DesktopDefault.aspx

The Women's Sports Net provides the most up-to-date sporting news for women in sport.

Glossary

amateurism   From the Latin meaning "love of," specifically is associated with love of sports.

athletic trainer   Health care professional who works with doctors to prevent and diagnose athletic injuries so that patients recover fully and in a timely manner.

bidding scandal   When representatives of the host city provide incentives supplementary to the traditional perks during the selection of host cities for such mega-sporting events as the Olympic Games, Super Bowls, or World Cups in return for votes.

blood doping   The practice of removing the blood from an athlete so that her/his body is forced to replenish the red blood cells by making more blood, after which the blood is reintroduced into the body. Such a practice provides an overabundance of red blood cells, increasing the athlete's endurance by increasing the capacity to move oxygen to muscles. It is a banned practice.

boycott   Refusing to participate in a sport event based on ethical or political reasons. The act is meant to serve as a symbolic act in protest of a human injustice.

character education   Instruction in learning about, valuing, and doing what is morally right.

chronic traumatic encephalopathy   A progressive degenerative disease that impairs brain function in individuals who were persistently subject to brain injuries through sport.

code of ethics   A written set of guidelines, values, and principles that serve to direct actions in an organization.

collective bargaining agreement   A document that sets forth such conditions of employment as wages, working hours, training, health and safety, and grievance mechanisms. Most major leagues establish these documents to provide security for both owners and athletes.

commercialization   A term used to mean the sale, display, or use of sport or some aspect of sport so as to produce income.

commodification   Sometimes used interchangeably with "commercialization." this term refers to when ideas, products, or entities not normally associated with revenue production become associated with revenue production.

competitive balance   A situation in which no one sports team has a large or unfair advantage over other teams. This idea leads to the belief that any team has the potential to win at any given time, thus making the outcome unknown.

competitive impulse   The innate drive that humans have to compete with each other. This term extends from the belief that early in human history, there was a natural condition that humans were in competition with other animals for survival, which later emerged into a competitive impulse against one another for survival.

concussion   A traumatic brain injury that shakes or jars the brain because of a blow to head or body.

discrimination   The unjust or prejudicial treatment of different categories of people often based on race, ethnicity, gender or sexuality.

drug testing   Technical analysis of urine, blood, sweat, saliva to determine the presence of a prohibited substance in a person's body.

ethnicity   The identification of belonging to a particular group based on heritage, language, or cultural values.

female athlete triad   A syndrome when women experience three interrelated health issues. These issues are eating disorders, amenorrhea, and osteoporosis.

feminism   A term to describe a collection of movements aimed at defining, establishing, and defending equal political, economic, and social rights and equal opportunities for women.

flow   A term coined by psychologist Csikszentmihalyi that describes the state of being fully present, aware, and immersed in an activity. It is often referred to as being "in the zone" by athletes.

gender equity   A goal of having gender be inconsequential to equal access to rights and social status.

global   Of the world.

globalization   The process of increasing global relationships with respect to economics, culture, and people. In sport, it refers to the ways in which sport facilitates these global relationships.

"glocal"   A combination of the words "global" and "local" to indicate the tendencies for local communities to reshape global ideas, culture, and sports into local and unique practices in sport.

hegemonic   Of or describing when the dominant group exerts social, cultural, ideological, or economic influence.

homophobia   An irrational aversion to, contempt for, anger toward, fear of, and discrimination against homosexuals or homosexual practices.

ideology   A comprehensive vision, belief system, and way of seeing the world that affects understanding, meanings, and actions.

inclusive masculinity   A term coined by Dr. Eric Anderson used to describe the behaviors and attitudes of men that constitute a softer form of masculinity, which includes a wider range of acceptable behaviors for heterosexual men.

intercollegiate athletics   Sport competitions between universities and colleges.

international sport organizations   Sport organizations that govern the general rules, policies, and for a particular sport event or multisport event in which countries all over the world compete. They have no allegiance to any one country.

lifestyle sports   Sports that emphasize immersion in a particular sport for the love of it, the feelings it evokes. It is a term employed by those participating in a sport that implies one's life centers around participation in it. While it often refers to sports that refuse commercialization, regulation, and institutionalization, there are often evidence of some of these in most lifestyle sports.

marginal revenue product (MRP)   The salary at which if the team paid more would reduce its profit or below which it would increase its profit.

masculinity   Behaviors and attitudes associated with being masculine and which contribute positively to one's masculine capital such as displays of power and dominance, demonstrations of strength and muscularity, suppressing emotions, expressing misogynistic attitudes, and overt displays of heterosexuality. Sport is one area of life that promotes and reproduces these behaviors.

media rights   The condition that a media company has to broadcast sport events in a number of ways. The media companies pay for the privilege of broadcasting sporting events.

new media   A type of media that refers to user-generated media or social media, such as Facebook, blogging, YouTube, and Wikipedia, which allows consumers to control and personalize access to and production of information and knowledge.

new racism   A term used to describe the growing positive media attention given to athletes of color while ignoring other social inequities.

politics   The acquisition, distribution, and use of power.

prosthetic   An artificial device or extension that replaces a missing body part.

race   A socially constructed term to categorize people based on physical characteristics. There is no biological basis for categorization of people.

racism   A belief that humans are hierarchically arranged by certain skills and traits based on stereotypical physical characteristics. This belief leads to irrational differential treatment of people based on "race."

related party revenue   Income received based on the fact that sport team owners also own the networks who broadcast the team. Income from the broadcasting company is considered related party revenue. Team owners often try to increase the related party revenue in accounting so that the team revenue appears low, which increases the amount the team will receive because of revenue sharing agreements.

revenue sharing   The practice within leagues to redistribute total league earnings from high-revenue teams to low-revenue teams. This practice is meant to preserve competitive balance by controlling the amount that teams can earn from regular league play.

salary cap   Viewed as a way to preserve competitive balance, it is an agreed-upon maximum monetary value that teams can spend on player salaries. It can be per player, team roster, or both.

senior woman administrator (SWA)   The NCAA designated name for the highest-ranking female in an athletic department. The designation is intended to bring visibility, credibility, and decision-making involvement to those women administrators in intercollegiate athletics.

sex testing   The practice of verifying the gender of athletes. It is also known as gender verification testing.

sexism   Irrational beliefs about gender and the capabilities associated with gender that infer inferior capabilities of females or people who act feminine.

sport for development   The movement that assumes sport can be used to ameliorate economic, social, and political injustices in developing countries.

sport franchise   A term used in North American sport to refer to an individual team that has exclusive rights over a particular geographical territory. North American sport organizes leagues as groups of franchises, which remain closed unless the league decides to admit a new team.

sport league   A group of sports teams or franchises that compete with each other throughout regular season play.

sport medicine   A branch of medicine that specifically deals with the treatment and prevention of athletic injuries related to sports participation and physical activity.

sport psychology   A branch of psychology that is concerned with helping athletes attain peak performance.

sport science   A discipline that applies insights from technology, physiology, psychology, and other sciences in order to improve and enhance athletic performance.

sport sociology   The study of sport as a social practice. It looks at sport as a practice of socialization with respect to cultural values, role modeling, and organizational structure.

sport sponsorship   The marketing practice of corporations paying money to sports teams, events, and organizations for the privilege of being associated with those entities to increase revenue for their corporations.

sports agent   A person who negotiates on behalf of an athlete specific employment contracts and endorsements.

stock car racing   A type of auto racing that uses automobiles that have some resemblance to standard production line cars. While current stock cars have many modifications and cannot be considered production line autos, they still stem from a production line car.

ultrarunning   A running event in which the distance run is more than a marathon or 26.2 miles.

white privilege   The condition of having benefits and advantages because of being white.

youth sport   Sport that serves young children, adolescents, and young adults.

Index

About the Author

Maylon Hanold is a full-time lecturer in the Sport Administration and Leadership program within the Center for the Study of Sport and Exercise at Seattle University. She holds a BA from the University of Washington, an EdM from Harvard University, and an EdD from Seattle University. She specializes in sport sociology, sport leadership, and organizational behavior. In addition to teaching in the masters program, she advises graduate students on various research topics regarding sport organizations, social issues, and leadership. Her research interests remain grounded in sport cultures, embodiment, and leadership. She has published two articles titled "Beyond the Marathon: (De) Construction of Female Ultrarunning Bodies" and "Leadership, Women in Sport, and Embracing Empathy." Currently, she is engaged in an ethnographic study of ultrarunning—examining how this particular subculture of distance running maintains its identity in a period of rapid growth. She was a member of the U.S. Whitewater Kayak Team from 1984–1992 and was an Olympian in 1992. She was head coach of the U.S. Junior National Whitewater Kayak Team from 1994–1996. Maylon remains active and enjoys trail running, ultrarunning, snowboarding, and wilderness paddling with her family.